*Image and Power
Women in Fiction* ... *eth
Century*

Image and Power

Women in Fiction in the Twentieth Century

Edited by

Sarah Sceats and Gail Cunningham

Longman
London and New York

Longman Group Limited,
Longman House, Burnt Mill,
Harlow, Essex CM20 2JE, England
and Associated Companies throughout the world.

*Published in the United States of America
by Longman Publishing, New York*

First published 1996

ISBN 0 582 255376 CSD
ISBN 0 582 255368 PPR

British Library Cataloguing-in-Publication Data

A catalogue record for this book is
available from the British Library

Library of Congress Cataloging-in-Publication Data

Image and power : Women in Fiction in the Twentieth Century / edited by Sarah Sceats and Gail
Cunningham.
    p.   cm.
    Includes bibliographical references and index.
    ISBN 0–582–25537–6. — ISBN 0–582–25536–8 (ppr)
    1. English fiction—Women authors—History and critism.
2. Women and literature—Great Britain—History—20th century.
3. English fiction—20th century—History and criticism. 4. Power
(Social sciences) in literature.   5. Women in literature.
I. Sceats, Sarah.   II. Cunningham, Gail.
PR888.W6I43   1996
823′ .9109352042—dc20   95–24401
                                                     CIP

Set by 8 in Ehrhardt 10/11.5pt
Produced by Longman Singapore Publishers (Pte) Ltd.
Printed in Singapore

Contents

Section 4: Public power

Acknowledgements

We would like to thank Longman for their vision and confidence in supporting this project.

We thank Kingston University for facilities provided, and especially John Ibbett for his good humoured support.

We owe a most particular debt to those friends and colleagues whose comments, suggestions and recommendations were so helpful. John Mepham, Peter Conradi and Elizabeth Maslen deserve special mention, and we thank also Suzanne Raitt, Julia Hallam and Sandra Kemp for recommending contributors.

On a more personal note, we want to express our deepest gratitude to Doron Swade and Joe Bailey for their unfailing support, involvement and willingness to listen and make suggestions. Our thanks and appreciation are due, too, to Saul, Emily, James, Matthew and Anna, for their interest, enthusiasm and tolerance over the long period of the book's gestation.

Notes on contributors

Lucie Armitt is a lecturer in the Department of English at the University of Wales, Bangor. She is the editor of *Where No Man Has Gone Before: Women and Science Fiction* (Routledge 1991) and is currently finishing a book on the interrelationship between critical theory and the fantastic. Other research work focuses upon contemporary women's fiction, feminist theory and the gothic.

Stephen Benson is currently a doctoral student and teaching assistant at Queen Mary and Westfield College, University of London. His thesis involves a study of the role of folk tales in recent fiction and theory.

Peter Conradi has taught at the University of Colorado at Boulder, the Jagiellonian University, Krakow, Poland, the University of East Anglia, and is currently Professor of English at the Kingston University. He has written numerous articles and reviews, and the books *John Fowles, Dostoevsky* and *Iris Murdoch: the Saint and the Artist*. He is currently working on a book on Angus Wilson and a collection of reminiscence by British Council lecturers in Poland from 1936 onwards.

Julian Cowley taught English at King's College, London before joining the University of Luton, where he is Senior Lecturer in Literary Studies. He has published essays on contemporary British and American literature and culture including articles published this year on Bruce Chatwin, Ishmael Reed and Lord Berners.

Gail Cunningham read English at Oxford, where she subsequently took her DPhil. She has taught English at several universities, among them Oxford and the Open University, and is currently Dean of the Faculty of Human Sciences at Kingston University. She has written extensively on women in nineteenth and twentieth-century fiction. Publications include *The New Woman and the Victorian Novel* and a number of essays on Margaret Drabble.

Anne-Marie Fyfe was born in Cushendall, County Antrim in 1953. She lectures in English at Richmond-upon-Thames College and is currently researching critical aspects of contemporary women's writing. Her stories and poems appear in various literary journals.

Philippa Gregory has a BA degree in history from the University of Sussex and a PhD from Edinburgh University. She has worked as a journalist for newspapers and BBC Radio and has tutored at universities and for the WEA (Workers Educational Association). In 1987 she published the internationally successful novel *Wideacre* and has since published five other novels, four books for children and a screenplay for BBC Television. She is a Fellow of the Faculty of Human Sciences, Kingston University.

Julia Hallam teaches film and visual communication in the Department of Communication Studies, University of Liverpool. A former nurse and community health worker, she has recently completed a doctorate on the relationship between popular images of nursing and professional identity.

Elisabeth Mahoney teaches in the English Department at Aberdeen University. Her research and teaching interests are in contemporary women's fiction, speculative fiction, twentieth-century women poets, and feminist critical theory. Current research projects include work on Amy Lowell's poetry, and an interdisciplinary project on gender and representations of the twentieth-century city. She has edited an edition of Jane Austen's *Northanger Abbey* for Everyman (1994) and is currently preparing an edition of Thomas Hardy's *A Pair of Blue Eyes* (forthcoming 1996).

Merja Makinen is a principal lecturer in the English Department at Middlesex University, teaching mainly women's writing, contemporary feminist genre fiction and feminist theory. She has published *Joyce Cary: A Descriptive Biography* and, with Lorraine Gamman, *Female Fetishism: A New Look*. She is currently working on Angela Carter.

Elizabeth Maslen is a senior lecturer at Queen Mary and Westfield College, University of London. Her book on Doris Lessing (in the new series on Writers and their Work) has recently been published by Northcote House in association with the British Council, and she is now working on the politics of novels written by women after the granting of Universal Franchise in 1927.

John Mepham studied at Oxford and Princeton Universities. He has had both academic and non-academic careers. He taught philosophy and literature at Sussex University and also in colleges and universities in Australia and the USA. He also worked as a consultant for the GLC, for the Harvester Press and for European Nuclear Disarmament. He was for many years associated with the Radical Philosophy Group and in the 1970s was co-editor of the four-volume *Issues in Marxist Philosophy*. His publications include *Virginia Woolf: A Literary Life* and articles on contemporary film and television. He is now Reader in English at Kingston University. He lives in London.

Nickianne Moody has undertaken postgraduate studies at the Universities of Warwick and Wisconsin-Madison. She lectures in Media and Cultural Studies at Liverpool John Moores University where her teaching interest is predominantly in popular fiction. She has researched popular representations of new technology, and is currently embarking on a research project, to include a major component of oral history, on Boots Booklovers' Library.

Terry Phillips lectures in English at Liverpool Institute of Higher Education. Her major research interests are in the nineteenth and twentieth-century novel, and particularly in the relationship of women to modernism. She is currently working on the philosophical aspects of the work of Dorothy Richardson and May Sinclair.

Sarah Sceats took her first and masters degrees as a mature student, and now lectures in English Literature at Kingston University. Publications include a book describing the reconstruction of a wooden oyster smack which she also illustrated (Batsford 1983), magazine articles and biographical literary references (Bloomsbury 1989). She is currently completing a doctorate on the literary and cultural significance of food and eating in contemporary fiction by women, with special reference to Angela Carter, Doris Lessing, Alice Thomas Ellis and Michèle Roberts.

Trudi Tate is a lecturer in English at the University of Southampton. She is currently completing a book on modernist fiction and the First World War, and has recently edited a collection of short stories: *Women, Men and the Great War* (Manchester University Press 1995). She is co-editing, with Suzanne Raitt, a collection of new academic essays on women writers of the First World War (Oxford University Press forthcoming). Other publications include an edition of Dorothy Richardson's short fiction, and *That Kind of Woman*, an anthology of modernist stories by women, co-edited with Bronte Adams (Virago 1991).

Introduction

Introduction: Image and Power

Raison d'être and genesis of Image and Power

This volume has been a long time in the making. We first conceived of it when teaching a course on images of women, and found ourselves casting around for a collection of critical essays to put on the reading list. We wanted something more than a trot through the classics, envisaging a collection that would strike out into the manifold aspects of women's lives, that would encompass a wide range of fictional genres and that would include a variety of critical standpoints, of differing degrees of theoretical sophistication. We did not find such a volume. And so was born, initially the tiniest of ideas, the determination to create one of our own.

To set out with the deliberate idea of producing a critically and generically eclectic multi-contributor volume of essays is to give oneself obvious difficulties, most notably in terms of cohesion. While our purpose was to display range and diversity, at the same time we wanted to avoid randomness. Just as ferreting out 'images of women' in canonical literature gave way to more complex feminist approaches to less traditional texts, so our ideas became focused on women's writing, predominantly in the twentieth century. As the conception grew, we designed the unifying themes of image and power to reflect the combination—both within individual essays and across the collection as a whole—of readings which examine the idea of gendered image and those which give a challenging perspective on the relations between sexuality, culture and power. Sadly, we could not, in one volume, be wholly inclusive: the collection is concentrated largely on English writers, does not tackle ethnicity and omits significant areas of popular fiction, such as the detective story. These, and other areas, we hope to tackle in a future volume.

Structure of the collection

The collection is organised not chronologically but thematically, in four sections. The first, 'Usurping the male', brings together essays on women writing about subjects or in genres which are conventionally assumed to be male territory. The intellectual, explorations of space and time, eroticism: all have traditionally tended to be thought of or treated as predominantly male concerns, but are here examined as they have been constructed—or deconstructed—by women writers and with female subjects. 'Endorsing the female', by contrast, looks at fictional forms which are normally associated with a female readership or with concerns mainly relating to women. Pony books, the supernatural, nurses and fairy tales are all associated either exclusively or to a large degree with the female, and the essays in this section examine areas of fantasy, sexuality and social involvement in fiction by or for women. The final two sections, 'Private power' and 'Public power', contrast the broad arenas in which women may find expression for, exercise or experience power. 'Private power' takes areas of the intimate or domestic, often assumed to be female territory—food, motherhood, love, the home—and the chapters in this section examine some twentieth-century women writers' approaches to the power relations within these areas. In 'Public power' the concerns of history, war and politics, nationalism and narrative itself are examined through female voices which can disturb and challenge male traditions.

The sections should not, of course, be seen as discrete or exclusive, for there is an abundance of fruitful cross-connection and overlap between the chapters. We draw attention to some of these below, but we hope that part of the volume's stimulus to readers will lie in its provocation to drawing their own.

Section 1: Usurping the male

The entire collection is framed by two essays (the first one, in this section, by John Mepham and the final one, in 'Public power', by Elizabeth Maslen) which stress political commitment and the responsibility of the intellectual. John Mepham's opening chapter investigates the question of gendered reading, through which he examines the role and importance of the intellectual heroine, a figure who offers something of a world view, a way of looking that will make sense of the reader's experience both in terms of gender and in general. What happens, he asks, when the reader, who identifies in a 'gender-blind' way with such a protagonist, is of a different gender, especially when the heroine's truth-telling includes specifically female emotional and physical experience, as in Lessing's *The Golden Notebook*? Part of the answer, Mepham suggests, lies in the very project of inquiry into the obstacles or impediments that obstruct the way to truth-telling, obstacles that make us cling rigidly to fixed meanings for fear that the alternative is chaos. Through her heroines, Lessing, he claims, endorses the need to give up rigid traditions of thought and feeling, to give voice to what is hidden or unspoken and to acknowledge changing responsibilities. Here, perhaps, are projected utopian possibilities which lie beyond gender, or which are non-gendered—notwithstanding their location in a gendered context.

The utopian, or its opposite, is unspoken in much writing of a broadly political kind. Elisabeth Mahoney embraces *dystopia* as offering 'potentially radical fictional space in which women can unravel and re-imagine existing power relations'. If Lessing offers, in part at least, the possibility of moving beyond obstructive gender categories, Mahoney's argument and the texts she chooses to examine are clearly concerned with usurping the male, with claiming narrative space, by means of what she terms 'acts of genre subversion'. Her emphasis is on textual space; she takes deconstructive texts, texts which undermine their own 'master' narrative, inserting alternative, disruptive, more 'open' female narratives in the interstices. Using Barthes and Derrida she examines how these texts work to offer alternative feminist perspectives, opposing women's non-linear narratives to the 'master discourses' of the male narrators' texts. Suggesting a parallel within these texts to the feminist project of uncovering neglected women writers, Mahoney's view of the feminist dystopia presents both supplementary writing 'in the spaces' and a specifically feminine idiolect as facilitating the emergence of new, 'self-represented' textual identities.

Merja Makinen probes sexual difference. Seeking to explore how contemporary women's writing challenges ideologies which emphasise passive female sexuality, she takes on cultural definitions of women's sexuality since the eighteenth century, Freud, Lacan and the popular pseudo-medical (and hence 'scientific') discourses of the sex manual. Clearly, there is some considerable usurping of male territory going on here. Taking a number of fictions of desire, both heterosexual and lesbian, Makinen examines the active/passive polarisation of sexual power, specifically in relation to orthodoxies of 'doing' and 'being done to' (which, interestingly, she notes are challenged in the 'consensual and non-oppressive' role-plays and fantasies of sado-masochism). The question of space recurs, but here it is the phallocentric space of desire that is claimed by the 'power and danger of erotic desire in the feminine mode'. Though she finds a number of the popular novels wanting—uncovering 'old-fashioned male phallocentrism' masquerading as liberation—Makinen suggests that two writers offer a 'feline devouring energy . . . a potent orgasmically-desiring force'. This realisation of female desire is, she says, 'unnamed in more theoretical discourse'. Just as the first two essays focus on ways in which the writers in question break through established discourses, so here Makinen discovers a challenge which is mounted fantastically, subversively outside the legitimating discourses of theory.

But theory has its own part to play in articulating the challenges to masculine space, and Lucie Armitt's essay makes clear the productive symbiosis between theory and science fiction. Like the dystopian novels, feminist science fiction challenges and even subverts genre boundaries; indeed the essence of science fiction might be said to involve the transgression of boundaries and borders. The parallels between its concerns and those of psychoanalysis (with, for example, the borders of reality or personality, abjection, psychic journeys) are quite startling, as Armitt illustrates in her reading of *Kindred* and *The Incomer* in relation to the work of Julia Kristeva. Following Kristeva's claim for the formative importance of space (especially in relation to women) relative to time, Armitt posits the interplay (and dislocation) of space and time in science fiction as productive of textual or narrative space for an alternative feminist view on politics and ideology, and explores how this is worked through in the novels. Time travel allows the coexistence of or conflict between 'patrilinear' historical time and the maternally cyclical, and the women's travelling mentality provides for an exploration of the mental and bodily spaces of female desire—though it

5

should perhaps be stressed that this is not simplified, and Armitt draws attention to paradox and contradiction in both texts and theory.

The search for space *and* time here relates specifically to sexual difference, but the connections with the earlier chapters are obvious. What is hidden, what is unspoken, what is denied or marginalised, analysed or subsumed within 'master' discourses is being uncovered, articulated, given voice, obliquely in the spaces in subtle, complex and informed acts of expropriation.

Section 2: Endorsing the female

Gail Cunningham identifies a highly gender-specific endorsement of female endeavour and achievement in her investigation of constructions of women's power and its representation in relation to horses. Working from the premise that horses represent or provide a combination of independence, power, emotional satisfaction, practical achievement, gender equality and sublimated sexuality, she traces their symbolic and literal significance from nineteenth century fiction, through girls' stories to contemporary popular fiction.

Drawing attention to themes of submission and domination in relation to women in literature, Cunningham also highlights the more unusual emphasis on practical, physical and competitive female ability in the girls' pony books, where gender equality, and even female superiority, are evident. As the characters progress through puberty towards adulthood, however, differentiation in gender roles begins to appear, with the suggestion that men will replace horses as the focus of female interest in adult life. Some contemporary popular fiction, Cunningham suggests, gives sexuality overt expression, but nevertheless offers an adult version of the pony book, in which a woman's ability to love and care for her horse brings its own rewards. The mild endorsement of women's capacities here contrasts with the much more adventurous association of horses with sex, power and independent capability in the fiction of Philippa Gregory (author of our chapter on victim heroines), who combines the raunchy potential of women and horses with a distinctly feminist agenda.

If the domestic is displaced in the realm of horses (and nurses), it is very much in the centre of women's ghost story writing as surveyed by Nickianne Moody. Ghost stories, she says, enable the exploration of difficult transitional states (such as marriage and divorce) and re-examination of domestic and familial pasts. Voices suppressed or unheard in life are given the capacity or licence to speak of life experience from beyond the grave. She quotes Ellen Moers as claiming that the fantastic allows women to draw on their own experience of fears provoked by patriarchy, and claims, too, that the transgressive nature of the fantastic also provides for experiment and self-expression: the ghost story offers a specific *space* for alternative viewpoints, for examining the hidden stresses in women's lives, for the exposure of injustice and for retribution and reversal. Twentieth-century women writers' ghosts are, she points out, active, even enticing, not just representing hidden desires, and thus enact a parallel with twentieth-century women.

Clearly, women's ghost story writing is concerned both with endorsing the female and usurping the male, as indicated by the annexing of generic space. Unpleasant and powerful emotions can be explored, expressed and endorsed in relation to the commonplaces of women's lives, especially where there is a lack of social acknowledgement for their importance. Most tellingly, Moody suggests, women's ghost stories reveal the destructive nature of patriarchal marriage.

The expectations of patriarchal marriage inform and underpin the apparently female realm of the Sue Barton nursing novels explored by Julia Hallam. Focusing on the images of femininity in these nursing novels, with their combination of career and romantic interest, she examines their ideological role, suggesting that their roots lie in the sentimental didactic tradition, directed as they are at girls in transition from girlhood to womanhood. She identifies a kind of 'Nightingalism' in the novels, characterising a 'moral warfare' in the inculcation of vocational values through the display of 'ideal types' of femininity. Unsurprisingly, perhaps, these vocational values stress forbearance, self-sacrifice and obedience— the ability to love and care for the patient/doctor bringing its own rewards.

The ideological force of these nursing novels is clearly evident in Hallam's observation that they make no distinction between public and private lives, the 'potentially political' space of the hospital being presented as a shared personal living space that effectively replicates the traditional family. Thus the doctor becomes the father, the nurse the mother, and patients the children. Here, women prevail through subterfuge and manipulation in the face of existing power relations. Contrasting the enduring success of these stories with the demise of Cherry Ames (a more independent-minded single-woman nurse), Hallam comes to the conclusion that the 'separate spheres' philosophy, in which nurses were expected to be single and vocationally committed, did not survive the increasingly scientific culture of medicine from the 1950s, as a result of which doctors became seen as prestigious experts and nurses were relegated to a supporting caring role. The fact that Sue Barton combined marriage and career, Hallam suggests, offered some possibilities for institutional change, whereas the single and independent Cherry Ames remained outside the 'medical family'.

Up to this point our contributors have written of genre subversion, genre appropriation and even the creation of new genres or subgenres. Stephen Benson tackles the question of genre head-on, revealing varieties of modern romance as embedded in the folk and fairy tale traditions. These traditions in themselves resist narrative fixity (and orthodoxy), he says, offering numerous alternatives to the 'culturally sanctioned utopian vision of the ideal fictional romance'. His emphasis on the intertextuality of genre suggests the possibility of a simultaneity of differing readings. Thus no particular 'story patterns' or 'life stories' may be seen as more 'natural' than others. Such an approach opens out what has become narrowed and closed, so that culturally endorsed, accepted readings of fairy tales involving male secrecy and female subordination are seen to be constructions, suggesting an interpretive closure. Other readings, claims Benson, might draw out and indeed endorse 'submerged, partially silent narrative voices'.

Such other 'readings' are evident in the writing of Angela Carter and Margaret Atwood, as Benson illustrates, and it is a significant coincidence that these two writers appear elsewhere in the collection, specifically in the context of challenging the culturally authorised: alternative voices in Atwood's writing are discussed in Elisabeth Mahoney's chapter on dystopia; Carter's radical female sexuality is highlighted in Merja Makinen's chapter on the erotic and her anarchic portrayals of appetite explored in Sarah Sceats's discussion of food and power. Benson suggests that, culturally, it is the utopian and didactic elements of the fairy tale romance which have been retained. As he demonstrates, however, these two writers reclaim the fantastical elements that were suppressed by realism, and in doing so emphasise the complexity and multiplicity of narrative voices. If romance and folklore both transmit cultural institutions and provide a release from them (in much the same way, perhaps, as the *unheimlich* both recalls the homely and threatens it), these modern writers emphasise the release aspect, confounding traditional stereotypes of confinement, curiosity and desire, and substituting 'multiple alternatives' which endorse those unheard, denied, subsumed —and frequently female—voices.

Section 3: Private power

Both 'usurping the male' and 'endorsing the female' involve reassessing, readjusting or undermining existing power relations. The essays in the following sections address the vexed question of power quite explicitly, both in the private or domestic spheres and in terms of public and political life.

Sarah Sceats focuses on the essentially private domain of food and its surrounding activities, drawing upon Foucault and psychoanalytic theory to examine the power relations of appetite, cooking and eating in contemporary women's writing. She suggests that the line between empowerment and enslavement is difficult to draw, particularly where nurturing mothers or mother-types are concerned, and claims that care and nurturing—and indeed neglect—are in any case inseparable from issues of power. She indicates how cooks may be portrayed as infinitely powerful, by reference to one of Angela Carter's more malignant cooks (a point Peter Conradi also makes, in relation to Alice Thomas Ellis), but suggests that, at least in Carter's writing, it is appetite that manifests power most energetically. Insisting on the complexity of the power relations connected with food and eating, however, her analysis draws attention to the paradox that the most powerful and predatory appetites are often the most insatiable, sabotaged by their own internal dynamic of loss and nostalgia. Mothers, daughters, carers, cannibals, victims, anorectics and the rest of the world portrayed in the texts discussed all engage in the risky business of constant jockeying for positions of domination, for the blissful satisfactions of eating are all too transient.

Much of the maternal provision, cooking, feeding and nurturing that Sceats discusses involves thinly-veiled attempts at possession and control. Terry Phillips engages with something of the same power/love conflict when she investigates May Sinclair's portraits of mothers emulating Woolf's (and Patmore's) figure of the 'Angel in the House'. Her discussion is illuminated by Nancy Chodorow's analysis of the enduring significance of the pre-oedipal and oedipal mother/daughter bond, a bond whose immeasurable significance is evident in so much women's writing, and explicit in the early novels of Michèle Roberts, touched upon in Sarah Sceats's chapter.

Phillips draws attention to contradictions between male idealisations of motherhood and the 'lived experience' of mothers and daughters portrayed by Sinclair, and highlights some of the contradictions inherent in the Angel-mother's position, for example the impossibility of realising women's sexuality when it is simultaneously unacceptable and necessary to fulfil the maternal role. Above all, she suggests, the desire for power is problematic in this social set-up. It must, like sexuality, be masked, because inappropriate for the Angel, and thus takes highly manipulative forms (cf Julia Hallam's depiction of the nurse, another 'Angel' figure). Since women's power at the time in which Sinclair's novels are set can only be exerted in the private sphere, it is largely visited upon daughters, so perpetuating the stresses and contradictions of the mother's experience.

Mothers are, of course, archetypally powerful figures, and consequently loom large in private spaces. But sexual relationships, and particularly heterosexual ones, undoubtedly take up more textual space, particularly so in popular fiction. Philippa Gregory makes a bold leap to compare the literary and especially the moral conventions of contemporary popular, commercially successful novels with those of eighteenth-century fiction, finding, disturbingly, that despite huge changes in terms of independence—political, economic, sexual—women are still shown as desirable *because* of their feminine vulnerability. Depictions of employment in contemporary bestsellers are, she says, sketchy, and suggest no real satisfactions. Even in the case of supposedly powerful heroines the women are generally shown as either dependent or the beneficiaries of inherited power or even as failures.

Women, in short, are portrayed not as producers but as consumers. They also enjoy—or endure—sex, though Gregory makes the point that liberation breeds no equality here either, both because of the depicted emotional inadequacies of men (which compares neatly to the double standards of the uncommitted eighteenth-century hero) and because of the deviant and frequently harmful sexual abuse to which women are subjected. This contrasts with the view put forward by Merja Makinen of the practices of sado-masochism (and especially lesbian sado-masochism) as consensual, egalitarian and safe. The excess of women's distress in current popular fiction, suggests Gregory, is in a direct line of descent from the eighteenth-century morality tale, where adventure is portrayed as dangerous and painful for women and in which saint-like suffering transforms the erring hero and ensures his subsequent protection of the heroine.

What is surprising, says Gregory, is the persistence of these conventions of female powerlessness, vulnerability, and suffering. Women, it seems, now as in the eighteenth century, are punished in fiction for transgressing the boundaries of private spheres, occupying 'male' spaces or challenging the discourses of power.

One alternative to such problems is simply not to engage with 'male' discourses or invade their cherished spaces at all, and this is one of the claims that Peter Conradi makes for Alice Thomas Ellis. Drawing attention to the wit, commonsense and self-sufficiency of her heroines, he suggests a relation of some sort to feminism, if only for her systematic mockery and denigration of men. He insists (as she does), however, on her being an 'outsider': opposed to the value currently accorded to sex, unashamedly old-fashioned in her Catholicism, a fervent non-joiner, resisting what she sees as the doctrine or dogma of feminists and the '*bien pensant*'. Most importantly, he identifies what he describes as a 'cult of self-sufficiency' in her writing, the evocation of a pragmatic though fanciful 'woman's realm' that celebrates its own lack of masculinity.

Conradi points out the dangers of this approach. What is in effect a withdrawal from engagement with a large part of the world promotes a sterile view of sexual love, and encourages a concomitant pessimism that verges on despair. At the same time, however, Ellis can be very funny, particularly about men, and about the absurdities of sexual behaviour and what one of her characters memorably calls 'lerve'. Her view of sex diverges not a little from those discussed by Merja Makinen and Philippa Gregory. A consequence or concomitant feature of self-elected distance from the 'male realm' is increased emphasis on the domestic world, on the mother-child bond and the caring and nurturing roles traditionally assigned to women. Here Conradi's chapter interconnects with several others, most notably with Sarah Sceats's on food, as he focuses on Ellis's witty evocation of the power of cooks; her attitude to mothering is also interesting to read in conjunction with Terry Phillips's chapter on mothers in the work of May Sinclair.

Section 4: Public power

A collection that focuses on women's writing is bound to reflect recurring preoccupations with motherhood, and it is significant that the first chapter of our 'Public power' section should also begin with the effect of the 'public' on this most personal of areas. Trudi Tate uses as her starting point the fact that HD believed the stillbirth of her child in 1915 to have been caused by 'shell shock' or war neurosis—not in the form of direct violence, but because of the brutally related news of the loss of the *Lusitania*. In effect, says Tate, HD attributes the loss of her child to a story, a dramatic claim for the power of narrative that may be seen to reverberate through this collection, with powerful implications for the reciprocal relationship between fiction and the world. The instructive aspect of pony books or nursing stories, or the more questionable sexual dynamics detailed by Philippa Gregory offer only the most overt examples of textual persuasion; every chapter has as its subtext the effect of the fiction discussed, though none makes so dramatic a claim as the work of HD.

HD's fiction, according to Tate, is concerned with damage caused particularly to civilians in the war, and she cites Belgium, Edith Cavell and the loss of the *Lusitania* as three incidents specifically framed as violated 'femininity' for propaganda purposes, so as to work on the imagination, in the same way as fiction does. The 'imaginary' effects of war are thus a highly important factor. But Tate rejects a simple gender/violence parallel, for this, she says, denies the specific *historical* experience of war. Nor, she says, is this '*women's* experience', since there is no such thing as a common experience to women, and anyway men were similarly damaged.

The important question, she stresses, is how gender is constituted in relation to war. The problem for both men and women is that of being a witness, and how this inter-acts with gender. There is, perhaps, an unusual equality here, inasmuch as men and women are *both* seen as non-combatant, rather than being polarised once again into 'doing' and 'done to'. But the character Julia, in *Bid Me to Live*, shifts the balance, seeing her maternal suffering as comparable to or even worse than men's. Contrary to popular conceptions, men's sufferings from the war are shown as not indescribable; the unrepresentable horror is rather that of women. *Bid Me to Live* 'problematises' just this, says Tate: who, precisely, are the victims and who the victimisers? This question, too, resonates through the chapters of this volume.

Tate suggests that war, as 'experience and discourse, *interpellates* women and men differently, constructing them differently as gendered subjects', and perhaps this is true of violence generally, of history and of public life. Julian Cowley's study of Janette Turner Hospital focuses on a similar area and the central questions: in what sense is culture and history shared, what is inheritance and how in a postmodern world is authority established and preserved? He says that Turner Hospital opposes storytelling and 'talk' to the monologic, authoritative discourses of (generally male) power voiced by specialists, professors, priests and the like; where patriarchal author-ity speaks in monologue, Turner Hospital's women, says Cowley, seek situations that allow meaningful exchange through the reciprocity of dialogue.

The detachment that comes with monologic authority may be seen to underpin acts of violence proceeding from lack of mutual understanding or recognition (cf. the chapters by Elisabeth Mahoney, Philippa Gregory, Trudi Tate and others), and women's discourse is presented by Turner Hospital as a kind of antidote to this. In a postmodern world in which specificity has given way to uncertainty, says Cowley, the need to recover human contact assumes a 'moral urgency'. Turner Hospital offers storytelling as a way of locating the self in the present by grasping the past through narrative—and there is a need for versions of the past 'responsible to the present'.

On the assumption that it is the telling of historical events that gives them mean-ing (and again this intersects with Trudi Tate's argument), Turner Hospital interrogates key narratives of patriarchal society that tacitly sanction violence. In par-ticular, the critical distance of colonisers is seen as voyeuristic, controlling and sadistic, just as photographs limit and falsify without the dynamic of narrative or talk to provide meaning. The Australian frontier-woman represents the need to cross conceptual and narrative boundaries, and the combination of her transgressive nature and the Scheherazade model emphasises the transactional capacity of narrative to promote change.

The combination of breaking down fixed meanings and categories, the search for ways of telling that incorporate hidden or unheard voices, and the acknowledgement of changing responsibilities is highly reminiscent of John Mepham's observations about Doris Lessing, and connects, too, with the final chapter by Elizabeth Maslen. More apposite to Anne Marie Fyfe's survey of Irish women writers is the conception of exclusive patriarchal and traditional narratives, in this case constructing a literary tradition or canon that includes women only as images and figureheads, not as authors. The potency of images of women, she suggests, is in inverse ratio to their degree of power in a society, and in this case is responsible for a relative dearth of women writers and for the marginalisation or even suppression of much of what they do write.

Tracing the place of Irish women writers from Maria Edgeworth to the present, Fyfe identifies a cultural equation of womanhood with nationality which reduces women to mere abstractions, thus neatly avoiding the need for recognition of gender realities. Women's identities are subsumed within a rhetoric of nationalism, with the consequence, amongst others, of the rejection of a substantial strand of 'Anglo-Irish' women's writing. Women's voices, claims Fyfe, have been silenced by state and church, particularly by the Censorship Board. She also cites women's lack of educational opportunities as a possible explanation for their failure to explore experimental modes (as exemplified above all in the work of Irish male writers such as Joyce, Beckett, Flann O'Brien).

Fyfe's essential point is that alternative views (diverging from largely male-dictated, culturally sanctioned, religiously or politically inspired agendas) have been given little space, and that only recently have alternative versions of the past been able to be accommodated. In an interesting parallel with Julian Cowley's concept of Australian women writers as doubly marginalised, she observes that the renaissance of writing in Northern Ireland is almost entirely male, and suggests a direct parallel in the failure of Northern Ireland to develop a women's movement.

Irish women's writing is, understandably, a critically neglected area: banning, repression, puritanism, small-mindedness, and the use of women as images having taken their toll. Irish women writers are, it seems, only slowly untangling themselves from these traditional constraints and structures, and are beginning to search for 'new language and new forms to represent [Irish] women's experience'. This survey, putting together a history of relatively little-heard voices, itself provides an alternative to the canonical 'patriarchal narratives' of nationalism and literary tradition.

In the final chapter of this volume the opening themes of political commitment and responsibility in women's writing, always running as an undercurrent through the collection, are reinforced as central concerns of the intellectual, as Elizabeth Maslen considers the ways in which women writers of the late 1920s and 1930s engaged with contemporary history.

Touching on debates about what women's writing is, or 'ought' to be, and citing attacks by feminists on realism, Maslen adopts an essentially pluralist line. Like a Doris Lessing heroine she avoids clinging rigidly to fixed meanings and categories; noting that 'realism' may refer either to storyline or narrative mode, she makes the claim that realism itself is perfectly capable of accommodating undercurrents in a changing society, and comments tartly that 'it is the definition of the term that needs continual revision, if it is to keep pace with what is acceptable as the reality of any period's modernity'.

The point is specifically about form, but it is closely related to John Mepham's argument about truth-telling, Julian Cowley's and others' about change and definitions, and Trudi Tate's about the importance of recognising both genders, as against seeing women as gendered and men as simply 'human'. This is partly a question of balance, but crucially concerns a willingness to retain flexibility and openness in the face of change and difficulty.

Maslen's examination of 1930s women writers focuses on the realities they portray and the use of a varied and dynamic realism. Though most of the writers she discusses are committed to parties of the Left, they offer very different views of socialism and of feminism, echoed in the fierce debates about narrative mode, realism being seen by some as essentially conservative. Maslen argues in relation to these texts, however, that in many cases realism embraces fantasy and intertextuality, especially in the employment of outcast women from the past. Here again timelessness, or imaginative leaps in time, can make illuminating connections between one age and another.

The difficulties of engaging with history—past and present—are not merely formal, however, and the novels discussed break political ground and political silence. They do not gloss over the pressures and difficulties for politically engaged women (and in at least one case men), especially in conflicts between their 'public' lives and their capacity as 'private individuals'. The diversity in form reflects political diversity, not just between movements but within them, and personal diversity, between individuals and within each person. Few people 'fit in' exactly, whether with socialism or feminism or conservatism, and Maslen draws attention to the revealing conflicts and confusions of personal engagement with the public world in these novels.

Her final point about form will certainly ring bells with the acknowledged aims of popular fiction: realism is also used to lure readers. For writers with a political or moral agenda—if not all writers—this must surely represent an important consideration; after all, how do you begin to convince people if they don't read you? Having said this, however, Maslen does not overlook other modes, mentioning in particular the dystopias of Storm Jameson and Katherine Burdekin, thus reinscribing by example the practice of pluralism.

Conclusion

Having introduced the collection, and indicated some of the interconnecting threads, themes and preoccupations which link the chapters and sections, we want finally to switch direction and celebrate the differences of subject, approach, perspective, voice, narrative. The point we made at the very beginning of this introduction about its eclecticism is, we believe, borne out in its very subject matter. Not only do the contributors interrogate and go beyond various cultural and critical orthodoxies, but they insist upon the concern in many women's writing, in diverse genres, to endorse pluralism and the need to give space and ear to a multiplicity of voices and perspectives not of the mainstream. Such, indeed, is the guiding principle of this volume.

1 Usurping the male

1 The intellectual as heroine: reading and gender

John Mepham

I have two themes. The first is the representation of the intellectual in women's fiction, and as my main example I will take Anna Wulf in Doris Lessing's *The Golden Notebook*. My second theme is 'gender-blind' reading, when the reader unself-consciously accepts the world as it is experienced by a fictional character, and to that extent identifies with that character, regardless of gender.

The kind of intellectual I have in mind is one who takes upon him or herself responsibility for questioning and producing social meanings, values and projects. Because the figure of 'the intellectual' is so central to everything I have to say, I begin with a lengthy quotation, in which Edward Shils proposes a definition which fills out and begins to make richer and more precise what is involved in being an intellectual in this sense:

> In every society . . . there are some persons with an unusual sensitivity to the sacred, an uncommon reflectiveness about the nature of their universe, and the rules which govern their society . . . [who are] enquiring, and desirous of being in frequent communion with symbols which are more general than the immediate concrete situations of everyday life, and remote in their reference in both time and space. In this minority, there is a need to externalise the quest in oral and written discourse, in poetic or plastic expression, in historical reminiscence or writing, in ritual performance and acts of worship. This interior need to penetrate beyond the screen of immediate concrete experience marks the existence of the intellectuals in every society.[1]

It is in discussing Virginia Woolf as an intellectual that Edward Said cited this passage, in his Reith Lectures on representations of the intellectual, and certainly both Woolf and some of her characters were intellectuals as they are conceived here. The intellectual as heroine is central to many of her works, both fiction and non-fiction.

I will spell out in more detail the idea of the intellectual, emphasising the importance of *responsibility*, for this is the central concept for the heroine of *The Golden*

Notebook. The intellectual's role might include: the responsibility to encourage people to live with an eye to more than their own narrow interests and pleasures, to live for something larger than themselves; the responsibility to name, refine, revitalise those values in attachment to which we make our lives transcend the narrowness of self-interest, values of equality, democracy and freedom; the responsibility to contribute to the process of political dreaming, which means the formulation through political imagination of aspirations and projects for alternative futures; and, underlying all these, the responsibility of truth-telling, of 'naming', of finding vocabularies and creating perspectives through which hidden or unspoken things can be voiced.

Other women writers who have, in their own lives or through their characters, created images of the intellectual as heroine, and who have thereby played an important part in the lives of their readers, are Simone de Beauvoir and Christa Wolf. One thing that all these authors have in common is that, in creating intellectuals as heroines, they offer to their readers models of alternative versions of self. This is why they have such a profound impact, for they raise questions of self-definition. They identify and clarify possibilities of self in which readers may recognise images of who they might be. They all also explore questions of gender, specifically the question of what it is or might be to be a woman. It is this combination of seriousness about issues of social and political value, and about the projection of alternative futures, with their opening up of visions of possible lives for women, that has given their work its particular cultural place and which lies behind the unusually intense relationship they have with their readers. They make possible an intimate and highly valued relationship between reading and the achievement of self-definition. It is very striking, for example, how many women readers of Woolf have testified that over and above any academic and aesthetic interest she may have had, she has seemed also to offer something else, something crucial to the shape of their lives. For example, Sara Ruddick writes that 'Virginia Woolf was the personal, direct agent of change in my life; it was she who freed me from dependence on men's judgment, who made women real for me, who helped me recover my own mind, eyes, and voice'.[2] It is significant in connection with my themes here that what reading Woolf made possible for her was a life not only as a scholar but also precisely as a politically or socially responsible intellectual.

For another example, we can look at Elizabeth Wilson's comments on what reading Simone de Beauvoir and Doris Lessing meant to her in the 1960s. She says that 'in the strange cultural landscape of 1960 they loomed up, Cassandras of women's experience, an experience that was everywhere silenced, concealed and denied'. They were heroine-authors with whom she could then, as a young woman, identify 'as heroines and alternative selves'.[3] She quotes Margaret Walters, writing in 1976:

> When I first read *The Second Sex*—about fifteen years ago, before the present
> women's movement—it struck me with the force of a genuine revelation. It helped
> me make some sense of my confused and isolated depression. Since the book
> appeared in 1949, de Beauvoir has received thousands of letters from women all
> over the world, grateful for the way her book helped them to see their personal
> frustrations in terms of the general condition of women.

These comments highlight the connection I want to emphasise between reading and the reader's quest for self-definition, a connection forged by the writer's illumination of what it is to be a woman.

The Golden Notebook played this same cultural role. Michèle Roberts is quoted as saying that it was 'the book that every feminist woman kept on her bedside table' (*The Guardian*, 25 July 1994). It made available unprecedented descriptions not only of women's sexuality and erotic dependency but also of the life of the political intellectual. Jean McCrindle's account of her reading of it confirms this: the book appealed because of its 'detailed descriptions of things which I had never seen written down before'.[4] Its appeal was its truth-telling (its 'naming', finding the right names for things, as Anna Wulf herself calls it) about being a woman: '. . . no one before *The Golden Notebook* had so accurately captured the different moods and ambiguity of women's sexual feelings'.[5] Moreover, the book's treatment of the relations between men and women, its precise depictions of ambivalence, of instability of feeling, of all the contradictions and deceptions of feeling and language that were so accurate to that historical and cultural moment of England in the 1950s, gave voice to things which otherwise left women feeling alone and going mad by themselves. Reading the novel sparked recognition and identification: '. . . I certainly didn't read *The Golden Notebook* as a rarefied literary text. I read books as a way of finding out about the world and who I was and where we stood in the world and what love and emotions were all about'.[6] It is not uncommon, I suppose, for young readers of either sex to ask themselves as they read, as does Doris Lessing's character Martha Quest, 'What has this got to do with me?' and to wish 'for books which might explain this confusion of violent feeling she found in herself'.[7] But perhaps there is something more involved. The heroine figures I am talking about are not just fantasy figures. They also suggest a world view, a language and way of looking at things, which helps to make sense of the reader's experience both in general and in gendered terms. Areas of experience previously unspoken and unrepresented find, through the voice of the heroine, author or character, a way into language and become a common cultural and psychological resource. The enrichment is a collective one of vocabulary, images and narratives which articulate and illuminate women's experiences, choices and aspirations. In doing this they not only provide images in which the reader can recognise a possible version of herself (an alternative self), but also provide a framework of meaning in terms of which that self can be understood culturally and historically.

The most familiar statement of this potential of literature is Virginia Woolf's discussion of the possible future of women's fiction in *A Room of One's Own*. In Woolf's metaphor, fiction can shine a light into the dark cavern of women's friendships and women's work:

> [if the woman author] knows how to express it she will light a torch in that vast chamber where nobody has yet been. It is all half lights and profound shadows like those serpentine caves where one goes with a candle peering up and down, not knowing where one is stepping . . . That is a sight that has never been seen since the world began . . .[8]

When light is thrown into the dark chamber, it illuminates questions of ultimate value which are also questions of politics: what is it that makes life worth living, what possible futures are there and what obstacles stand in the way of their being realised? Implicitly or explicitly, the heroines give voice to projects of emancipation and not just dreams of individual desire.

At this point I want to focus on the idea of 'identification', which seems to be crucial to how these works that I have in mind are read. What if the gendered reader of these women's writings is a man, and he too enjoys a sense of recognition and self-clarification? My approach to this will be a detour via a discussion of the opposite case, as discussed by Kate Soper in her subtle and intriguing essay 'Stephen Heroine', which is about her own identification, in reading *Ulysses*, with the young intellectual Stephen Dedalus.[9] This young man is of crucial interest in the context of my argument because he first appears in *Portrait of the Artist as a Young Man*, which was, says Seamus Deane, 'the first novel in the English language in which a passion for thinking is fully presented'.[10] For Stephen, he goes on, 'thinking is a mode of experiencing the world'. In this Stephen stands, as far as the English novel is concerned, at the beginning of a line of affiliation which will run to those intellectual authors and heroines, Woolf and Lessing and their creations. These two, the evidence suggests, were both conscious of fretting in the shadow of Joyce's portrait of Stephen. They were both interested in the specific conditions of life of women intellectuals as compared to those of the comically arrogant and bad tempered young man Dedalus, and it would be interesting to contrast him in this respect with, say, the fictional author Mary Carmichael of *A Room of One's Own* or Rose Pargiter in *The Years*. Stephen is in a tradition of intellectuals for whom selfhood seems to be incompatible with relationship, and he grows to selfhood by putting up barriers between himself and family, nation and Church, and eventually by cutting links and choosing exile. He must develop, says Said, 'a resistant intellectual consciousness before he can become an artist'.[11] His quest for the conditions in which he can be an intellectual is a quest for freedom, just as, of course, are those of Anna Wulf (with whom I will contrast Stephen below) and Simone de Beauvoir.

It is the figure of Stephen Dedalus as he appears in *Ulysses* that is at the centre of Kate Soper's argument, and her focus is on her sense of identification with him. In reading the novel she feels close to his consciousness and sensibility, his way of perceiving the world. 'There is,' she says, 'no female character in modernist fiction with whom I feel the empathy I do with Stephen.'[12] But this identification works only within limits.

Her observation is, to put it somewhat in my own words, that in reading there is a tension between the version of the reader's self which identifies with the protagonist (or protagonists, since she feels at ease also in the world as lived by Leopold Bloom) and the version of the reader's self which is gendered, and active in the gendered world of her everyday life. These two selves come most clearly into conflict at certain moments when she cannot sustain her gender-blind identification with the male hero's manner of making meanings. In particular, there are those moments when she is reminded that in the world of these heroes women are always perceived externally, as being of the opposite sex. Women's legs and women's clothing are perceived erotically, and the words used in designating them are pungent with erotic charge, in ways that are quite at odds with the perceptions and the language of the heterosexual woman reader. The words *flower*, *drawers*, *naughty*, *stocking* and so on are Bloom's words before they are hers, and at those moments when fictional heroes most force-fully place women apart as objects of their erotic gaze, of erotic fascination and desire, at those moments she recoils and cannot sustain her habit of identification, of unselfconsciously sharing the protagonists' meanings.

Her capacity to fall comfortably into sharing Stephen's meanings (and Joyce's and Bloom's) does not, she points out, derive from their being feminine men, for to say this would be to arbitrarily accept a distinction between feminine and masculine qualities which the experience of reading and of identification is there to challenge. As a reader, Kate Soper says, 'I forget I have a sex', and this experience reminds us precisely of the ways in which we do, at least potentially, as a real possibility, share experiences and meanings across gender lines. A celebrated passage in *Portrait of the Artist as a Young Man* tells of Stephen's ambiguous relation to the English language, that it is both the language in which he lives and writes and yet also one from which he feels to some degree excluded. As he speaks with his English Dean of Studies he reflects:

> The language in which we are speaking is his before it is mine. How different are the words *home*, *Christ*, *ale*, *master* on his lips and on mine! I cannot speak or write these words without unrest of spirit. His language, so familiar and so foreign, will always be for me an acquired speech. I have not made or accepted its words. My voice holds them at bay. My soul frets in the shadow of his language.[13]

This is, no doubt, such a celebrated and much quoted passage because the ex-perience to which it gives voice is one with which so many readers, especially intellectuals proud of their linguistic autonomy, can identify, and it is one which falls squarely within the terms of Kate Soper's remark that 'there is a considerable range of sensibility or critical response to the world which it is mistaken to categorise in gender terms'.[14] If she can identify with Stephen's experience of simultaneously living in and yet being exiled from his language, this is neither because he is feminine nor that she is Irish (which she is not), but because of the fact that for all of us our language can seem to belong to somebody else, that in relation to language we are all to one degree or another outsiders, impotent and out of control.

The experience of reading *Ulysses* is therefore an experience of 'bi-location', of being both enfolded within a male protagonist's perspective and also exiled from it, of sustaining both a self forgetful of its sexuality and one for which its sexuality is central. The 'unreflective reading self which lies outside the space of gender apper-ception'[15] is the self, or the version of self, for whom the text offers 'a sustained mirror of' her own subjectivity, for whom the writer is performing the task which I have mentioned above, of articulating meanings in the world which the reader shares, though in her world those meanings remain latent and unvoiced. Thus, in the mode of identification, we both recognise our own experience, or potential experience, but also hear it spoken, articulated perhaps for the first time.

I will now return to my discussion of heroine-intellectuals, and specifically to *The Golden Notebook*. For while Kate Soper identifies more easily with Stephen Dedalus than with any female character in modernist fiction, I myself identify more easily with Anna Wulf than with any male character in post-1950s English fiction. Of course, there are limits to this; there are moments of recoil, or indeed extended

21

passages, when I can no longer unselfconsciously, as a gender-blind reader, enter into this character's world. Obviously, this is most definitively so when it is the character's body and her sexuality that are in focus (or those of her counterpart Ella in the 'Yellow Notebook' sections of the novel), that is, at some of those moments which were especially prized by women readers as being without precedent as truth-telling about women's experience.

As for male characters in *The Golden Notebook*, there is no question of identifying with them at all. Not many men would be willing to see themselves in the appalling Richard. He combines undiluted self-preoccupation with a minimum of self-insight and his obtuseness and his insistence on monopolising power are dangerous and destructive forces for those around him. He is, unlike most real men, an un-complicated personification of patriarchal attitudes. Equally unappealing, though, is his rebellious son Tommy, who is humourless and judgemental and rather pathetic.

Doris Lessing's male characters, and not only in this novel, are rarely appealing. In *The Golden Notebook* there is no narration from a male point of view and the con-sciousness of male characters is only presented indirectly, through dialogue. There is, perhaps, something of a parallel here with *Ulysses*. In that novel there is, of course, a female point of view, in the monologue of Molly Bloom, but as Kate Soper con-vincingly argues, Molly is 'no exception to the absence of the consciousness of the "feminine erotic" in *Ulysses* but rather the culminating confirmation of a presiding masculinity', since 'very little happens to her . . . which is not refracted through the male gaze and orchestrated around the sexual desire of the men in her life'.[16] One might say that whereas we only perceive Molly, even in her own words, as she is seen by men, so we only perceive the men in *The Golden Notebook* as they are heard by women. The view of them that we are offered, even when they speak for themselves, is limited to how they are taken to be in terms of the presiding femininity of the book.

My gender-blind recognition of self in Anna Wulf is centred on her life as a heroine intellectual, working in the room of her own in which she writes her note-books. Whereas Kate Soper's identification with Stephen is anchored in the image of Stephen sitting in a library studying Aristotle or working up a theory about Hamlet, my own identification with Anna is anchored in the image of her alone in her room, the walls papered with newspaper clippings headlining geopolitical events which defeat her capacity for making sense of the world. Daily narratives of Cold War, Stalinism, nuclear weapons and so on add up to global chaos and refuse to shape up into an intelligible narrative of world history on which she could draw in formulating her own intentions or with which she could align her sense of political responsibility. In this Anna's situation by far transcends the particular historical moment of the late 1950s. If I try to define what it is about this figure, about her perceptions of the world and about her own sense of value and aspiration, that appeals to me and seems to mirror a version of my own self, a starting point might be with the formula that she is a truth-teller who finds herself in cultural and political circumstances in which truth-telling seems to be fundamentally obstructed, and that she is an intellectual with a sense of responsibility who is disoriented by a mistrustful attitude to prevailing dis-courses of value and politics. The paradox is that this combination of alternative selves, the truth-teller and the sceptic, the 'legislator' and the liberal, in other words the assertive pluralist, seems to be necessary to the constitution of the writer-intellectual in our time.

Stephen's refusal to serve Church or country leads to his choice of exile. Stephen identifies exile with freedom, yet the reader might legitimately doubt whether he is right to do this, for geographical location does not necessarily remove the forms of unfreedom in the head that are the greatest obstacles to thinking and writing. Anna is already, in a manner of speaking, an exile, or at least she is an outsider, since she was brought up in East Africa and lives in London as an émigré. Anna's decision to exile herself is her decision to leave the Communist Party, and this is equally a cutting-off of self from the habitual source of political and personal meanings. But, unlike Stephen, she does not experience this divorce as liberating, in the sense of making possible the emergence of an authentic self and an autonomous voice. What results is a hopelessly fragmented self, fearful and without autonomous coherence, seeking expression in a variety of different voices, in her different notebooks, none of which she is prepared to trust to publication.

In every sphere her sense of self is undermined and her relationship to language is not just fretful but downright disabled, and this is represented as being a mark of her integrity. Anna is a stammerer. She has to abandon a lecture on the history of art because she finds herself stumbling with doubt and unable to continue. Once again, it is useful to contrast Anna Wulf with Stephen Dedalus. The thing about Stephen that most stands in the way of my identification with him (though this is, of course, not a clear cut, yes or no, matter; I also, like Stephen Dedalus and Kate Soper, have stayed late in the college library reading Aristotle, and Kate Soper has in fact had a highly respected life as a politically active intellectual) is precisely his verbal facility and the self-confidence that is rooted in it. As he walks the beach, phrases flow through his mind. The world becomes word with such easy pleasure. In *Ulysses* Stephen seems to be able effortlessly to transform the seashore into his mannered, over-rich discourse, interweaving perceptions of seaweed with thoughts of mortality:

> Under the upswelling tide he saw the writhing weeds lift languidly and sway
> reluctant arms, hising up their petticoats, in whispering water swaying and
> upturning coy silver fronds. Day by day: night by night: lifted, flooded and let fall.
> Lord, they are weary: and, whispered to, they sigh.[17]

The facility of this generates fascination rather than recognition. I cannot share his trust in metaphor. Nor could Doris Lessing, nor her heroine Anna Wulf. Their rather painstaking observation and plodding prose are slow and cumbersome by comparison. Anna is unwilling to be taken in by metaphor, and is constantly on guard against the power of language to falsify.

But while Anna is obstructed by her mistrustful relationship to her own voices, she remains committed to the values of the political intellectual and to the responsibility that is part of that role, in particular to the commitment to truth-telling. Tommy says to Anna '. . . you said the thing you'd learned from being a communist was that the most terrible thing of all was when political leaders didn't tell the truth. You said that one small lie could spread into a marsh of lies and poison everything.'[18] Anna Wulf continues in the line of her literary near-namesake Virginia (it is surely no accident that her author chose to call her 'Anna Wulf'). She is precisely the woman writer that Woolf, in *A Room of One's Own* and in her essays 'Women and Fiction' and 'Professions for Women', prophesied would, in the next generation, write about women's lives which have

> an anonymous character which is baffling and puzzling in the extreme. For the first time, this dark country is beginning to be explored in fiction; and at the same moment a woman has also to record the changes in women's minds and habits which the opening of the professions has introduced. She has to observe how their lives are ceasing to run underground; she has to discover what new colours and shadows are showing in them now that they are exposed to the outer world.[19]

For, she goes on, the English woman has become 'a voter, a wage-earner, a responsible citizen' and this has 'given her both in her life and in her art a turn towards the impersonal. Her relations now are not only emotional; they are intellectual, they are political.' In 'Professions for Women' Woolf pointed to another area of truth-telling that, she foretold, women's fiction would soon be able to open up, namely, telling the truth about the woman's passions and about her body. This is something that Woolf herself failed in; the obstacles were just too great: '. . . telling the truth about my own experiences as a body, I do not think I solved. I doubt that any woman has solved it yet. The obstacles against her are still immensely powerful and yet they are very difficult to define.'[20] Doris Lessing is one among many women who have met this challenge. *The Golden Notebook* can be read as an inquiry into the obstacles to truth-telling, the forms of unfreedom, both objective and subjective, which stand in the way of truth-telling for the heroine-intellectual, both at that historical moment of 1957, but also more generally, so that we can still see the heroine's predicament as one with which we can identify today.

I see Anna Wulf as the woman writer, installed in her own room, but plagued by her own internalised prohibitions and taboos, restraints and demands, ghosts and phantoms, equivalent to Woolf's 'Angel in the House', the ideal of Victorian femininity, who stood at her shoulder and prevented her from writing freely anything that would weaken a man's ego or offend his respectability. The writer, while seeking a critical perspective on society and culture, is nonetheless its creature, certain to be tormented by inner ghosts (as is Stephen Dedalus by the image of his dead mother), who remind her of ways of thinking, feeling and evaluating the world that cannot be got rid of by going into exile or by shutting oneself in one's own room.

The novel within a novel in *The Golden Notebook*, which is ironically called 'Free Women', concerns the lives of two women who are, in conventional terms, free of the forms of dependency which most obviously impede free intellectual life, namely marriage and lack of financial independence. It poses the problem of the forms of unfreedom of 'free women' and the struggles of the intellectual committed to truth-telling in circumstances in which the conditions for truth-telling cannot be assured. The external obstacles to Anna Wulf's writing have been removed. She has a room of her own and she has an income, enough to live on, from royalties from her successful first novel. What are the obstacles which still block her writing? The impediments to truth-telling, as they show themselves to Anna in her room alone, are both gender-specific and specific to the historical circumstances of her experience, but they also transcend gender and immediate circumstances. We can recognise, in the seductions, ghosts, invasions and taboos to which she is subject in her room, patterns of impediment that plague us all. As a writer she is pressured by the offers of media people, satirised in her black notebook; she is tormented by the pressure to conform to dishonest and deceptive political discourses, a pressure which can be experienced ironically as political conscience or solidarity. More subtly, she wrestles with the problem of literary form, for example, the way in which her novel about her experience in Africa, by conforming to conventional models, lays down a false patina of nostalgia upon the story. More generally, she suspects that writing has a self-dramatising and falsifying effect so that even her diary entries read falsely: 'I keep trying to write the truth and realising it's not true' (GN 272). The only way in which she can hope that a meaningful pattern will emerge in what she writes is by separating off the various parts of her life from each other into the different notebooks, and yet that very division is itself falsifying. If, instead, she wrote everything in one book, no significant pattern of connections and relationships would show up at all and she would be left with chaos. So is her problem fear and cowardice, in that she cannot tolerate the chaos that an honest account of her life would reveal?

It is when her friend's son Tommy invades her room and reads her notebooks that she is forced to try to state more precisely for herself just what it is that impedes her writing. Tommy plays the part of the Angel in the room: his presence helps her to see more clearly the nature of the fear and shame that impede her writing. She cannot bear the thought of him reading about her sexual experience, and she cannot tolerate his reading about those moments when she loses control and flips temporarily into despair or even madness. She hates to expose to him the image of herself as out of control.

Tommy taunts her with her fearfulness, her unwillingness to take the risk of self-exposure. But even more damagingly, Tommy takes offence because she will not do what he wants her to do: he demands that she take responsibility for his life precisely by writing as a traditional intellectual, setting herself up, in Shelley's words, as an 'unacknowledged legislator' for the world, defining values for him, making choices for him, resolving the moral ambiguities of the world for him. It is her feeling of incapacity to take on this role that most torments her, especially after Tommy, unbalanced by uncertainty, tries to kill himself:

> During the last months she had been haunted by the memory of Tommy standing over her notebooks, turning page after page, on the evening he had tried to kill himself. She had made few entries recently; and then with effort. She felt as if the boy, his hot dark eyes accusing, stood at her elbow. She felt that her room was no longer her own. (GN 373)

The most paralysing obstacle to free thought for Anna is the fear of admitting political failure, and the fear of the chaos of mind that will result from that admission:

> Why do our lot never admit failure? Never. It might be better for us if we did. And it's not only love and men. Why can't we say something like this—we are people, because of the accident of how we were situated in history, who were so powerfully part—but only in our imaginations, and that's the point—of the great dream, that now we have to admit that the great dream has faded and the truth is something else—that we'll never be any use. (GN 70)

In the 1960s, Jean McCrindle remembers, one particular part played by this novel was that of allowing, while fighting against, pessimism, of articulating doubt while avoiding despair:

> Now Doris Lessing dared have her characters say in *The Golden Notebook* what none of us dared say out loud—that it might have been futile after all, that the socialist dream had become too corrupted by the experience of the twentieth century to survive it. 'For our time at least a dream would be dead.' . . . I think Doris Lessing somehow allowed me the possibility of pessimism—allowed the possibility of failure and still surviving, because you could emerge somehow with a kind of bedrock of truth. So, for me, her pessimism was a kind of renewal of politics, that they could be more open and honest.[21]

This figure of pessimism and failure offers to the intellectual a model of self with which to identify, as one version of self, one way of relating to one's own categories and meanings. It is necessary to be able to view one's own meanings with detachment or even scepticism, and to be able to allow other voices, other ways of deploying meanings in the world, a tolerant trial. Categories, and this is of course true of gender categories, are socially constructed (though my soul frets in the shadow of that metaphor). It is a paradoxical condition of truth-telling that though we have to use 'constructed' categories, we also have to overcome great resistance to changing them. Lessing's metaphor of the breaking down of barriers between our different selves and voices, which is a prerequisite of intellectual honesty, hints at the stratagems we use to protect our categories from change and to preserve their comforting simplicity, by compartmentalising our experience. Anna says to Molly:

> '. . . it occurred to me—if we lead what is known as free lives, that is, lives like men, why shouldn't we use the same language?'
> 'Because we aren't the same. That is the point.'
> Anna laughed. 'Men. Women. Bound. Free. Good. Bad. Yes. No. Capitalism. Socialism. Sex. Love . . . ' (*GN* 63)

This is, says Doris Lessing in her 1971 'Preface' to the novel, a statement of the central theme or essence of the book. Lessing's view is that we must overcome the fear of chaos that holds our categories too firmly within their various separated places, the fear that without fixed meanings truth-telling and moral evaluation will be impossible and thereby the whole edifice of moral responsibility and meaningful political aspiration would be swept away.

Writers in their own rooms are of different genders and, living in different historical and cultural circumstances, share their rooms with historically specific Angels. Yet, as I have been arguing in agreement with Kate Soper, there can be recognition between reader and character across historical distance and gender boundaries. Just as one does not need to be Irish or a man in order to feel at home in the world of Stephen Dedalus, so one need not be a communist nor a woman to recognise one's anxieties and possibilities in Anna Wulf. That fear of chaos which plagues Anna Wulf is not gender-specific and the difficulty in admitting failure is something common to many generations of progressive writers. It was not only the communists of

1956 who suffered the realisation that they needed to give up their traditions and habits of thought and feeling.

Nonetheless, the figure of the intellectual heroine needs to be constantly re-written, recreated for new readers in new times. In Doris Lessing's career we find that she has invented a whole series of new images of the writer and intellectual as a challenge to our perceptions of ourselves and as ways of testing the limits of our self-definitions. Different Angels inhabit her heroines' rooms and the burdens of responsibility take different shapes. With her most recent version, the heroine of *The Diaries of Jane Somers*, Lessing has altogether emigrated from the tradition of the political intellectual as we found it not only in *The Golden Notebook* but also in *The Children of Violence* series and in later novels such as *The Memoirs of a Survivor*. Jane Somers, editor of a women's fashion magazine, author of popular romance fiction, was the first of Lessing's heroines written, in a manner of speaking, 'irresponsibly'. Lessing wrote in her 'Preface' to these novels that 'Jane Somers knew nothing about a kind of dryness, like a conscience, that monitors Doris Lessing whatever she writes and in whatever style'[22]. This 'conscience' has been the politicised Angel who has stood at Lessing's shoulder in her room, ensuring that she and her heroines conformed to a certain definition of responsibility. One wonders whether Lessing has killed her Angel, or merely tricked her, by writing under another name, into looking temporarily the other way. In either case, Jane Somers, for all her lack of interest in politics, is a heroine who, like Martha Quest and Anna Wulf before her, insists on forcing us to focus on questions of ultimate value: what is it that makes life worth living and what are our responsibilities towards each other? In whatever mould, this is what the heroine-intellectual is for.

I would like to thank Kate Jones, Jean McCrindle and Kate Soper for the help they have given me in the preparation of this essay.

NOTES

1. Cited in Edward Said, *Representations of the Intellectual: The 1993 Reith Lectures*, London, Vintage 1994, p. 26.
2. Sara Ruddick, 'New combinations: learning from Virginia Woolf', in C. Ascher, L. De Salvo and S. Ruddick (eds) *Between Women: Biographers, Novelists, Critics, Teachers and Artists Write about their Work on Women*, Boston, Mass., Beacon Press 1984, p. 138.
3. Elizabeth Wilson, 'Yesterday's heroines: on rereading Lessing and de Beauvoir', in Jenny Taylor (ed.) *Notebooks/Memoirs/Archives: Reading and Rereading Doris Lessing*, London, Routledge and Kegan Paul 1982, pp. 57, 70.
4. Jean McCrindle, 'Reading *The Golden Notebook* in 1962', in Taylor (ed.) *Notebooks/Memoirs/Archives*, p. 43.
5. Ibid., p. 51.
6. Ibid., p. 49.
7. Doris Lessing, *Martha Quest*, London, Paladin 1990, p. 79.
8. Virginia Woolf, *A Room of One's Own*, Harmondsworth, Penguin 1945, pp. 83–4.
9. Kate Soper, 'Stephen Heroine', in *Troubled Pleasures: Writings on Politics, Gender and Hedonism*, London, Verso 1990.
10. Cited in Said, *Representations of the Intellectual*, p. 12.
11. Said, *Representations of the Intellectual*, p. 13.

12. Soper, 'Stephen Heroine', p. 250.
13. James Joyce, *A Portrait of the Artist as a Young Man*, New York, Viking 1969, p. 189.
14. Soper, 'Stephen Heroine', p. 253.
15. Ibid., p. 250.
16. Ibid., p. 261.
17. James Joyce, *Ulysses*, New York, Vintage 1961, p. 49.
18. Doris Lessing, *The Golden Notebook*, St Albans, Granada 1973, p. 58. Subsequent page references will be cited parenthetically in the text with the abbreviation *GN*.
19. Virginia Woolf, 'Women and fiction', in *Women and Writing*, London, Women's Press 1979, p. 50.
20. Virginia Woolf, 'Professions for women', in *Women and Writing*, p. 62.
21. McCrindle, 'Reading *The Golden Notebook*', p. 49.
22. Doris Lessing, *The Diaries of Jane Somers*, London, Penguin 1985, p. 6.

2 Writing so to speak: the feminist dystopia

Elisabeth Mahoney

Why . . . not add a supplement to history? calling it, of course, by some inconspicuous name so that women might figure there without impropriety?

Virginia Woolf[1]

We must always keep open a supplementary space for the articulation of cultural knowledges that are adjacent and adjunct but not necessarily accumulative, teleological, or dialectical.

Homi K. Bhabha[2]

A 'supplementary space' where 'women might figure': the space delineated in an ironic fashion by Woolf and positively by Bhabha aptly describes the feminist dystopia, the future fiction set in a 'bad place' for women. In this chapter I will argue that the dystopia offers a potentially radical fictional space in which women can unravel and re-imagine existing power relations. My interest here is in one particular sphere of authority—that gained through control of narrative and articulation—but the formal tension contained by the genre (at a distance from the socio-political real, but always in relation to it) ensures that the dystopia is *always* concerned with the workings of power at different historical moments. When women subvert the generic tradition in feminist 'bad place' narratives, these networks of power can be seen through 'a different lens', as Christa Wolf puts it, one which has gender as its focus.[3]

Two recent feminist dystopias—Margaret Atwood's *The Handmaid's Tale* (1985) and Vlady Kociancich's *The Last Days of William Shakespeare* (1990)—self-consciously foreground relations of gender and power in inherited, established types of discourse, and speculate on ways in which women might begin to challenge such authority. *The Handmaid's Tale* is set in the Republic of Gilead, a right-wing religious regime, occupying the former United States. Women are divided into three groups according to their reproductive potential and class position: wives, econowives and handmaids who act as surrogates for barren women. *The Last Days of*

29

William Shakespeare depicts a 'Campaign for Cultural Reconstruction' in a South American state, focusing in particular on the fanaticism of the politicians who impose a ban on all non-indigenous cultural production. Each novel includes two competing, gendered narratives (narrative authority coded as masculine, silence as feminine) which clash in a power struggle within the fictional space: a masculine spoken or written discourse (the Historical Notes section of *The Handmaid's Tale* and the chapters of Kociancich's text which focus on the prize-winning author, Santiago Bonday) and a feminine, autobiographical text (Offred's story and Renata's letters and diary). Although these cover the same ground and are linked to the same plots, different narratives emerge from these antithetical spaces; this difference is crucially connected to power. While the dominant masculine text is the site of plot detail, history and tradition, the women's narratives occupy a much more tenuous, marginal place. As well as describing the cultural place occupied by the dystopia (as a conventionally popular, non-realist form), I want to suggest that the term 'supplement' can also be used productively in a reading of Offred and Renata's texts; they write in a supplementary representational place from which binary oppositions (such as masculine and feminine, articulation and silence) can be confused and destabilised:

> The supplement is one of these 'undecidables'. In French, as in English, it means both an addition and a substitute. It is something added, extra, superfluous, above and beyond what is already fully present; it is also a replacement for what is absent, missing, lacking, thus required for completion or wholeness.[4]

Derrida argues that it is the in-between status of the supplement—something 'added' and 'what is absent'—that makes it threatening: 'Its slidings slip it out of the simple alternative presence-absence. *That* is the danger.'[5] Thus the power relations between any discourse and its supplements are not fixed but fluid ('slidings'), and this is because the supplement occupies a position beyond interpretation or containment. My reading of these two dystopias will focus on the 'slidings' of power within the texts and, in particular, the site of this battle: narrative authority and control. The struggle which we witness in these texts has, of course, a symbolic value: Offred and Renata's attempts to construct their narratives represent in microcosm feminist projects to uncover neglected women writers and to voice a different perspective from that articulated by the literary and historical canon. Roland Barthes's *The Pleasure of the Text* (1973) offers a strikingly suggestive theoretical and metaphorical parallel to the power struggles represented in these narratives, as it develops gender-specific components (*plaisir* and its supplement *jouissance*) in an erotics of reading. I want to begin by looking at the representatives of control and authority in each text, aligning them with Barthes's notion of *plaisir* or 'pleasure', before moving on to examine the narrative supplements: the women's writing which threatens existing textual order and brings *jouissance* or 'bliss' into the narrative. I conclude with an examination of the clash between these two orders and the uneasy resolution offered by each.

The male protagonists of these dystopias occupy central positions within literary and historical establishments:

> . . . the tall elegant figure, the attentive gray eyes, the pipe held in his hand like a small intellectual torch; the prize-winning writer, Santiago Bonday, or 'The Master' as he is known.[6]

Keynote Speaker: Professor James Darcy Pieixoto, Director, Twentieth and Twenty-First Century Archives, Cambridge University, England.[7]

The 'Master' and the 'Professor' are at one with tradition and culture, part of the academic or literary mainstream: 'prize-winning', 'Director', 'Keynote Speaker'. Pieixoto works with archive material at Cambridge and has 'Darcy' as his second name, while Bonday invents himself in the text as the sensitive artist with his 'tall elegant figure', 'attentive gray eyes' and pipe. Each of these details aligns them both with Barthes's description of the reader/text of *plaisir*, and situates them absolutely within dominant discourses:

> Text of pleasure: the text that contents, fills, grants euphoria; the text that comes from culture and does not break with it, is linked to a *comfortable* practice of reading.[8]

Such texts reaffirm some archaic order; they reinforce values and systems of dominance rather than challenging them. In this definition of the text of pleasure we begin to see that this 'pleasure' includes power: these texts 'fill', '*grant* euphoria' and 'come from culture'. Perhaps unsurprisingly, this power is gender-specific: throughout *The Pleasure of the Text*, Barthes describes a male reader taking 'his pleasure' (*P* 3); both the spectator and the pleasure are delineated as specifically masculine. The trope of 'voyeur' is introduced to describe the reading subject of criticism or commentary, and a voracious reader who skips passages of a text is compared to:

> . . . a spectator in a nightclub who climbs onto the stage and speeds up the dancer's striptease, tearing off her clothing, *but in the same order*, that is: on the one hand respecting and on the other hastening the episodes of the ritual. (*P* 11)

Although Barthes replaces the usual 'I' or 'he' of his text with 'we', so that 'we resemble' this spectator (and become implicated in the violation of the 'tease'), 'we' tear off the dancer's clothes (or perhaps 'unknot' from *dénouement*, which is presumably what 'we' are hastening towards), this 'spectator' is unquestionably male; the female dancer is also *in the same order*, trapped and objectified in ritual. Thus within *The Pleasure of the Text*, the woman is contained by an 'order' of sexual and textual exploitation, and it is this same order that is in place—then contested—in Atwood and Kociancich's texts.

Both Pieixoto and Bonday knowingly occupy a position of mastery and their texts are constructed to *perform* this mastery—of history and literature, but also of the feminine subjects (or objects) of their narratives. This is clearest in Professor Pieixoto's academic paper entitled 'Problems of Authentication . . .' within the Historical Notes coda to *The Handmaid's Tale*. Like the voracious reader of *plaisir* who 'speeds up the dancer's striptease', Pieixoto's text moves obsessively towards a dénouement, a denuding of the handmaid's text. The 'pleasure' of this text is inextricably linked with interpretation, and this act of historical interpretation is an attempt to keep the handmaid and her narrative in 'the same order' of supplementarity or subservience. Pieixoto is concerned only with definition, rationalisation, finding and demonstrating 'proof' or truth, essentially epistemic questions. Much of his paper is taken up with trying to establish the handmaid's identity so that 'we might be well on the way to an explanation of how this document—let me call it that for the sake of brevity—came into being' (*HMT* 315). Pieixoto's performance is driven by a desire for closure, to 'arrange' (314), 'to make some decision' (314), to 'understand' (315), to 'deduce' (323) or 'decipher' (324) the handmaid's tale. His irritation at the text's resistance to this process of interpretation, both in terms of what is said and the way in which it is spoken, is clear: '*we had to go over it several times*, owing to the difficulties posed by accent, obscure referents, and archaisms' (*HMT* 314, emphasis added).

This division also structures Bonday's narrative in *The Last Days of William Shakespeare*:

> I do not answer him as Santiago Bonday, the writer, but as Santiago Bonday, the man.
>
> After a lifetime dedicated to art for art's sake, I feel it unnecessary to justify a body of work translated into more than fifteen languages, which, over the past decades has won every major national literary prize and even the congratulations . . . of our country's Presidents. However, I wish to correct your critic's crude interpretation. (*LD* 95)

In this rare example of first person narration which, as in Pieixoto's paper, appears only within a context of formulaic, clichéd language (epitomised by 'art for art's sake'), 'I' is used to signify the writer's claims to intellectual superiority. As with the sudden change of pronoun in Barthes's text, we should be immediately suspicious; the textual effect is not what we might expect: the use of 'I' actually serves to *de*personalise and distance Bonday's discourse further. The 'I' here is a universal subject, which can transcend all cultural and historical specifics, 'translating' into any language—and one which can unquestioningly assert itself as both the 'writer' and the 'man'. Bonday's main, hyperbolic sentence aligns his 'body of work' with both the literary ('every major national literary prize') and political establishment ('our country's Presidents'), and it is this alliance with dominant discourses which empowers him to state, 'I wish to correct . . .'. Bonday writes in confidence; it is a formal, rhetorical, polished text (thus the use of 'I' is to produce a specific rhetorical, textual effect, marking this text as that of a man of letters).

His status as literary 'master' is performative and self-conscious:

> As happened for a few minutes every day, the contents of his workroom injected Bonday with a dose of literary adrenalin. The armchairs upholstered in soft fragrant leather; the exquisitely bound books that lined the walls; the table piled with the Greek and Latin classics for easy, though always postponed, reference. In his office there was his electric typewriter, half a ream of A4 paper, notebooks full of jottings . . . (*LD*, 7)

Bonday masquerades as artist, surrounding himself with signs of artistry and success. He spends much of his time maintaining what he considers to be an appropriate public image, carrying with him (rather than reading) Dante in winter and Shakespeare in summer: 'Both fitted his image as a man of letters, but above all they helped him to believe in his passion for the classics . . . He didn't often actually read the book' (*LD* 65). However, he is bored by his own success and the ease with which he writes, and this is confirmed by the details of his workroom: the 'few minutes' of enthusiasm each day, the full notebooks, the half-used ream of paper. We rarely see Bonday write anything at all, and it increasingly seems as if his work emerges effortlessly, almost slides from literary tradition itself, rather than from 'The Master'. The attention to sensual and surface detail here reinforces this feeling; the upholstery, binding, lining, books used as accessories foreground material and domestic possessions, rather than the introspection and reflection we might expect and which we come to associate with Renata, the struggling woman writer in Kociancich's text.

Yet this effortlessness is a sign of authority, and in both texts the control of language and utterance is mirrored structurally in the division of the novels: it is in Bonday and Pieixoto's narratives that we find the 'controlling' elements of plot and time foregrounded. For example, in the Historical Notes we get most of our detailed information about the Gileadean regime, and through this Offred's tale is placed in an historical and cultural context. Bonday's narrative details the 'Campaign of Cultural Reconstruction'—both the escalation of power and his involvement in it—in a thinly-disguised future Argentina. This political fanaticism is only obliquely referred to in Renata's diary and letters. It is important that both of these dominant discourses—the 'Master's' and the 'Professor's'—are shown to have survived the 'bad place': Pieixoto's paper is a commentary on the historical past of Gilead, and Bonday returns from exile after the Campaign has been defeated.

However, it is clear from the titles *The Last Days of William Shakespeare* and 'Problems of Authentication' that the power of Bonday and Pieixoto's discourses is challenged by Renata and Offred's antithetical narratives; the masculine texts are threatened with extinction by the supplements. I want to move now to these voices which threaten to dislocate existing textual power relations, or in Barthes's terms from the realm of pleasure which is delineated as masculine, to that of 'bliss' or *jouissance*, which is implicitly feminine. This involves a shift of attention from that which 'grants euphoria' to 'the absolutely new' (*P* 40); from the voyeur/spectator tearing his way towards control of discourse to that which disrupts 'the order' through a relocation; to the women who speak from a different place:

> I knelt to examine the floor, and there it was, in tiny writing, quite fresh it seemed, scratched with a pin or maybe just a fingernail, in the corner where the darkest shadow fell: *Nolite te bastardes carborundorum.* (*HMT* 62)

> . . .this dry husk of a world that closes in and chokes you before you find your real voice. Here we don't mature, we just grow old in darkness and silence . . . It's the flow of a river not its origins that interests me, so I'll never find the fountainhead.(*LD* 96–7)

In these excerpts from Offred and Renata's texts it is immediately clear that we are outside 'master' narratives. Here, a supplementary perspective and voice is articulated and an *idiolect*, the language of the individual subject, replaces the language of the establishment or institution. This 'tiny writing' occupies a tenuous place; it is only 'scratched' skin-deep, almost tattooed 'with a pin' in the darkest corner. The tools for writing, a pin or fingernail, are the antithesis of Bonday's 'exquisite' and 'fragrant' study and his typewriter; the women are writing *primitively*. Despite being hidden in darkness, the feminine voice is under threat before it has spoken from a 'dry' world which 'closes in and chokes' the beginnings of its 'flow'. For the woman whose 'tiny writing' Offred discovers it is already too late: she hanged, choked and silenced herself. In her text, which translates as 'don't let the bastards grind you down', she has, however, managed to appropriate and subvert dominant and oppressive language. Because of where it is written or how it is spoken, the message becomes potentially radicalising. Renata and Offred's texts are written and spoken in the shadows, through 'darkness and silence' and it is their origins in this darkest corner which marks them as texts of 'bliss'.

Barthes associates *jouissance* more with creative or writing *processes*, than with the activity of reading which is aligned with pleasure (we can note here that Bonday and Pieixoto write little or nothing, while Renata and Offred are constantly concerned with issues of narration and pulling their texts together from the dark corners). Barthes also seems to designate 'edges' and 'shadows' as feminine:

> There are those who want a text (an art, a painting) without a shadow ... but this is to want a text without fecundity, without productivity, a sterile text ... The text needs its shadow: this shadow is a bit of ideology, a bit of representation, a bit of subject. (*P* 32)

That this 'shadow' should be both fecund and fragmented in discourse ('a bit of representation') signals it as a space in which a feminine *spectre*, 'a bit of subject', can be located. If we consider for a moment the places in which the feminine texts are written, this link becomes even clearer. The Historical Notes suggest that Offred's tapes may have been recorded in attics or cellars of 'safe houses'; the message in Latin is found closeted in the wardrobe; and some of Renata's letters and diaries are written from the 'red office'. Atwood and Kociancich's protagonists both produce fragmented texts: Offred's account is divided into the speculative 'Night' sections and other chapters dealing with the daily, lived reality of life in Gilead; Renata's narrative is composed of letters to a writer in exile, Emilio Rauch, and private (and again, more speculative) diary entries. While these divisions are not fixed—and indeed they begin to dissolve as the texts progress—the narrating subjects emerging from these texts *are* fragmented. Each narrative posits a feminised idiolect being constructed in the margins, away from the mainstream. The women's narratives are constructed in a safe place, a supplementary cultural space; for Renata this is in the form of letters that will never be sent—'I write you letters which aren't real letters' (*LD* 71)—and for Offred, the 'supplement' is rendered possible by the freedoms of anonymity and the random, spoken word in her autobiographical tape-recordings.

One of the most striking ways in which these feminine texts declare their otherness is by exposing the very moments of their construction:

> I'm all beginnings. Here I am, docile and lazy, into the first lines of a blank notebook . . . I've nothing to say. Perhaps there's no such thing as a writer's destiny and it's all just a pathetic exploration of loneliness, a search for an escape route out of all the confusion and silence.
>
> . . . Good grief, I've actually started the diary. But nothing I do comes out right. This doesn't read like a page in a diary. (*LD* 5, 6)

It isn't a story I'm telling.

It's also a story I'm telling, in my head, as I go along.
. . . I wait. I compose myself. My self is a thing I must now compose, as one
composes a speech. What I must present is a made thing, not something born.
(*HMT* 49, 76)

We see Renata and Offred at the moments of composition, moments which are
screened in the Professor's and Master's narratives: at the 'beginnings', 'blank', with
'nothing to say', exploring, searching through confusion ('It isn't a story . . . It's also
a story . . .'), in *composition*. It is not only the texts but the subject which is in crisis;
the self is seen as other: '*I'm* all beginnings', 'I compose *myself*', 'I call up my memories and see myself' (*LD* 52). Subjectivity is 'composed' in language, in the text,
moving from 'confusion and *silence*' to a *narrative* identity. Offred's statement that
she composes herself 'as one composes a speech' suggests that these compositions are
not only synchronous, but the *same process*; 'language, or the signs of language, or
subjectivity itself are put into process'.[9]

The self-reflexive quality of Offred and Renata's narratives foregrounds both the
act of narration itself—'I've actually started the diary', 'a story I'm telling'—and the
unease experienced in this position. This unease manifests itself in subjects and texts
which are contradictory and unstable; Offred uses the space of her text to wonder
whether or not she is 'telling' a story. Renata's narrative also posits a problematic
relationship between speaker and text and subjectivity. From the beginning of her
text she details obstacles to her writing and, unlike Bonday, has no image of herself as
a writer. As the oppression escalates in the novel, her hold on textuality and subjectivity becomes increasingly precarious: 'I can't find the words to express myself' (*LD*
160), becomes 'I slowly drift further and further away from myself' (*LD* 205). She
even describes the emptiness of her life in a textual analogy: 'It's like a novel without
a plot, a short story without a story' (*LD* 11). Thus writing and narrating in these
texts are inextricably bound up with *being*; rather than using the centripetal discourse
of Pieixoto (interpretation) or Bonday (plot), Renata and Offred attempt to move
through or beyond the text to subjectivity.

Thus far we have seen how the feminine discourses distance themselves from
those described as dominant; they eschew traditions not recognised as their own and
attempt to speak or write another. However, it is particularly through their resistance
to closure and to the interpretative filter of 'plaisir' that these narratives present their
greatest threat:

. . . you'll repeat your name, in nights to come, in your dream of another struggle,
alive and writing in the sun, Renata, tomorrow . . . . (*LD* 230)

Whether this is my end or a new beginning I have no way of knowing: I have given
myself over into the hands of strangers, because it can't be helped.
And so I step up, into the darkness within, or else the light. (*HMT* 307)

The most obvious manifestation of this resistance is the way in which the women's
texts end. Indeed, both refuse to end, referring speculatively to the post-narrative;
Offred and Renata 'step up' and out of the narrative, to the unknown, to 'strangers',
a dream, 'tomorrow . . .'. The openness of these final sentences, epitomised by the
classic antitheses in Offred's text and the obscurity of meaning at the end, coupled

35

with the possibility that this is in fact 'a new beginning', radicalise the women's narratives. These endings can be compared to Pieixoto's and Bonday's texts, which end, respectively, with 'Any Questions?' and 'The Master' back at the top of the literary establishment, literally back where we started. Renata and Offred's narratives resist any dénouement, and thus they are not allowed to have the final word (they are not 'the end' of either novel); as we shall see in a moment, the dominant discourse asserts itself and attempts to fill in, to speak/write the ending.

However, it is not only the endings which work against closure; the women's texts as a whole are non-linear, at once self-conscious of narrativity and at the same time denying and disrupting narrative. As we have seen, they refuse to give the reader an ending; we, with Offred, 'have no way of knowing', not just at the end but throughout the text. These discourses foreground reconstruction, layering, 'flashback', spoken or written by an anonymous narrator: 'It didn't happen that way either. I'm not sure how it happened; not exactly. All I can hope for is a reconstruction . . . ' (*HMT* 275). Narrative works here as 'a frame, the arrangement of shapes on a flat surface' (*HMT* 153); this reminds us of the handmaid carving out her Braille-like message on the smooth wood of the wardrobe, and emphasises the arbitrary narrative identity of these texts: indistinct, indefinable 'shapes'. Spatial metaphors predominate in both texts; Renata is drawn to labyrinthine spaces such as the National Theatre: 'There's so much *mystery* in its empty rooms, in the spaces opening out onto *nothing*. I admit it: I love these long *random* walks, these *inexplicable* voids' (*LD* 37, emphasis added). It is within such textual and subjective spaces that they arrange the 'shapes' that constitute their narratives. Offred's most speculative narration comes in the series of chapters simply entitled 'Night' in which she seems freed from the constraints of chronology, place and narrative order: 'But night is my time out. Where should I go?' (*HMT* 47).

The non-linearity of these narratives is further emphasised by the surfacing of memory:

> All I have left now is my memory . . . In the memories that keep me poised on the edge of the abyss, until they open the door, I seem such a stranger. (*LD* 221)

> Are they old enough to remember anything of the time before, playing baseball, in jeans and sneakers, riding their bicycles? Reading books, all by themselves?
> . . . after that they won't. They'll always have been in white, in groups of girls; they'll always have been silent. (*HMT* 231)

Renata makes explicit the role memory plays in stabilising a dangerously precarious subjectivity, keeping her from 'the abyss'—the confusion and silence which threatened her early texts. Offred too recognises that memory may prevent women from being pushed back to the 'edges', losing their idiolect, being 'silent' in groups. Memory is linked with both textual and political resistance for women; indeed Offred's entire narrative is marked by memory, and her fragile hold on subjectivity is under threat from what she calls 'attacks of the past' (*HMT* 62):

> . . . a palimpsest of unheard sound, style upon style, an undercurrent of drums, a forlorn wail, garlands made of tissue-paper flowers, cardboard devils, a revolving ball of mirrors, powdering the dancers with a snow of light. (*HMT* 13)

This excerpt, from the opening paragraph of the novel, shows Offred's text starting from memory and is also suggestive of the textual identity of the women's narratives in the novels. The notion of palimpsest, a text whose original inscription has been replaced, making space for a second writing and another meaning, is crucial not only for Renata and Offred, but also for Atwood and Kociancich who are engaged in acts of genre subversion.[10] The feminist dystopia, a 'style upon style', transforms the 'bad place' to a space for a feminine and transforming narrative, previously 'unheard', 'forlorn', an 'undercurrent'. Like memory in the texts, such supplementary writing (Offred, Atwood, Renata, and Kociancich) occupies a tenuous textual position, remaining fragile, a 'wail', 'powder', 'snow', 'tissue paper'. Yet within this fragility lies a power: through genre subversion, new textual identities emerge which allow women to move towards self-representation.

I want to look finally at the clash of the dominant discourse and the feminine idiolect, at the moments at which *plaisir* and *jouissance* come into conflict. Two moments in particular are of interest here: the first is when the feminine text disrupts the text of pleasure to such an extent that 'a state of loss' (*P* 14) is engendered; the second sees the restoration of the dominant discourse.

> Bonday had imagined that writing this letter would be one of the few pleasant moments he would enjoy at this time, but now he was having real difficulty finishing it. (*LD* 187)

Increasingly, in *The Last Days of William Shakespeare*, it is Renata's text which becomes central, moving from the shadows to assume control of the whole narrative. Plot, which had been found only in Bonday's text, relocates to hers, his sentences begin to fragment, breaking down into series of dots, which we might associate rather with Renata early in the novel. Bonday is also suffering from sexual impotence and thus in both senses his 'small intellectual torch', which first aligned him with the text of pleasure, has been replaced by that 'dissolve' which bliss brings. He has recurrent nightmares, linked to his impotence; the divide between unconscious and conscious is that which dissolves. When he looks at himself in the mirror he sees not only a grotesque image, but, importantly, sees himself as other:

> The man in the mirror made him feel indignant, ashamed. 'I drank a whole bottle, what an animal.' Fixed by the frame of gilt garlands, he observed himself with horror and fascination. 'A sick, slobbering wolf.' (*LD* 101)

This perception of self-as-other is something we associate very much with Renata in the early part of the novel, and this contrasts sharply with Bonday's seamless performance as the prize-winning author. Crucial points in his breakdown include his first sighting and subsequent infatuation with Renata, and his conversations with a child who later dies, leaving Bonday in a 'daytime nightmare' (*LD* 173). Both are outside dominant discourse; both, from the margins or 'edges', prevent 'The Master' from writing and eventually push him into exile—literal and metaphoric—from discourse and from himself.

The 'state of loss' in *The Handmaid's Tale* emerges as Pieixoto realises he will not be able to complete the desired interpretative process on the feminine text:

> . . . many gaps remain. Some of them could have been filled by our anonymous author, had she had a different turn of mind. She could have told us much about the workings of the Gileadean empire, had she had the instincts of a reporter or a spy. What would we not give, now, for even twenty pages or so of printout from Waterford's private computer! (*HMT* 322)

His irritation is made clear by the 'had she had . . .' clauses, established earlier on by a sentence which begins, 'She does not see fit . . .' (318). It is also obvious that the historian would be happier with a text of pleasure, a masculine narrative, from a 'spy', 'reporter' or, better still, the Commander—all discourses of pleasure, which would fill those 'gaps'. Offred's discourse itself is of no value, as it cannot, despite their reconstruction and arrangement, offer the editors detail or fact; it cannot be pinned down. The moment at which *jouissance* surfaces, however, comes when Pieixoto names her text as other, as beyond his interpretation:

> Voices may reach us from it; but what they say to us is *imbued with the obscurity of the matrix out of which they come*; and, try as we may, we cannot always decipher them precisely in the clearer light of our own day. (*HMT* 324, emphasis added)

The denotation of 'matrix' as linguistic register here, which is presumably what Pieixoto intends, is immediately replaced by the connotations of matrix as womb, as maternal space. This has already been set up in Offred's own narrative, at the 'Birth Day' ceremony: 'Smell of matrix' (*HMT* 133). He is unable to interpret the text of bliss, citing the matrix as that which prevents closure, that which disrupts and opens up the gaps. The maternal associations continue with 'out of which they come' and 'imbued', implying saturation, moistening, fluidity.

Plot and interpretation break down when faced with the non-linearity and 'obscurity' of the matrix. Pleasure is replaced by bliss and the masters of discourse are displaced by new voices, and yet, at the end of these novels, who is speaking? In both cases, the women have been silenced once more and it is the historian and the prize-winning author who have the final word. Bonday, rather interestingly, ends with, 'Ah yes, for all their faults, one must recognize they've left their mark' (*LD* 233), signalling that the feminine voice has been suppressed, but that it has 'marked' discourse. This restoration has come about through a second clash of bliss and pleasure (alternative and dominant, feminine and masculine), only this time pleasure has asserted itself though the violence alluded to earlier, in Barthes's trope of the spectator/voyeur at the striptease:

> Without shouting, or struggling, without even any fear, I let him undress me and rape me. I keep my eyes wide open. (*LD* 230)

> We may call Eurydice forth from the world of the dead, but we cannot make her answer . . . (*HMT* 324)

Renata is finally silenced through specifically masculine violence: if a woman's voice cannot be silenced, *plaisir* brutally re-asserts itself. Renata's final journal entry retells the quest for dénouement from the other side, from the victim's rather than the voyeur's gaze. Pieixoto's allusion to Eurydice provides a paradigm for the textual violence, which is of particular concern here; Eurydice was killed by Orpheus looking back at her, just as the handmaid's tale has been edited, rearranged, named and interpreted by the historian looking back. The rape and murder of Renata in the 'red office' and the textual suffocation of 'Offred' show the same desperate masculine discourse, re-asserting dominance through the only means it has left. These are, then, the 'last days' of such discourse and the 'problems of authentication' will not simply go away.

For the moment, however, the dominant discourse is able to assimilate Renata and Offred's texts to silence the disruptive narrative, that 'something without a shape or name' (*HMT* 13). Barthes's distinction between pleasure and bliss seems to suggest that this might be the case, bliss as a transitory, ecstatic moment, pleasure as order which must reassert itself: 'it is a veritable *époché*, a stoppage which congeals all recognized values' (*P* 65). Yet these 'recognized values' are called into question within the space of the fictions, and Pieixoto and Bonday—the spokesmen for such discourses—can never quite escape the shadow of the supplementary narratives: Pieixoto admits defeat in his interpretative quest and Bonday retreats into exile. Although at the end of the dystopias we are left with their presence and speech, both of these have been destabilised; the power and authority associated with the words of the professor and the prize-winning author have been challenged and marked by other voices: '. . . speech, silence, absence and presence operate contrapuntally so that the traces of absence and silence are always latent in speech and presence'.[11] These 'traces' are foregrounded in each novel by a textual *shock*, a moment of horror within the reading of the text which makes clear the entrapment of the women's words: in *The Last Days of William Shakespeare* we realise that none of the letters Renata compulsively writes are ever sent ('the letters never sent, intact, fresh, dead', 221); in *The Handmaid's Tale* there is the shock of realising that Offred's narrative is a reconstruction, edited and arranged by Pieixoto. Thus Atwood and Kociancich do not show us a battle won; their texts include women's voices which remain only 'adjacent and adjunct', but the textual identity of the dystopia is irrevocably altered. The non-real fictional place is opened up to include other 'cultural knowledges' and the *possibility* of future feminine fictions. The woman's supplementary narrative occupies a crucial position: '[it] exists as a shifting, intermediary state, caught between its representations of its own appropriation and its enactment of an "otherness" it can only adumbrate, a "fiction" of what it might become'.[12] The feminist dystopia offers a supplementary place for the multiplying of textual identities, making space for an alternative feminine idiolect and subjectivity to be inscribed in the 'opened' text:

> All I can hear now is the sound of my own heart, opening and closing, opening and closing, opening. (*HMT* 156)

NOTES

1. Virginia Woolf, *A Room of One's Own*, Harmondsworth, Penguin 1945 edition, p. 39.
2. Homi K. Bhabha, *Nation and Narration*, London, Routledge 1990, p. 313. Chapter title 'Dissemination: Time, narrative, and the margins of the modern nation'.
3. Christa Wolf, *Cassandra: A Novel and Four Essays*, London, Virago 1984, p. 271.

4. Joan Scott, 'Women's history', in Peter Burke (ed.) *New Perspectives on Historical Writing*, Cambridge, Polity Press 1991, pp. 49–50. Scott uses the 'contradictory logic' of the supplement to analyse the discourses of women's history.

5. Jacques Derrida, 'Plato's pharmacy', in Peggy Kamuf (ed.) *A Derrida Reader: Between the Blinds*, Hemel Hempstead, Harvester Wheatsheaf 1991, p. 134.

6. Vlady Kociancich, *The Last Days of William Shakespeare*, London, Heinemann 1990, p. 2. All further page references will be cited parenthetically in the text, with the abbreviation *LD*.

7. Margaret Atwood, *The Handmaid's Tale*, London, Virago 1987, p. 311. All further page references will be cited parenthetically in the text, with the abbreviation *HMT*.

8. Roland Barthes, *The Pleasure of the Text*, Oxford, Basil Blackwell 1990, p. 14. All further page references will be cited parenthetically in the text, with the abbreviation *P*.

9. Julia Kristeva, 'A question of subjectivity—an interview', *Women's Review* 12, pp. 19–21. Reproduced in Philip Rice and Patricia Waugh (eds) *Modern Literary Theory, A Reader*, London, Edward Arnold 1989, p. 129.

10. Atwood is engaged in a very specific act of genre subversion. *The Handmaid's Tale* subverts the Orwellian dystopia in a number of explicit ways (for example, the use of an historical 'Appendix'), but is also littered with clues to and signs of the re-writing: for example, the hotel bedroom at the brothel is Room 101 and Atwood's novel (whichever edition is consulted) begins on page thirteen, just as the clocks are striking thirteen as an ominous note at the very beginning of *Nineteen Eighty-Four*. For a discussion of the genre subversion, see Amin Malak, 'Margaret Atwood's *The Handmaid's Tale* and the Dystopian Tradition', *Canadian Literature* Spring 1987, pp. 9–16.

11. Dympna Callaghan, *Woman and Gender in Renaissance Tragedy*, Hemel Hempstead, Harvester Wheatsheaf 1989, p. 74.

12. Bette London, *The Appropriated Voice: Narrative Authority in Conrad, Forster and Woolf*, Ann Arbor, University of Michigan Press 1990, p. 133. London is describing the possibilities which French feminist theory offers for theorising the feminine voice.

FURTHER READING

There has been little critical consideration of women's experimentation with the dystopia, even within recent work on feminist genre fiction. However, each of the texts listed below includes some discussion of the feminist 'bad place'.

Barkowski, Frances, *Feminist Utopias*, London, University of Nebraska Press 1991.

Barr, Marlene, *Alien to Femininity: Speculative Fiction and Feminist Theory*, Westport, Greenwood Press 1987.

Lefanu, Sarah, *In the Chinks of the World Machine: Feminism and Science Fiction*, London, Women's Press 1988, chapter 7.

Mahoney, Elisabeth, 'Writing so to speak: the feminist dystopia', unpublished doctoral thesis, University of Glasgow, 1995.

Russell, Elizabeth, 'The loss of the feminine principle in Charlotte Haldane's *Man's World* and Katherine Burdekin's *Swastika Night*', in Lucie Armitt (ed.) *Where No Man Has Gone Before: Women and Science Fiction*, London, Routledge 1991, pp. 15–28.

Wolmark, Jenny, *Aliens and Others: Science Fiction, Feminism and Postmodernism*, Hemel Hempstead, Harvester Wheatsheaf 1993.

3 Embodying the negated: contemporary images of the female erotic

Merja Makinen

Between the late seventeenth century and the early nineteenth century, the image of women's sexuality was reversed from that of a lustful, impassioned craving to that of a passive, lustless sanctity: 'the mutation of the Eve myth into the Mary myth' as F. Basch put it.[1] Freud, creating in the nineteenth century his model of the female and male psyches, reinforced the Mary myth for femininity. Using the image of the passive egg with the active sperm swimming to penetrate it, Freud argued that women were naturally passive and men active, in sex. His model of children's shift to sexuality, from their polymorphously perverse babyhood via the castration complex, has both sexes valuing the penis as the desired object. Boys turn from their mothers in disgust at discovering her 'lack' of one and, in allying themselves with their fathers, assume heterosexuality. A denigration of women as lacking and inferior is thus 'normal'. Girls, becoming aware of their inferior clitoris, desire the father's penis ('penis envy'), and turn towards heterosexuality by desiring the father to give them a baby as a penis substitute.[2] Following from this model of men as possessing the penis while women passively desire it, masochism is seen as the expression of the 'feminine essence' and linked to a passive narcissism, while the masculine erotic drive is conceived as essentially sadistic and vigorous.

In the twentieth century, Lacan revised the Freudian model to take account of the structuralist analysis of how language works, but his more sophisticated psychoanalytic model left female sexuality still further out of the active arena, even while it opened masochism to both sexes. The symbolic phallus ruptures the relationship between mother and child and allows the male baby access to language (the symbolic) as well as to his gendered self. 'Anatomical difference comes to *Figure* sexual difference, that is becomes the sole representative of what that difference is allowed to be.'[3] Girls are defined as lacking the phallus, the symbol that sets language in motion (through a recognition of difference) and so their relationship to it can only be negative. Women's experience is outside language, cannot be spoken, and so they can only exist as enigma (the other) or as the object of the male gaze.

41

Freudian definitions influenced medical discourse and its popular offshoot, the sex manual. Margaret Jackson, in her essay ' "Facts of life" or the eroticization of women's oppression', studies the sex manuals from the late nineteenth century of Van de Velde and Marie Stopes, through to the twentieth century of Kinsey and Masters and Johnson.[4] Jackson argues that, though ostensibly written to teach men how to give their wives pleasure, sex manuals in fact reinforce masculine 'supremacist' notions of man as the active hunter and woman as the passive prey. As such, they deny women any sexual autonomy and tie their pleasure to men's desires. Such quasi-medical books, portrayed as liberating women's desires (by admitting she has them), actually eroticise women's oppression, Jackson concludes. And the fact that women writers promoted this model of active male and passive female sexuality illustrates 'how pervasive the ideology was and also how powerful science was (and still is) as a legitimizing force'.[5]

Elsewhere, I have challenged on theoretical grounds the notion of female sexuality as being passive, and the object of desire as being solely the penis or phallus.[6] What I am interested in doing here is exploring how such a pervasive ideology has affected the way contemporary women have written about female sexuality. Within a culture that negates a positive feminine erotic, what kinds of symbols of desire do women writers create?

Clearly one agenda of feminist theoreticians has been to challenge the essential passivity of women's sexual desires, to question the active/passive dichotomy and at times even the theory of penis envy, although the symbolisation of a female erotic is still largely untackled.[7] Contemporary fiction writers, both heterosexual and lesbian, have increasingly been creating fiction about erotic experience and do construct images of female desire. Positing women as sexually active, as creating a female *subject* of desire, can destabilise the gender variables of which one does and which is done to, and envision a less aggressive pairing where both do and are done to.

However, this is more complicated than might at first appear. Alice Echols warns against a radical feminist polarisation of male sexuality as driven, genitally oriented and potentially lethal, and female sexuality as diffuse, interpersonally oriented and benign—a simplistic dichotomy that argues 'Men crave power and orgasm, while women seek reciprocity and intimacy'.[8] Such a polarisation places women still within sainthood, men as the orgasmically desiring, and so denies for women a free sexual pleasuring. Esther Newton and Shirley Walton, discussing the way lesbianism was initially assumed to be more egalitarian than heterosexuality, argue 'unfortunately . . . things are not so simple. Power and sexual desire are deeply, perhaps intrinsically connected in ways we do not fully understand.'[9] Lesbian sex acts were not necessarily more caring and non-oppressive. Indeed, as Paulina Palmer has recently argued, the whole debate around lesbian sado-masochism erupted out of a reaction to such bland muting of lesbian desire.[10]

E. Ann Kaplan, in an essay questioning whether the gaze is necessarily male, or whether it can be appropriated by women, asks is there such a thing as a female subject of desire? And, behind such questions, she argues, lie the bigger ones concerning female desire and female discourse: 'Is there any escape from the overdetermined, phallocentric sign?'.[11] For Kaplan, so long as the structures of sexual attraction are locked into defining the masculine as dominance—'cold, driving, ambitious and manipulating'—and the feminine as the submissive—'kindness, humaneness, motherliness'—the fact that some women are allowed to step into the masculine role leaves the structure intact: the gaze is not male but masculine and phallocentrism remains. Questioning the films of such feminists as Laura Mulvey and Claire Johnston who sought to embody a feminine discourse within the Lacanian framework, Kaplan further argues that they have simply left women trapped in a negative position from which they can subvert but never posit.

What of feminist writers as opposed to feminist film makers and artists? Have they too left women in a negative position in trying to articulate a fiction of feminine desire? Perhaps the mode that most exemplifies the dynamics of who does what to whom, the active-passive model, comes in the sado-masochistic act. I have chosen to look at three texts that claim to be about and for the 'liberated' woman reader: Julie Birchill's *Ambition*, the Black Lace edition *The Captive Flesh* by Cleo Cordell, and Pat Califia's *Macho Sluts*. All three, written as erotic fiction for contemporary women readers, invoke the sado-masochistic dichotomy. Two of these texts, *Ambition* and *The Captive Flesh*, adopt a mode not so far from the conventional Mills and Boon or Harlequin romance plot; *Macho Sluts* is very different but still raises the question of appropriating the phallocentric position.

The conventional romance has a hero who is ten to fifteen years older than the heroine, of a higher social class, economically successful, saturnine, sexually expert and arrogantly domineering. The younger, poorer and sexually more innocent heroine reacts to his contradictory actions which veer between tenderness and aggression, and struggles to evade the rape fantasy encoded in the text (a violence that is reified as natural to masculinity). The romance ends happily when the hero declares his love for the heroine and elevates her socially by marrying her.

In *Ambition* the character of heroine Susan Street is very different.[12] She is worldly, sexually experienced, and a fiercely competitive journalist. As such, she is apparently the epitome of the young, brash superwoman of the late 1980s. Yet, where the text may ostensibly challenge the overt construction of femininity, it reinforces the usual relative construction of masculinity—if the heroine is hard, the hero gets harder.

The novel opens with Susan contemplating the corpse of her editor, whose heart has given out under the strain of her sexual supremacy. She believes herself next in line for his job but the callous owner, Tobias Pope, disabuses her. He devises six tasks for her: if she agrees and succeeds in accomplishing them all, the job is hers; if she fails she loses everything. Pope's motivation is a sadistic love of humiliating others, and breaking a strong woman is a worthy challenge. The six tasks involve Susan having 'sold' tattooed on her forehead; an orgy in Brazil (three men and three women); sex with two black men; a gang-bang in a New York dyke bar; performing in a Thai sex club and taking on any trade. Pope dies of a heart attack before the last ordeal—drinking a Margarita spiked with semen and thus playing Russian roulette with AIDS.

But Susan experiences a strange affection for Pope, whose lust for power she recognises as shared by herself; he finally in true romance style says he loves her and wants to marry her because she is able to take the humiliating scenarios and turn them into sites for her own pleasure. In doing so, she earns his respect because her pleasure makes her appear the winner, not the victim. Here the heroine earns the hero's love by her persistence for pleasure, rather than her persistence in virtue, but in both cases the woman has to prove herself worthy of the powerful, aggressive male.

43

It is true that the various tasks succeed in turning the usual sexual stereotypes on their heads: it is the women in Rio who give more satisfaction than the well-hung men; the 'black studs' turn out to be considerate lovers appalled at the idea of Susan being tied up; lesbian sex is not caring and non-invasive but penetrative and dominating. But beyond these constructions, the heroine is still being initiated into this sexual odyssey by the powerful, experienced male and he instigates the abuse which she cannot refuse. The 'ambition' of the successful superbitch, the text underlines, is to be dominated by an even stronger supersadist: 'When would men discover the obvious fact that strong women wanted strong men?' (39). Female desire is an unstoppable force that can take any sexual humiliation and transcend it simply by enjoying the orgasm.

That women want rough trade is underlined by the two supporting male characters, Matthew and David. Matthew is the handsome, intelligent successful doctor whom Susan lives with and despises for trying to please her. Sex with him is uninteresting because he is 'weak'—considerate and concerned to be the good lover. David, Pope's son and heir, combines an emotional respect with brutal, inconsiderate sex that Susan finds irresistible (one scene briefly invokes the aftermath of her flagellation). He too tells her he loves her and wants to marry her but she leaves him to go to his monstrous father whom she concedes she will probably marry. Only on Pope's death is she free to marry the heir who can now offer her both marriage *and* the editorship.

The text invokes a femininity that is seen as transgressive because it is ruthless, competitive and individualistic. But though the construction may challenge the nurturing, caring stereotype, the character of Susan Street simply steps into the masculine role of cold ambition while Matthew becomes the 'girlie' invoking E. Ann Kaplan's scenario of a 'masculine' phallocentrism. Feminine sexuality is illustrated as reinforcing the older, seventeenth-century stereotype of woman as whore, who can take any humiliation because of her insatiable appetite—indeed can take any humiliation because ultimately that is what she wants. Even the indomitable 1980s career woman is reassuringly masochistic between the sheets. Behind all the 'bonkbuster' sex-and-shopping glitz we have the same old reinforcement that sexually women are masochistic and desire to be dominated by their men.

The Captive Flesh is remarkably similar.[13] This novel is part of the 'Black Lace' series claiming to be 'erotic fiction for women' of the 1990s. In a recent *Late Show* programme, the editors of Black Lace claimed to have sold over a million books in their first year and argued that they saw their task as dispelling the myth that women wish simply to lie back and be all wanting.[14] The book that they cited as indicative of dispelling this myth was *The Captive Flesh* and they read out the scene of the slave, Gabriel, being beaten naked in the town square:

> As the phallus stiffened and stood proud, the crowd went wild. Gabriel's hair was released, his head grasped and his neck bent forward so that he could watch while the thick set man worked his glowing member up and down.
>
> How does he stand it? Marietta thought appalled. But like the crowd she could not take her eyes from the rigid stem, crowned by the tight swollen bulb. (30)

But this scene of beautiful man as the object of the female gaze is not typical of the book as a whole. And even here, the construction of man as sexual object is clearly humiliating and shameful to his masculinity. The main plot involves the incarceration in his harem of two French convent-girls by the powerful Algerian, Kasim.

Claudine does not resist becoming his latest acquisition but Marietta, resisting out of pride, is a worthy heroine to be tested and initiated into a variety of sexual scenarios until the moment when she chooses the aggressive power-figure over her love for the gentler Gabriel (just as Susan would have chosen Tobias Pope over the son she loved). Love and consideration are no reward in comparison with sexual domination by a powerful sadist who 'respects' the women's ability to enjoy their masochism. In this text the sado-masochistic scenario is about pain as much as power. And it includes the feminine narcissistic pleasure of being seen by the male gaze. Half the sexual scenarios are related through Kasim's view, the other through Marietta's experience of being viewed by him. So the text reinforces the phallocentric gaze of woman as object, but broadens out to allow men as well as women to become the object of the powerful Kasim who commands all he surveys.

The book invokes the conventional erotic plot of the reluctant libertine who must have her true nature revealed to her by the experienced male, who 'names' her desires for her. The 'Eve' stereotype is deliberately invoked in chapter one when Marietta senses Kasim's ruthless cruelty as 'forbidden fruit. The temptation of Eve' (22). By the end he has shown her that she longs to abase herself before him, to be whipped, abused and then taken. Women's ultimate pleasure, the text implies, is to serve 'the master's' pleasure with no thought for themselves; his granting them orgasm is the final reward.

> Kasim . . . knew that the moment when he inserted his penis into Marietta would be deeply significant. For him there was a kind of sacredness inherent in the particular act. He allowed his favourites only the full use of his body. (214)

The use of the male gaze allows a reinforcement of the primacy of the phallus to grant value. The text invokes Marietta as privileged for being so favoured and the thing that privileges is the phallus of the powerful male. The heroine comes to desire her 'utter compliance' and this is underlined when she chooses between her powerful abuser and the loving and beautiful Gabriel, and the novel ends with the words:

> 'On your knees Marietta. Free my phallus.'
> Marietta felt a strong swimming desire in her loins as the welcome submission gathered in her belly. She sank to the carpet in front of Kasim and said softly, huskily: 'Yes. Master.' (235)

Female desire in *The Captive Flesh* is the desire to be forced to admit to oneself the need to be utterly compliant to the cruel, phallocentric male. Such a text is not masculine in its phallocentrism, in E. Ann Kaplan's terms, but old-fashionedly male. Stating that women have sexual desires, in such a context, is disruptive of nothing. It simply reinforces the Freudian formula of female inferiority, female masochism and female narcissism and gives it added cultural weight by being invoked in an erotic novel written by women for women in the 1990s.

Neither of the two 'popular' texts challenges the passive eroticism of female sexuality; Pat Califia's lesbian text, on the other hand, certainly does, at least on the surface. When there are two women enacting the aggressive-passive roles then at least one of them cannot be categorised as passive and masochistic. The unequal gender relations at play in the sado-masochistic liaison take on a new twist when the interaction is between the butch and the femme. Where the two heterosexual popular texts have proved unable to deconstruct the 'naturalisation' of the definitions of masculinity (aggressive) and femininity (passive) predicated on unequal power relations, this lesbian text, by transplanting the strong/weak, powerful/dependent on to two women, at least brings into question the whole 'naturalisation' of gender roles based solely on sexual difference. Potentially, women are freed from subjugation to men's sadistic and patriarchal drives and are shown with a sexuality unmediated by male desire—when the heroine's sights are no longer set on the powerful phallic male, then there is the potential to challenge the phallocentric idealisation of masculinity. For the powerful 'other' being desired and idealised is yet another (and hence transgressive) form of femininity. As Bonnie Zimmerman points out, a lesbian perspective allows a vantage point from which to see how gruesomely abnormal 'normal' heterosexual relationships actually are.[15]

But does *Macho Sluts* subvert phallocentric power structures or does it simply reinforce them within a lesbian context? Is the 'butch' simply masculine and the 'femme' feminine?[16] Within the lesbian sado–masochist scene, is the 'top' a phallocentric sadist or a 'feminine' sadist? *Macho Sluts* most clearly of the three texts presents a whole sado-masochistic subculture unmediated by romance or a fuzzy wish-fulfilment. As such, it is the most disturbing to read. The collection of short stories does not mystify the aggression, it presents it clearly, and spells out the pleasures to be gained by giving or receiving pain. Such a representation, I would suggest, disturbs all readers who are not part of the sado-masochistic sexual subculture. Paulina Palmer argues that such sado-masochist erotica is often aimed more at shocking the reader and challenging a 'feminist moralism' than truly exploring a lesbian erotics.[17] And there are plenty of side-swipes at censorious feminist moralising in Califia's stories, especially 'The Hustler', set in a future ruled by women who outlaw sado-masochism since its power-play undermines the edict of equal opportunities.

But there is a level of role-play and fantasy involved in the stories that many sado-masochism advocates argue is precisely what divides their consensual practice from more misogynistic social oppressions. In 'Surprise Party', for example, the menace of three cops who kidnap the narrator and subject her to an apparently phallocentric worship of their cocks, is annulled by the fact that the macho cops are not only gay but friends acting out a surprise fantasy for her birthday. Even in the more straight-forward fiction, the gaze of the texts keeps switching so that the reader is implicated in both the sadist's and the masochist's role and shares the pleasures of each. The fact that both are female experiences clearly complicates Freud's thesis that all women are masochists—there are plenty of lesbian sadists and dominatrixes here—but the insights of the practice complicate the apparent power structures even more. This book highlights, as the other two do not, that in a consensual sado-masochist transaction it is the masochist who is in control, who can stop the scenario at any time by withdrawing her consent. As the femme in 'Jessie' acknowledges, 'she was checking me out constantly. I could have said no any time' (61). One dominatrix in 'Calyx of Isis' comments 'Everyone knows it's really the bottom who runs the scene' (115), while another confesses 'I'm such a chickenshit, I *have* to be a top' (148).

These stories are less about cultural domination, and the narcissistic degradation of inhabiting the despised position as 'woman' inherent in a phallocentric masochism, than discussions of a sexual stimulation that comes from experiencing pain:

Unless you love pure pain, for its own sake, it is difficult to see that deliberately administered, controlled agony retains its own severe sensuality. ('The Vampire' 249)

Under severe and continuous pain, the soul reaches a certain kind of clarity. ('The Surprise Party', 237)

Further, in 'The Spoiler' a distinction is made clear between submissives, who are excited by humiliation, and masochists, who are excited by pain. The submissive in 'Calyx of Isis', for example, experiences herself as the focus of the 'amphitheatre' of the five dominatrixes where 'there was no shame, only a playful facsimile that was a spice to heighten her excitement' (146).

So far, I have been arguing that these texts do negate the concept that women are sexually masochistic by insisting that they can be sadistic too, that sadism and masochism are often interchangeable (the sadist in 'The Spoiler' is a masochist who has made himself into his own fantasy-figure) and that in the power-play of the scene, it is not the sadists who in fact wield the power, though they may wield the pain. By shifting the narrative gaze from men to women, from tops to bottoms, the texts could be argued to reinforce the role-play inherent in the transactions and so destabilise the erotic gender roles. In all of these aspects, *Macho Sluts* can be argued as less phallocentric, less masculine in its positing of the sadist, and of women's erotic desires.[18] However, within the texts there are elements that question so clear-cut a reading: the top in 'Calyx' is called 'Daddy' by her bottom, reinforcing a paternalism of power; while in 'The Vampire' which mystifies the 'blood sports' of heavy sado-masochism, the top is seen as chivalrous for not hitting a woman, since she despises 'feminine wiles and plots and foibles', choosing only male victims. This clearly is misogynistic, and is not altogether undercut by the woman managing to outsmart her in order to become her victim.

Obviously any discussion of sexual domination-submission is problematic for libertarian feminism which argues for less oppression and less domination. Power and sexual desire do at times seem intrinsically bound, since to simply censor a femme's desire to be dominated with the cry, 'No, no, it is the prick in your head; women should not desire that act,' is to tyrannically reinforce a phallocentric reading of the lesbian scenario.[19] However, to argue that sexual politics does not interconnect with cultural politics is also naive, and ignores that the bottom being dominated enacts an epitome or masquerade of femininity—as femme—that links into a cultural misogyny that touches deep roots. Lesbian sado-masochist texts will continue to raise problems and questions about gender representation and gender relations to culture, sexuality and power. But in so doing, they at least unsettle the more popular 'bonk-buster' representations of sadism as an essential element of masculinity which women desire to accommodate.

In moving from an exploration of female masochism in contemporary literature to the issue of whether women writers have succeeded in creating a symbol of feminine erotic desire, I do not wish to anchor the sign too closely to the female body and thus link it to an essential biologism. There are feminist texts that reify the vagina as erotic object, but this strategy simply challenges the centrality of the biological penis and is open to reappropriation. R. Parker and Griselda Pollock, discussing the artist Judy Chicago's 'The Dinner Party' assemblage with its assertion of a feminine vaginal iconography, argue that it does not 'rupture radically meanings and connotations of woman in art as body, as sexual, as nature, as object for male possession'.[20] Rather, I am looking for a symbolism that could signify the power and danger of erotic desire in a feminine mode to counter the claim that the phallus is the only signifier of desire within language and culture.

My first chosen text in this search, *Rotary Spokes*, creates a lesbian narrative that, incidentally, rejects the domination/submission transactions of Pat Califia, in order to posit a relationship of mutual power. The eponymous biker heroine, Rotary Spokes, rejects a sexual liaison with the young and impressionable Carolee, seeking a relationship where the power of sexual desire is matched (as it will be with Jessimer) but matched for mutual delight, not a wrestling match for domination, as it would be with Aurelia Bontemps.

The symbol that Fiona Cooper creates for female desire in *Rotary Spokes* is that of 'The Hug'.[21] The text posits a need for this new symbolisation because there is no expression for the desire of one woman for another:

> I have a dream of a Hug. And I ain't never been hugged that way. And I have a dream of a woman. And I am a woman. And what the damn hell can I make of that? (37)

The Hug is imaged as warm and powerful, with a 'leonine tail'. The image is of a powerful and dangerous large cat, that purrs with contentment when it is satiated but can become ravenous and dangerous when starved. Fighting off Carolee's weakling advances, Rotary has to cage its hunger. Only when she meets Jess does the Hug recognise a mutual power and become unstoppable:

> The Hug awoke, unreasonable vibrant, and started to purr down its jungle-fed muscles . . . Rotary Spokes' head throbbed a message of blood and sinew strength . . . She groaned inwardly at the power The Hug wished on her, flexing its claws, itching for someone to tangle with its thick fur . . . the two great cats circling each other in one corner of the lounge. (199)

This image of female desire incorporates power and danger, but it is an aggression that can be held in check and wishes for a reciprocation of its own strength in the other. It holds all of the erotic potency of that male signifier of desire, the phallus, but it does not seek to dominate/penetrate the object of its desire. The feline Hug allows for an element of femininity that is allied to one of power, of potency.

Interestingly, it is the same image that Angela Carter employs in *The Bloody Chamber* in the stories that evoke the pubescent girl's awakening to her own erotic potential: that of the tiger or the big cat.[22] Carter's tales challenge the stereotypes of women as passive and demure and encode a whole gamut of feminine sexual experiences, including those of the masochist victim of 'The Bloody Chamber' and the preying vampire of 'The Lady of the House of Love', where the successful negotiations of feminine desire involve some form of reciprocity with the chosen partner. The two big cat tales, 'The Courtship of Mr Lyon' and 'The Tiger's Bride' turn the young girl's negotiating of erotic desire inwards, to symbolise the potency of her own feminine desire. And once again, feminine desire is feline. In 'The Courtship of Mr Lyon', Beauty visits the Beast only to please her father and constructs herself as prey, as Miss Lamb. From this guise, the lion's 'bewildering difference from herself [is] almost intolerable; its presence choked her' (45). His touch as he kisses her hands evokes only his otherness and makes her shrink nervously 'into her skin'. But at the end of the icy coldness, when spring arrives and Beauty finds herself emerging from adolescence, she discovers herself strangely joyful to be summoned back to the Beast. The house she now enters is an objective correlative of her own spoiling freshness, with its air of despair and physical dissolution. Now she acknowledges her promise to the Beast, for the first time seeing him rather than herself narcissistically reflected through him, and she acknowledges a similarity:

> How was it she had never noticed before that his agate eyes were equipped with lids, like those of a man? Was it because she had only looked at her own face, reflected there? (50)

Able to acknowledge this otherness, rejecting the cultural construction of woman as innocent lamb who must shrink from the touch of desire, Beauty reciprocates the Beast's earlier gesture by flinging herself into his lap and kissing his paws. The otherness is thereby transformed into an ordinary human emotion, as the Beast becomes a man.

Where the heroine of 'The Courtship of Mr Lyon' identifies with her feminine desire by humanising it, the narrator in 'The Tiger's Bride' identifies with it by animalising it, by keeping the uncanny otherness of desire intact. In this story, beasts and women are both categorised as 'other' by patriarchy because, according to the Bible, they do not have souls. This Beauty is more knowing, and since she does not construct herself as innocent lamb, she is not fearful of the 'carnival figure of papier mâché' that is the socially acceptable face of desire (the tiger dressed in gown and mask). Brought up with the nursery bogeyman of the tigerman who will gobble her up, Beauty will not be humiliated into sexual object and refuses to strip naked for the Tiger until he is first forced to do the same. Only then will she reciprocate the gesture and reveal herself. In all the successful relationships in these tales, there is a reciprocity of doing and done to, that prevents a relationship of submission–domination.

When the tiger disrobes and desire is revealed to Beauty, she feels a panic that she will not be able to bear the sight, but 'the lamb must learn to run with the tigers':

> A great, feline, tawny shape whose pelt was barred with a savage geometry of bars of colour of burned wood. His domed, heavy head, so terrible he must hide it. How subtle the muscles, how profound the tread. The annihilating vehemence of his eyes, like twin suns.
> I felt my breast ripped apart as if I suffered a marvellous wound. (64)

Learning to run with the tigers, Beauty strips off her clothes and reveals to the animals 'the fleshly nature of women' (64). Rejecting the patriarchal culture she allies herself with the tiger, hoping his appetite will not bring her extinction, and finds instead that his tongue strips the patriarchal skin to reveal the beautiful fur of her real, desiring self beneath. In both tales, set in lands held by frigid ice and seen as 'introspective regions', the adolescent girls confront and identify with a feline desire that is denied to women within patriarchy.

The potency and otherness of a feminine erotic is given the same symbol as that of the Hug in *Rotary Spokes*, and the feline devouring energy works in all three texts to encode a potent orgasmically-desiring force unnamed in more theoretical discourse. Where representations of lesbian sado-masochism can at times free sexual transactions from the phallocentric sign, the feline appetite of the large cats can successfully embody the negated hunger of a female erotic, a positive feminine desire that stands for itself, rather than as a mere reflection of phallic desire. Disappointingly, many popular texts purporting to be for the modern woman still subscribe to a negative, passive construction of female desire, legitimated by psychoanalytic discourse. In Cooper and Carter, on the other hand, we find at least two contemporary writers offering an infinitely more positive, active female erotic.

NOTES

1. See Introduction to Pat Caplan (ed.) *The Cultural Construction of Sexuality*, London, Tavistock Publications 1987, p. 3.
2. Sigmund Freud, 'Three essays on the theory of sexuality', *The Standard Edition of the Three Works*, translated James Strachey, London, Hogarth Press 1953–64, Vol. 7.
3. Jacqueline Rose, 'Introduction II', in Juliet Mitchell and Jacqueline Rose (eds) *Feminine Sexuality: Jacques Lacan and the Ecole Freudienne*, London, Macmillan 1982, p. 42.
4. Margaret Jackson ' "Facts of life" or the eroticization of women's oppression? Sexology and the social construction of heterosexuality', in Caplan (ed.) *The Cultural Construction of Sexuality*, pp. 52–81.
5. Ibid., p. 66.
6. Lorraine Gamman and Merja Makinen, *Female Fetishism: A New Look*, London, Lawrence & Wishart 1994, especially Chapter 3 'Women and sexual fetishism'.
7. See Luce Irigaray, 'When our lips speak together', translated C. Burke, *Signs* 6(1), Autumn 1980. Irigaray posits the double lips, oral and vaginal as challenging the phallic signifier.
8. Alice Echols, 'The Taming of the id: feminist sexual politics 1968–83', in Carol Vance (ed.) *Pleasure and Danger: Exploring Female Sexuality*, London, Pandora 1989/92, pp. 50–72 (p. 59).
9. Esther Newton and Shirley Walton, 'The misunderstanding: towards a more precise sexual vocabulary', in Vance (ed.) *Pleasure and Danger*, pp. 242–50 (p. 246).
10. Paulina Palmer, *Contemporary Lesbian Writing: Dreams, Desire, Difference*, Buckingham, Open University Press 1993, pp. 25–7.
11. E. Ann Kaplan, 'Is the gaze male', in Ann Snitow, Christine Stansell and Sharon Thompson (eds) *Powers of Desire: The Politics of Sexuality*, New York, Monthly Review Press 1983, pp. 309–27 (p. 313).
12. Julie Birchill, *Ambition*, London, Corgi 1990. Originally published 1989.
13. Cleo Cordell, *The Captive Flesh*, London, Black Lace 1993.
14. *Late Books*, BBC 2, 8 June 1994.
15. Bonnie Zimmerman, 'What has never been: an overview of lesbian feminist literary criticism', in R. Warhol and D. Herndl (eds) *Feminisms: an anthology of literary theory and criticism*, London, Macmillan 1991, pp. 117–37.
16. Pat Califia, *Macho Sluts*, Boston, Alyson Publications 1988.
17. Palmer, *Contemporary Lesbian Writing*, p. 25.
18. Parveen Adams in 'Of female bondage' argues that lesbian sado-masochism can posit a female desire detached from the phallic reference, in Teresa Brennan (ed.) *Between Feminism and Psychoanalysis*, London, Routledge 1989.
19. Joan Nestle, 'The fem question', in Vance (ed.) *Pleasure and Danger*, pp. 232–41 (p. 234).
20. Shirley Ardener, 'A note on gender iconography: the vagina', in Caplan (ed.)*The Cultural Construction of Sexuality*, pp. 113–42 (p. 134).
21. Fiona Cooper, *Rotary Spokes*, London, Black Swan 1990.
22. Angela Carter, *The Bloody Chamber*, Harmondsworth, Penguin 1981.

4 Space, time and female genealogies: a Kristevan reading of feminist science fiction

Lucie Armitt

In 'Women's time', Julia Kristeva argues that one of the functions of literature is to operate as 'a game, *a space* of fantasy and pleasure . . .',[1] an approach clearly indebted to the work of Sigmund Freud, with his predilection for what she refers to as '*imaginary* formations' (*WT* 197) and whose early work 'Creative writers and day-dreaming' makes use of very similar terminology to that drawn upon by Kristeva here.[2] More recently such approaches have gained added impetus from the work of cultural theorists, whose own interests in the interrelationship between fantasy, ideology and constructs of cultural space have enabled the development of a broader, more interdisciplinary understanding of the role played by the spatial in the realm of textual studies. And yet as Henri Lefebvre warns:

> . . . any search for space in literary texts will find it everywhere and in every guise: enclosed, described, projected, dreamt of, speculated about. What texts can be considered special enough to provide the basis for [such] a 'textual' analysis?[3]

In answer to Lefebvre's question, Kristeva's definition of textual space seems, per-haps, particularly relevant to the 'special' case of popular fiction, with its prioritisation of pleasure, desire and consolationist wish-fulfilment and its situation of these within a defined spatial/formulaic enclosure. Narrowing the parameters fur-ther, it also seems fair to claim that no single popular mode offers a more sustained treatment of the relationship between fantasy, pleasure and concepts of the spatial than that of science fiction.

Clearly in 'Women's time' Kristeva demonstrates a sustained interest in the com-plex intermeshing of time and space and the implications of this for feminist thought more generally. That these are also the concerns of feminist science fiction (as are her preoccupations elsewhere with strangers, borders and the abject) implies that psy-choanalysis, for all its patrilinear inheritances, may also have something of value to say to feminist (re)appraisals of the science fiction mode. After all, psychoanalysis itself is a (perhaps fantastic) 'journey into the strangeness of the other and of

51

oneself'.[4] Indeed, as the recurrent fascination with space and time suggests, it may even be true that space *itself* is the ultimate 'stranger to ourselves' and psychoanalysis merely the means by which its journey is mapped out. As the epigraph to Margaret Elphinstone's science fiction novel *The Incomer* reads:

We shall not cease from exploration
And the end of all our exploring
Will be to arrive where we started
And know the place for the first time.[5]

Kristeva's intrepid voyager through space, the *sujet-en-procès*, is also perhaps a subject at play, for it is through Kristeva's early work on the importance of the free-playing counterstructures of textual pleasure and desire that she embarks, science fiction-like, upon a metaphorical journey into the psyche, prioritising as she goes '[a]ll functions which suppose a *frontier* . . . and the transgression of that frontier . . .'.[6]

However, rather than 'free'-play, in Octavia Butler's science fiction novel *Kindred*, projection into the rigidly structured ideological system of a nineteenth-century American slave culture seems less than liberating for Butler's black woman subject on trial/in process.[7] Her interventionist aims find themselves foiled by a reactionary *re*-playing of submission and denial. As the protagonist recognises, the space of 'pleasure' here merely functions to coerce black children into displacing their fantasies onto a slave-market game narrative (*K* 99–100) in which wish-fulfilment fades in the face of 'real-life' futures (or the lack of them). But perhaps, as Kristeva herself would argue, acceptance of a symbolic law is the first step towards its transgression. To that extent, just as the very title of Kristeva's 'Women's time' implies the peroration this *could be* women's time (if only we recognised the fact), so Butler's narrative utilises a dystopian vision only in order to beg an overreaching of it. In this respect it actually allies itself with Susan Griffin's radical call for a redirection of the conventionally perceived relationship between space and play, thus allowing for women's futures to become creatively rather than negatively 'shaped by . . . the littlest girls', for whom 'Space [is] filled with the presence of mothers'.[8] This is a utopian reading of the maternal not dissimilar from Kristeva's own.

As far as the relationship between space and time is concerned, according to Kristeva: 'when evoking the name and destiny of women, one thinks more of the *space* generating and forming the human species than of *time*, becoming or history' (*WT* 190). She then goes on to clarify this in commenting that 'My usage of the word "generation" implies less a chronology than a signifying space, a both corporeal and desiring mental space' (*WT* 209). However, that 'Women's time' goes on to utilise these ideas as a means of (among other things) positing a female *genealogy* of political activism, demonstrates that the feminising of the spatial is inseparable from a reinvestment of it with a temporal dynamic of its own. Thus her term 'generation' becomes intrinsically active, referring in part to the process of stimulus and creation (including, presumably, the generation of narrative journeys). In this manner she reinvests its collective application to a group of people sharing the same relationship with a slice of temporality, with additional dynamic resonance. What we find in Butler's *Kindred* is a science fiction narrative that interrogates this interconnection between the two meanings, pushing towards a site of liminality which is also one of spatio-temporal and textual play.

Time travel and futurist projection are undoubtedly two of the most significant literary devices that science fiction has contributed to the conventions of the novel, and in texts such as *Kindred* and *The Incomer* this is put to especially powerful use. For here, as in Kristeva's work, attempts are made to utilise temporal dislocations primarily as a means of opening up narrative *space* for an alternative feminist perspective on politics and ideology (in this case as they impinge upon racial and environmental issues). Of the two of them *Kindred* comes closer to Kristeva's concerns in 'Women's time', working with the tension between two conflicting temporal patterns, the linear (historical) and the compulsively cyclical (obsessively maternal). Thus Dana, a black American woman, travels back in time from 1976 to the early 1800s in order to protect Rufus, a white male child, upon whose continued existence her own family genealogy depends. In the process she finds herself trapped in what Kristeva would call the 'all-encompassing and infinite imaginary space' of a *monumental* temporal disruption (*WT* 191). Alongside the temporal complexities involved here, the major moral conundrum facing Dana is how to reconcile herself to her desire to protect an oppressor of black slaves. Right from the start this is justified in maternal terms: 'I reacted to the child in trouble. Later I could ask questions . . . Now I went to help the child' (*K* 13). However, although the impact of temporal disruption is experienced in terms of a semiotic-like maternal desire, it is the patriarchal pull of the linear that remains the dominant structural force. For it is Rufus who determines when such disruption occurs and, as is made clear on more than one occasion, the continued pre-eminence of patrilinear time is never seriously under threat. As Dana herself acknowledges: '. . . there was history. Rufus and Alice would get together somehow' (*K* 40). But where, paradoxically, the cyclical does dominate is in the recognition that, like the mutual dependency of space and time, neither Rufus nor Dana has dominion over the other. For Rufus needs Dana to save his life, and Dana needs Rufus because he is not only her surrogate son but also the 'several times great grandfather' (*K* 28) upon whose continued existence her own birth depends.

From this cyclical point of view it is interesting that the narrative opens with a birthing that is both a homecoming and a severance, ritually embodied by the anatomical amputation of one of Dana's limbs. Nor should the fact that this takes place in her own time and (living) space go unnoticed. For a number of feminists have examined the problematics of interior enclosures as far as women's bodily freedom is concerned:

> She falls into this labyrinth . . . The room in which the women fear time. In which she is afraid of becoming her mother . . . The place that turns back upon itself . . . The room in which time is a mirror.[9]

In a microcosm of the life-death cycle, Dana gives birth to her own story in pain, nurtures the cause of that pain, but ultimately separates from it by 'passing on' through death into another world. In a parallel with Christ and the Madonna, her son pays for her life with his death and she, in mirrored martyrdom, finds herself branded by pain. In this respect the relevance of Tina Chanter's analysis of the relationship between Kristevan theories of sacrificial motherhood and temporality are worth considering *vis-à-vis Kindred*:

53

... the very marginality of women privileges them with respect to time ... [for it] gives them access to a future in a way over and above the special relationship to the future that all 'minority' groups maintain ...[10]

In *Kindred*, if anywhere, this finds its closest textual embodiment. Unlike at Calvary, here the son dies so that Dana can have access, not to a 'special relationship' with the Father in eternity, but to one with her 'Mother' in the dim and distant past. For after all, the aim of the quest is to

... retrieve that ideal and perfect union with our [fore]mothers ... to recover the pre-oedipal state of self-in-relation to the mother ...

that Sally Munt perceives to be so intrinsic to the readerly pleasures of popular feminist fiction.[11]

Kristeva's reconceptualisation of female subjectivity in terms of repetition and eternity raises the issue of whether such a rereading can usefully reclaim Freud's rather disturbing connection between the fascinating but forbidding compulsion to repeat, and the creative space of the maternal anatomy:

... neurotic men declare that they feel there is something uncanny about the female genital organs ... the place where each of us lived once upon a time and in the beginning. There is a joking saying that 'Love is homesickness'; and whenever a man dreams of a place or a country and says to himself ... 'this place is familiar to me ...' we may interpret the place as being his mother's genitals or her body.[12]

Undoubtedly the *unheimlich* severance that opens Butler's *Kindred* does ensure that the maternal remains intrinsically related to the uncanny here (even when defined by absence). In this respect Dana's words to her partner Kevin are Freudian enough: 'Going home does take a while, you know. I have to get through the dizziness, the nausea ...' (*K* 51). In part this is also due to the role played by her maternal representative Alice who, while being Dana's 'refuge' (*K* 37), is also her *alter ego*. However, while for Freud such perceptible doubling derives from a 'creation dating back to a very early mental stage',[13] here it derives from a character dating back to a very early *genealogical* stage. As a result, although the two do connect and the quest is successful, Alice's observation to Dana that '[Rufus] likes me in bed, and you out of bed' (*K* 229) is less an expression of rivalry for male attention than the articulation of a fear that, faced with the apparent erasure of difference in temporal terms, their distinct identities and anatomical limits must be reaffirmed in other ways.

According to Jenny Wolmark, such mistrust also characterises the response inflicted upon feminist science fiction by 'a genre with a solid tradition of ignoring and excluding women writers'.[14] But perhaps this is an imbalance capable of being redressed by theorists such as Kristeva for, as Alison Ainley argues, a combined reading of 'Women's time' and 'Stabat Mater' appears to site the mother almost as the *defining* space for temporal and textual reconceptualisation.[15] And yet Kristeva's later work in *Strangers to Ourselves* returns to a disappointing Freudian prioritisation of the significance of the grieving *son*, the foreigner/alien of this text being both 'a stranger to *his* mother' (*SO* 5, my emphasis) and a 'lover of a vanished space ...' (*SO* 9). Likewise in *Kindred*, the archetypal outsider is not so much the 'strange nigger'

Dana (*K* 24), as the white male Kevin who, in Kristevan terms, 'cannot, in fact, get over his having abandoned a period of time' (*SO* 9). In contrast, as if to prove Chanter right, Dana is more disturbed by the relative *ease* with which she fits into an alien space/time dynamic:

> I could recall walking along the narrow dirt road . . . and seeing the . . . yellow light showing from some of [Weylin's] windows . . . feeling relief at seeing the house, feeling that I had come home. And having to stop and correct myself, remind myself that I was in an alien, dangerous place. (*K* 190)

Dana's main fear, of course, is that Kevin's chronological uprooting and subsequent inability to feel 'at home' in the twentieth century will result likewise in his withdrawal from her, for his 'disgust' (*K* 65) at the situation also bears more than a little resemblance to that uncanny sickness of Freud's neurotic male. In that respect it seems that Ainley's optimism is sadly misguided. But as Wolmark also stresses, such texts locate themselves at ' "intersections" . . . cross-over points where discourses become openly contradictory', and to that extent we should no more expect them to be straightforward wish-fulfilment narratives than we can presume Kristeva to be free from any of Freud's misogynist tendencies.[16] Instead, the more interesting examples of feminist science fiction strive to articulate paradox and contradiction, taking up a position whereby they 'live on that border, crossroads beings, crucified beings' (*SM* 178L), uneasily siting themselves in terms of liminal territory.

Naomi, the protagonist of Margaret Elphinstone's *The Incomer*, whom we also first encounter at a crossroads is, as her name suggests, a nomadic traveller. This is a characteristic that Kristeva tends to dissociate from mothers (*SM* 178L), but which is common to the science fiction form. Significantly, both Butler and Elphinstone use it as the basis for their explorations of that aforementioned Kristevan corporeal and desiring mental space of a female genealogy. For Dana's journey takes her into motherhood, while the purpose of Naomi's is to leave it well behind. Indeed it is this travelling mentality that leads both, in patriarchal terms, to be considered 'bad' or rejecting mothers, Naomi in particular being perceived as an unsettling figure for some:

> She could see [Andrew] was upset to see her, almost horrified . . . 'Why are you here?'
> . . . She saw one of the other men make a sign with his fingers, a sign against evil. He did it covertly . . . (*TI* 164)

Freud, writing on 'The theme of the three caskets', comments upon the significance of an all-presiding masculine fantasy of maternal omnipotence, greater in power than the biological mother alone, a fantasy that determines 'the three inevitable relations that a man has with a woman—the woman who bears him, the woman who is his mate and the woman who destroys him'.[17] Although undeniably borne out in the relationship Rufus has with Dana in *Kindred*, it is *The Incomer* that demonstrates most successfully the way in which Kristeva's belief that 'the exile is a stranger to his mother' (*SO* 5) depends upon a fulfilment of this Freudian paradigm. For among this narrative's catalogue of foreigners it is Patrick the rapist who, in destroying the second of these three maternal facets, finds himself alienated from the first, who will also become the third of these—Mother Earth herself:

> The forest was foreign to him now, another place. He had loved it all his life, and cared for it, and now he was cast out, blinded, staring at familiar forms and shadows, recognising nothing. There was no exile more bitter than this, to be no longer part of the land. (*TI* 168)

However nomadic, none can escape the vigilant (even at times *vigilante*) watchfulness of this omnipotent Mother. But while Clachanpluck, the ecofeminist community that Naomi enters, appears to bask in Mother Earth's approval, what gives this book its creative edge is the latent but perceptible presence of an imprecise uncanny threat that, akin to Kristeva's semiotic, erupts and disrupts but is never clearly articulated. In this respect it mirrors the host/visitor dynamic which fosters the interesting generic mix of this text. For although it is at the 'soft' end of the science fiction spectrum, the parasitic (if symbiotic) undercurrent of the gothic lurks here, destabilising and unnerving the reader's generic expectations, and providing us with a restless narrative that confronts its own strangeness in true Kristevan terms:

> *Meeting* balanc[ing] wandering. A crossroad of two othernesses, it welcomes the foreigner without tying him down, opening the host to his visitor without committing him. (*SO* 11)

Also summing up Naomi's position, it comes as no surprise that, refused articulation in one form, this disruptive potential finds it in a visual manifestation emerging out of the bodily contours of this wandering protagonist: 'the dark seiz[ing] her form and elongat[ing] it, stretching it out behind her like a weird night creature, with grotesque long limbs' (*TI* 121).

This gothic challenge to the solidification of boundaries, definitions and identifications bears, in itself, more than a passing resemblance to the host/visitor dynamic of the intra-uterine child/mother bond and expresses itself in this novel (albeit euphemistically) from both sides of the bodily divide. Thus, as metonymic representation of the mother's genitals, the uncanny derives power from its status as 'the terror of the unseen' (*TI* 3). But as metaphoric representation of the child, it also manifests itself as a 'hideous progeny' in its own right: '*a monster . . . born in the dreams of people . . . [which] slunk into the world through a chink left in someone's thoughts . . .*' (*TI* 60, original emphasis). In other words, pursuing the subject of female genealogies, like Mary Shelley's own monstrous creation *Frankenstein*, *The Incomer* follows in its literary foremother's footsteps in striving to reconcile foreignness, bastardy and bad mothering by uneasily placing gothic dis-ease within an emergent science fiction form.

More recently, such textual challenges to patriarchal legitimation have been radically rethought in Donna Haraway's innovative postmodern reading of cyborg culture as a working metaphor for feminist politics. In similar vein to Shelley's bastardised construct, the cyborg is also a 'monstrous and illegitimate' creature whose anatomy is 'a hybrid of machine and organism'.[18] And yet the victim status often inflicted on Frankenstein's monster conceals the fact that Haraway's contemporary cyborg double is a creature who takes '*pleasure* in the confusion of boundaries' and demands the right to the sort of 'disturbingly and pleasurably tight coupling' denied its nineteenth-century counterpart.

Haraway would probably disagree as radically with the ecofeminist perspective of *The Incomer* as she does with any prioritisation of the 'organic' at the expense of the technological. Nevertheless, her work does provide us with a way of articulating the manner in which textual bastardy most closely links up with this narrative's own unacknowledged but omnipresent 'monstrosity' through a sidestepping of patriarchal legitimation. For a palimpsestic undercurrent of lesbianism slips through the gaps left in the outwardly heterosexual orientation of the text, a sub-text which, when permitted to emerge, seems far from ambiguous:

'I think I love you,' said Emily. 'But I know that I'm afraid . . . I don't know what I did when I began this . . . but I do know that it will make everything different . . .'
'. . .My love for you is the same as yours for me.'
Emily sighed. 'I knew it could be no different . . . *There is too much the same.*' (*TI* 116, my emphasis)

In this respect Naomi's need to rush, a few pages later, back into the safe consolations of heterosexual romantic discourse, is not only an unconvincing, but also a rather banal facade:

The body of a man was something much more than she had remembered it . . .
. . .What she wanted was what he wanted, and there was no need to hold out on him at all . . . I have not been complete without this, thought Naomi, and never before have I been so much myself. (*TI* 127–8)

Unfortunately, such masquerades are nevertheless retained, even Naomi's invitation for Emily to join her in bed (*TI* 175–7) being articulated in the most euphemistic of terms. More euphemistic still is the (presumed) sexual encounter between the two teenagers Anna and Fiona, which communicates its erotic significance as much from the fact that it takes place in a *cave* within a *forest* as it does from the rather Kristevan 'whirl of words'[19] through which it is(n't) described:

. . . there was a distillation of colour that confused their senses . . . The sound was loud as blood pounding in their ears, swamping all other senses, overwhelming them. Their hands met and clasped . . . (*TI* 42)

Once again, it is only through the spaces opening up between the lines that desire and/or excess are permitted to emerge. Naturally this is a perspective not infrequently associated with lesbian narrative strategies, but neither is it incompatible with Haraway's own cybernetic textual structures. After all, they too look to the metaphors of perceived 'monstrosity' as a means of encoding the deconstruction of restrictive binary divides (including in this case the divide between silence and articulation).[20] Nor is this sublimation of clandestine desire structures incompatible with Freudian paradigms, despite the latter's difficulty with lesbian sexuality. For Emily, reluctant 'to bring dreams into daylight' (*TI* 203), recognises that the degree of control that the fantasist has over her own wish-fulfilments will always be compromised when called to acknowledge the presence of 'shameful secrets' and nocturnal desires.[21] Sadly, what does become clear at this point is the one major shortfall of Kristevan psychoanalytic theory as far as feminist science fiction is concerned. For while adding an important and liberating dimension to many of the defamiliarisation techniques so commonly applied to readings of the science fiction alien, her hetero-sexist reading of female genealogies leaves little if any room for the type of latent homoeroticism encoded in *The Incomer*.

Indeed Kristeva's reluctance to sanction what she perceives to be the 'extremely difficult' (*WT* 204) sexual choice of lesbianism, added to her belief that lesbian moth-erhood is 'one of the most violent forms taken by the rejection of the symbolic' (*WT* 205), tells us that, for her, there is clearly a 'good' and a 'bad' version of the mother/daughter bond. Somewhat inevitably, both also take up very different stances as far as the symbolic/semiotic dialectic is concerned. The lesbian bond, in wilfully turning its back on the symbolic, may sound 'fantastic', even Kristeva refer-ring to it as 'A "female society" . . . without prohibitions, free and fulfilling . . . an a-topia, a place outside the law, utopia's floodgate' (*WT* 202). But as she also reminds us, the price to be paid for this is one of eternal estrangement from the dominant ide-ology and thus from its attendant power. In contrast, Naomi settles for 'that language of the past that withers without ever leaving you' (*SO* 15), Kristeva's preferred 'posi-tive' but unavoidably melancholic escape route into the maternal dream-space of musicality and echolalias:

> Slow drift down into depths untouched by storm or winter . . . A long descent, forgotten images returning. Rocked by the sea, down in the darkness where there are no more words. Only the music, belonging to a place far beyond words, at the very roots of consciousness . . . all the music ever was was the sound of the sea. Rhythm of water, rhythm of blood, the whole music of the world within her . . . the long exile was over at last. (*TI* 208–9)

When Kristeva refers to writing as 'the ridge where the historical becoming of the subject is affirmed . . .', she uses an analogy that links the production of narrative quite explicitly with the birthing process and the mothering of a text.[22] This is a point she later works through more thoroughly, the split page of 'Stabat Mater' mir-roring the afore-mentioned state of the sacrificial, split maternal subject. As well as a splitting, however, we see that the role played/paid out by the fictional mother/mother of fiction can also be an unravelling, a psychoanalytic (indeed genealogical) piecing together of half-remembered fragments. In return, critics such as Munt have prioritised the importance of the role played by the daughter/reader in testifying to the power of the maternal as a site of narrative creation: 'I make my own narratives (over and over) of my mother's dying . . . I want to make meaning and cohesion out of this loss'.[23] In many ways Dana's quest in *Kindred* is to reconcile the daughter and the mother in this respect too. For, while storyteller to Rufus and first person narrator to us, this motherly unravelling combines with her own struggle to create 'meaning and cohesion' from her disoriented position as a split-subject torn, not between the two sides of a single page (as in 'Stabat Mater'), but far more radi-cally between time zones and worlds. That this is also a position from which she is 'untimely ripped', becomes clear as the thetic-like rupturing of 'flesh joined with plaster' (*K* 261) here connotes a shattering, rather than a healing conjunction within the 'dream-space' which is herself.

But if Kristeva's 'Stabat Mater' is a textual manifestation of the split maternal sub-ject, Dana's textual relationship to temporal subjectivity undergoes a number of shifts during the course of the narrative journey, including the optimistic midway belief that 'Some part of me had apparently given up on time-distorted reality and smoothed things out' (K 127). Later this develops into an embodiment of Sarah Kofman's reading of the absent or denying mother as a site of deferred desires. For as time-travelling mother to Rufus she can never, of course, in reality be 'present'. Instead, like Kofman's prohibitive mother, she becomes 'a myth, projected into the past, into the time of deferred action . . .'.[24] And for the reader too, her stalling tactics increasingly frustrate, stimulating a sense of urgency, drawing us compulsively through the text, because although we know *what* happens to Dana at the beginning (which is also the ending) of the narrative, we remain intrigued to discover *how and why* it happens.

But if both texts effectively deal with absent or partially absent mothers, neither suffers any lack of awareness of that presence of a substantial *literary* foremother in the shape of Shelley's own science fiction novel. In many ways like *Frankenstein*, *The Incomer* reveals and reveils its monstrous secret through the embedding of a number of storytelling voices, whose clashing fragments remythologise past tales of creation and creativity. Once more in cybernetic vein, however, Naomi herself remains a creature without origins. So she emerges out of nowhere, belongs nowhere, and moves on again into the unknown, having severed all her ties with the maternal and thus her own origins. Equally, although more ironically, while Dana's genealogical journey is set up as a quest to maintain and reinforce origins, the vicious cycle of dependency set up between Rufus and Dana actually denies the presence of *a priori* pre-existence in a manner that challenges the credibility of origins altogether. Ultimately this becomes a perspective fully embodied by the ritualised severance that begins, ends and indeed cuts through this temporal circle by which Dana is enslaved.

But here Kristeva's psychoanalytic and Haraway's postmodern perspectives most obviously part company. For although both the stranger and the cyborg function as bastardised aliens, Haraway's construct, as well as being a creature without origins, is also one with no sense of loss. In this respect it is denied any relationship with the maternal at all, whereas Kristeva's stranger as orphaned outsider is structured, paradoxically, via an absence dependent upon a past sense of maternal presentness. This is a point that actually allies both of these protagonists with the stranger rather than the cyborg, despite the fact that Butler is one of the authors Haraway connects most explicitly in her essay with cyborg narrative techniques. Indeed the importance that both novels place upon the function of the (psychoanalytic) journey also contributes to this. For unlike Kristeva's travelling stranger, the cyborg, through its complete lack of connection with both progression and repression, is perhaps as close to a time-less phenomenon as any cultural construct can be. Inevitably this affects their respective readings of time, space and feminist ontology. Haraway's belief that 'the boundary between science fiction and social reality is an optical illusion' presumably means that her ideal futurist narrative searches, like her political theory, for a world without gender,[25] an approach in large part challenged by Kristeva's sceptical enquiry 'is a society without foreigners possible?' (SO 127). More particularly one wonders if such a society would be desirable, not least for the foreigner herself. For implied in Haraway's argument is a challenge to the validity of a feminist science fiction which, like these two texts, takes pleasure in the depiction of women's role as *ongoing strangers* in a world searching not only for the space but also the time for cultural and sexual difference.

Undoubtedly postmodernism can open up a new understanding of our relationship to literary and cultural spaces and, in the process, make us radically rethink the nature of the role they play in our awareness of the structures of social and sexual relations. But psychoanalysis too, with its concentration upon the journey motif and its preoccupation with origins, permits a science fiction exploration of mothering and foremothering that delves back into and thus re-members the past in order to reconceptualise fantastic/future possibilities for women. Thus Naomi, beginning her journey with 'some [vague] sense of form, or lack of form, a possible obstruction in the path ahead . . .' (*TI* 2) finds, in the end, 'the road stretch[ing] away ahead of her, limitless . . . finding new ways and making [new] connections . . .' (*TI* 229). For *Kindred* and *The Incomer* are two of the most successful attempts to combine the popularity and the gratification of the pleasurable formulaic 'read', with a creative drive that, unapologetically engaging with a female tradition of monstrous mothers and patriarchal illegitimation, also, in the process, uncannily 'reveals a certain knowledge . . . about an otherwise repressed, nocturnal, secret and unconscious universe' (*WT* 207). This not only opens up future possibilities, but past and present ones too.

NOTES

1. Julia Kristeva, 'Women's time' in Toril Moi (ed.) *The Kristeva Reader*, Oxford, Basil Blackwell 1986, pp. 187–213 (p. 207, my emphasis). Subsequent quotations from this essay are referenced parenthetically in the text, with the abbreviation *WT*.
2. Sigmund Freud, 'Creative writers and day-dreaming' in *Art and Literature*, ed. Albert Dickson (The Penguin Freud Library Vol. 14), Harmondsworth, Penguin 1990, pp. 129–41.
3. Henri Lefebvre, *The Production of Space*, Oxford, Basil Blackwell 1991, p. 15.
4. Julia Kristeva, *Strangers to Ourselves*, Hemel Hempstead, Harvester Wheatsheaf 1991, p. 182. Subsequent quotations from this book are referenced parenthetically in the text, with the abbreviation *SO*.
5. Margaret Elphinstone, *The Incomer*, London, The Women's Press 1987. Subsequent quotations from this novel are referenced parenthetically in the text, with the abbreviation *TI*.
6. Kristeva, 'The system and the speaking subject', in Moi (ed.) *The Kristeva Reader*, pp. 24–33 (p. 29, original emphasis).
7. Octavia Butler, *Kindred*, London, The Women's Press 1988. Subsequent quotations from this novel are referenced parenthetically in the text, with the abbreviation *K*.
8. Susan Griffin, *Woman and Nature: The Roaring Inside Her*, London, The Women's Press 1984, p. 169.
9. Ibid., p. 156.
10. Tina Chanter, 'Female temporality and the future of feminism', in John Fletcher and Andrew Benjamin (eds) *Abjection, Melancholia and Love: The Work of Julia Kristeva*, London, Routledge 1990, pp. 63–79 (p. 73).
11. Sally Munt, 'The investigators: lesbian crime fiction', in Susannah Radstone (ed.) *Sweet Dreams: Sexuality, Gender and Popular Fiction*, London, Lawrence and Wishart 1988, pp. 91–119 (p. 106).
12. Freud, 'The "Uncanny" ', in Dickson (ed.) *Art and Literature*, pp. 335–76 (p. 368).
13. Ibid., p. 358.
14. Jenny Wolmark, *Aliens and Others: Science Fiction, Feminism and Postmodernism*, Hemel Hempstead, Harvester Wheatsheaf 1993, pp. 1–2.
15. 'Stabat Mater', in Moi (ed.) *The Kristeva Reader*, pp. 160–86. Subsequent quotations from this essay are referenced parenthetically in the text, with the abbreviation *SM* (the letter L following the page number indicates that the wording is taken from the left-hand column). See also Alison Ainley, 'The

ethics of sexual difference', in Fletcher and Benjamin (eds) *Abjection, Melancholia, and Love*, pp. 53–62.

16. Wolmark, *Aliens and Others*, p. 3.

17. 'The theme of the three caskets', in *The Standard Edition of the Complete Psychological Works of Sigmund Freud*, ed. James Strachey, Vol. 12, London, Hogarth Press 1913, pp. 291–301 (p. 301). Here cited in Sarah Kofman *The Enigma of Woman: Woman in Freud's Writings*, Ithaca, Cornell University Press 1985, p. 75.

18. Donna J. Haraway, 'A cyborg manifesto: science, technology, and socialist-feminism in the late twentieth century', in *Simians, Cyborgs, and Women: The Reinvention of Nature*, London, Free Association Books 1991, pp. 149–81, (pp. 149–54 passim).

19. This phrase, which Kristeva utilizes in connection with the 'homosexual-maternal facet' in *Desire in Language*, New York, Columbia University Press, pp. 239–40, is cited by Judith Butler as a perfect example of Kristeva's homophobic alliance of lesbianism with psychosis. See 'The body politics of Julia Kristeva' in Kelly Oliver (ed.) *Ethics, Politics and Difference in Julia Kristeva's Writing*, London, Routledge 1993, pp. 164–78 (p. 169).

20. Haraway, 'A cyborg manifesto', p. 181.

21. As Freud puts it in 'Creative writers and day-dreaming': 'Our dreams at night are nothing else than phantasies . . .If the meaning of our dreams usually remains obscure to us . . . it is because of the circumstance that at night there also arise in us wishes of which we are ashamed; these we must conceal from ourselves . . .' (p. 136).

22. See Julia Kristeva, *Desire in Language: A Semiotic Approach to Literature and Art*, Oxford, Basil Blackwell 1982, pp. 97–8.

23. Munt, 'The inverstigators', p.92.

24. Kofman, *Enigma of Woman*, p. 74.

25. Haraway, 'A cyborg manifesto', pp. 149–50.

FURTHER READING

Armitt, Lucie (ed.) *Where No Man Has Gone Before: Women and Science Fiction*, London, Routledge 1991.

Crownfield, David (ed.) *Body/Text in Julia Kristeva: Religion, Women and Psychoanalysis*, New York, New York State University Press 1992.

Meese, Elizabeth, 'Theorizing lesbian: writing a love letter', in Karla Jay and Joanne Glasgow (eds) *Lesbian Texts and Contexts: Radical Revisions*, New York, New York University Press 1990, pp. 70–87.

Mellor, Anne K , *Mary Shelley: Her Life, Her Fiction, Her Monsters*, New York, Routledge 1989.

Moers, Ellen, *Literary Women*, London, The Women's Press 1978.

Shields, Rob, *Places on the Margin: Alternative Geographies of Modernity*, London, Routledge 1991.

Wolmark, Jenny, *Aliens and Others: Science Fiction, Feminism and Postmodernism*, Hemel Hempstead, Harvester Wheatsheaf 1993.

2 Endorsing the female

5 Seizing the reins: women, girls and horses

Gail Cunningham

'She wished she were on horseback. . .'[1]

In this essay, I want to examine the role of the horse in relation to constructions of women's power. At first sight this may appear an unlikely subject, since few of us relate automatically to horses in the same way we do to, say, food or sex or violence— or even ghosts, science fiction or politics. For pre-industrial societies, indeed probably up to the First World War, the horse was such a commonplace and essential part of everyday life as to be virtually invisible to modern eyes. It blends into the period furnishings in much the same way as steam trains or open fires. In modern industrial societies, the horse has almost completely lost its earlier working or loco-motive role and has become confined to leisure and sport. And because of the expense and space required to maintain horses, equestrianism is a comparatively specialised activity in the way that tennis, running or football are not.

However, I will argue that the horse has, from the nineteenth century at least, occupied a unique and significant place in the empowerment of women. This can be both literal—what a woman could do on a horse which could not be achieved by any other means—and symbolic—what the idea or image of the horse can represent for women or (more usually in the modern period) girls. The header quotation to this section illustrates the point, for it captures exactly the combination of emotional yearning and practical ability which the horse uniquely symbolised for women in an age when horses were an integral part of life, and for the contemporary period when they are not.

The woman here wishing she were on horseback is George Eliot's Gwendolen Harleth, and she feels the lack of a horse for a very specific reason. Grandcourt has manoeuvred her into an isolated *tête-à-tête* and begins to press his suit 'with a touch of new hardness in his tone'. Her desire to postpone the moment of decision could be

65

fulfilled quite naturally if she had the independence and speed conferred by a horse, for then 'she might set off on a canter'. As things are, however, 'it was impossible to set off running'.[2] The scene also has strong symbolic overtones, to which I will return later; but on a purely literal level, it is a clear example of a woman trapped by a man's superior strength and will from which she could have escaped only on a horse.

On the emotive level, 'she wished she were on horseback' could almost serve as a title for one of the immensely popular pony book genre novels for girls which flourished particularly in the post-war years. Typical of such titles are *Wish for a Pony*, *I Wanted a Pony*, *If Wishes were Horses*. In their survey of girls' fiction from the nineteenth century to the present day, Cadogen and Craig refer somewhat dismissively to 'the odd tendency of certain young girls to identify strongly with horses'.[3] It is my contention that this tendency, far from being odd, represents a highly significant recognition of the ways in which the pre-pubescent girl's yearning for a horse or pony symbolises a desire for independence—even dominance—coupled with the traditional 'feminine' traits of caring and nurturing. A girl on a horse, as these books repeatedly demonstrate for their impressionable female readers, can link her skills of application, care and patience to the equalising power of the horse itself. She can at once love and dominate a creature bigger and stronger than herself which satisfies a latent sexuality unavailable to her future adult self; and she can be shown to win, both morally and physically, in open competition with boys and within a world of adult values demeaning to women.

Put at its simplest level, then, a girl or woman on a horse can go as fast, jump as high, last as long, as any male. The distinguishing factor is not inherent strength, but skill. This is not true of most other physical activities which are valued, either formally or informally, by modern society. Sports, as Jennifer Hargreaves argues, are 'an excellent purveyor of values', and the values purveyed have in the main been the traditionally masculine ones of 'physical prowess, courage, strength, endurance and aggression'.[4] Leaving aside for the moment the question of whether all these values actually are predominantly the province of men, the essential point here is that all can be displaced onto the horse rather than the rider: individual horses can be characterised as aggressive, courageous, strong and so on, while the rider's business is to harness these qualities to the task in hand. The issue of human gender is thus dissociated from values relating to the purely physical.

'Mother of three wins gold for US'[5]

As this headline illustrates, difference does not necessarily imply equality. Women on horses compete as equals, but are still not equally reported. But such casual chauvinisms remain common, and hunting down headlines of the 'Blonde wins Booker' variety is still comparatively easy game. More interesting in this case is the event itself, for Valerie Kavany won her gold medal not in any of the usual athletics or swimming sports, but for the 100 mile endurance championship in the World

Equestrian Games. She was competing in partnership with her horse, and against a field of both men and women. Uniquely amongst top international sporting events, equestrianism offers women the chance to compete on equal terms with men.

In modern Western societies, the progressive erosion of institutionalised inequalities between men and women has accelerated over the past three decades or so to the point where separatism now has to be argued for rather than against. Only in sport is it still widely—and largely unquestioningly—assumed that gender-based differences should inform almost every aspect of its organisation. And though the *prima facie* case for separating male and female competitors in, say, tennis singles may be so obvious as to require no justification or analysis, the implications are nevertheless worthy of investigation. For as Althusser argues, sport is one of those institutions in which dominant ideology becomes a 'lived condition'[6]; and in this instance, that lived condition, in contrast to the professed ideology of society in general, is one of female inferiority. Thus a woman on a horse, who is in the highly unusual position of being able to beat men in open competition, is vulnerable to the reminder from the unreconstructed male headline writer that in sport women cannot generally expect to be treated as equal to men.

Indeed, the history of women's struggle to be admitted to sport does not have the same ideologically clear parameters as their demand to be admitted to education, or politics, or the professions. Women could claim the right to become doctors not only on the grounds of natural justice, but also by pointing to the objectively measured successes of early women medical students. A woman could gain top marks in an examination against men, as Elizabeth Garrett Anderson did, notoriously, in medicine; no woman, on current performances, could hope to win the Olympic 100 metres against top male competition. This is an uncomfortable fact for feminists, and one which has historically been tackled by them through two different and opposing strategies. The first is to reject male sporting values entirely, and to substitute female-appropriate exercise. Thus in the earliest period of organised physical exercise for girls, Miss Buss at the North London Collegiate recommended musical gymnastics to the Schools' Inquiry Commission as activity which was 'easy, graceful and not too fatiguing . . . and has wonderfully improved the figure and carriage of the girls'.[7] The second, and dominant, strategy is to fight for male sports to be opened to women, and then to face the disadvantages of minimal media attention and, in professional sports, lower prize money.

Riding is a highly unusual activity in satisfying the criteria for both strategies. For women in the nineteenth century riding was valued both for its physically beneficial effects and its pleasing (to men) aesthetic qualities. On the competitive side, women were admitted to open Olympic competition in show jumping in 1956 and eventing in 1964. In the 1984 Olympics, eighteen of the forty-eight eventing competitors were women, and in both 1975 and 1983 Britain fielded an all-woman team in the European eventing championships and won the silver medal on both occasions.

Equestrian events are the main, but not the only, sports open to women and men equally. Some shooting and sailing events are also open, and it should in principle be the case that any sport in which the agents of power or locomotion are non-human (motor or speedway racing, for example) would have potential for female equality. Despite notable female contributions to activities like aviation or speed-boat racing,

67

however, both in fact and in imaginative representations horses have always provided the main outlet for women's physical power. Factors additional to the desire for competitive equality must clearly be involved.

'The body is brought into play, and masses move in concert of which the subject is but half conscious.'[8]

What is being described here, somewhat surprisingly, is not some form of erotic interaction, but hunting. Lady Greville's account of riding for women, written in 1894, ostensibly extols the virtues of fresh air and exercise, but unconsciously adopts a language which suggests an experience of deep sensuality. The additional factor which gives particular prominence to the appeal of the equestrian over other forms of power or locomotion appears to be sex.

In the nineteenth-century novel, indeed, women on horseback are frequently invoked in contexts which allow the writer to depict subtleties of sexual feeling which could not otherwise be described. The image of a woman on a horse was in itself erotic: riding habits were high-necked, tight in the bodice and waist, and flowing over the legs; the side-saddle posture necessitated a pleasing flexibility in the turn of the hips; boots and a whip were standard accessories. Add to this the picture of a woman, normally debarred from any demonstration of physical dominance, controlling a fast and powerful creature and the potential for sexual implication is clear. George Eliot notes the practical use of a horse in courtship rituals, but also invokes its sexual symbolism. When Gwendolen embarks on her solitary walk with Grandcourt, she instinctively snatches up her riding whip; on foot rather than on horseback, she nevertheless carries with her a comforting symbol of her earlier power and independence. Her unease at Grandcourt's attentions is signalled by her whipping the bushes surrounding them, and her escape is effected by 'accidentally' letting the whip fly from her hand. It is a false victory, of course, for while she can temporarily leave Grandcourt in pursuit of the whip the incident also prefigures her future powerlessness as the wife of a cold sadist: she surrenders the whip hand to her future husband. Dorothea Brooke in *Middlemarch* instinctively recognises the sensuality of her passion for riding when she makes it one of the first pleasures to be sacrificed in her programme of renunciation. And in *Mansfield Park* Fanny Price's sexual jealousy of Mary Crawford is first activated when Edmund borrows Fanny's horse to give Mary riding lessons. In contrast to the timid Fanny, Mary Crawford is 'active and fearless' and thus 'formed for a horsewoman'. Edmund's attentions move swiftly beyond those of a dispassionate instructor, and Fanny's feelings of neglect and rejection are comically transposed onto misplaced concern for the horse: 'if she were forgotten, the poor mare should be remembered'.[9]

Hardy, whose first wife was an accomplished rider, frequently uses the image of woman on horseback as indicative of the relations between his men and women. And almost always it is the woman, as object of the male gaze, who is displaying conventionally unfeminine qualities of power or independence. Gabriel Oak, for example, spies on Bathsheba from his hut in order to watch her equestrian acrobatics as she lies flat on her pony's back 'her head over its tail, her feet against its shoulder, and her eyes to the sky'[10]—a clear example of disguised sexual voyeurism. This 'abnormal attitude' is then tantalizingly compounded when Bathsheba, assuming herself safely unobserved, adjusts her seat from side-saddle to astride. And when a woman rides astride, she draws attention to the fact—so carefully disguised by Victorian conventions of dress and deportment—that there is considerable space and power between her legs.

As the horse became progressively displaced by the bicycle and subsequently the car as the preferred means of individualised transport, so its potential for naturalistically evoked sexual symbolism diminished in literature. Cars were annexed at the outset by men as requiring mechanical expertise and carrying phallic associations, and there is nothing remotely erotic about a bicycle. However, the horse did not entirely lose its special position as a potent image of female independence and disguised sexual power. It receded first into the specialised form of girls' fiction, and has recently re-emerged in contemporary bestsellers by, and predominantly for, women: a sort of sex-and-riding genre.

'I should have liked nothing more than . . . to have caught my fingers in their manes, felt them blowing warmly down my neck through wide nostrils and to have had the sweet horsey smell of their coats tickling my senses . . .'[11]

A pre-pubertal sexuality in girls' responses to horses is obvious in the above extract, and forms one recurrent aspect of the pony book genre which flourished in the post-war years. The emotional yearning for a beautiful, powerful and independent creature which nevertheless requires female nurturing gives an implicit dynamic to much of the I Wanted a Pony type of fiction. The intimate, quasi-domestic contact is as important as the riding. Horses are revered not simply for the power they confer on the rider, but also for the opportunity they provide for displays of physical and emotional intimacy:

> It was far better, I decided, to rub them down, to feed them and to be able to talk to them in the quiet sanctuary of their stables so that they learned to know you and to watch for you and you loved them for their companionship as well as for the ride they gave you.[12]

The potential for erotic deconstruction here is almost comically transparent, and may in part account for the loftily dismissive tone adopted by such critics as Cadogen and Craig when they refer to the 'absurd, exasperating connotations which the genre has acquired'. But this female reverence for power in the Other, combined with the woman's controlling domestic and personal skills, has a long and respected literary lineage. Jane Eyre's progressive taming of Rochester, for example, carries a similar charge of power and violence contained, of dominating patterns reversed, and of sensuality nevertheless remaining. A twelve-year-old female reader will recognise the same pattern in each.

But various means of combining submission and domination are familiar themes in the debates on women in literature, whether adult or child orientated. More interesting in the pony book genre, perhaps, is the practical, physical and competitive ability displayed by girls in an area where they can compete equally with boys while retaining specific and valued feminine characteristics. For this aspect of girls and horses I will concentrate on three novels by Josephine Pullein-Thompson published between 1951 and 1957, *The Radney Riding Club*, *One Day Event* and *Pony Club Camp*.

By the time the first of these appeared in the early 1950s, the pony book genre was already firmly established as a variant on certain familiar forms of girls' fiction. The Pullein-Thompson sisters (Christine and Diana as well as Josephine) were early practitioners in the field whose writings rapidly matured beyond the formulaic to a level of considerable sophistication. As early as 1947, indeed, Josephine Pullein-Thompson was able to incorporate ironic self-referentialism into her protagonists' reading:

> I hastily took one of Lucy's pony books from the bookcase ... This pony belonged to a nasty little rich girl who didn't appreciate him, and, after a few unfortunate adventures which proved she was unfit to possess a pony, he was given to her poor cousin, who, of course, won all the prizes in a horse show.[13]

This neatly encapsulates the routine promotion of readily acceptable values—honest poverty and effort measurably superior to self-serving riches and laziness—which are easily attachable to horsey pursuits but by no means unique to them. It is when the particular features of equestrianism become central to the depiction of female endeavour that the horse becomes most interestingly linked to implicit views on women's potential.

The novels I have selected for discussion form a loose trilogy based on the same broad set of characters but focusing mainly on the growth, in both equestrian and emotional terms, of the girl Noel and the boy Henry. They are remarkable both for their highly literate style (signalled by a pervasive irony, and a referential range covering various forms of art and literature) and for their sophisticated seeding of recondite knowledge into a conventional and thus acceptable structure of children's story. Peter Hunt, in his recent study of children's fiction, claims that 'children's books ... are fun and work is not'; on the whole, therefore, work has little place in 'the golden play-world of the child'.[14] As Hunt himself acknowledges, however, there are honourable and significant exceptions: Kipling can be both inspirational and morally stern (as in *The Jungle Book*) about the importance of hard and meticulous work, and Arthur Ransome repeatedly demonstrates the extent to which one's life can depend on the quality of one's own work. In the case of pony books, work is both a moral imperative—without it the animal suffers—and an incentive towards personal satisfaction and public recognition.

In Josephine Pullein-Thompson's trilogy, the three factors of the moral, the personal and the public are all explored, entertainingly but rigorously, through the equestrian medium. Henry Thornton, from a wealthy but emotionally and intellectually restricted background, is contrasted in childhood friendship with Noel Kettering, a comparatively poor professor's daughter, and the two are united through their joint desire to acquire advanced equestrian skills. 'I struggle and strive to leave the dismal abyss of ignorance,'[15] says Henry, and this struggle involves both characters in an immense amount of carefully documented hard work. The values which underpin this work are, moreover, interestingly linked to a construction of gender roles for which the horse is an essential focus. Noel and Henry strive jointly in an enterprise which of its nature allows the possibility of equality, even superiority, of the girl.

The values which these novels promote are laid out clearly at the beginning of *The Radney Riding Club*, sustained through *One Day Event*, and interestingly modified in *Pony Club Camp* to acknowledge the characters' growth into young adulthood in a social world of clear gender inequality. For the girl reader—and the genre is aimed exclusively at girls—these values are both challenging and reassuring. Henry likes Noel not merely for her expertise with horses, but primarily because 'she has an original mind',[16] and their conversation—witty, ironic, often based upon literary quotation—presents the reader with a high level of verbal sophistication. Noel is given characteristically 'feminine' qualities of self-deprecation, lack of confidence and denigration of her own abilities which are constantly counterpoised to the manifest knowledge and skill she can demonstrate through riding. It is she who is made the mouthpiece of expertise on the finer points of equestrian schooling, advising Henry early in the novel on how to handle his young and difficult horse: 'I think I know what I'd do with him if he were mine, but I'm probably quite wrong, and I don't suppose you'll agree, but if he belonged to me, I'd put him back in a snaffle'.[17] And the drawing-out of Noel's ability to recognise her own strengths, presented as a characteristic female difficulty, is a constant sub-theme of the novel:

> 'Have the courage of your convictions, my dear Noel.'
>
> 'I don't think that I have any convictions,' said Noel.
>
> 'Oh, yes, you have,' answered Henry. 'Look how you fly at poor unsuspecting persons who don't believe in dressage, ride with their legs in the wrong place, or who prefer the amenities and social life of towns to dwelling in primitive and unprogressive country districts.'
>
> 'Oh, shut up,' said Noel, 'you're only trying to be irritating, and I'm in no mood for argument.'
>
> 'That's the kind of remark women always make when they're being worsted in verbal contest,' said Henry, with a grin.[18]

As a role model, then, Noel reassuringly displays recognisable 'feminine' traits of uncertainty and self-denigration in a context which allows them to be objectively shown as at odds with the facts. On a horse herself, or teaching younger children to ride, Noel is manifestly superior to most of her contemporaries whether male or female. Her qualities of patiently acquired knowledge, and skill and courage in its application, enable the author to show her tested against competition which in the equestrian context can be both male and adult. At the end of the novel Henry, Noel, and her protégé Alex ride as a team in a one day event against adult competitors. Their inevitable win—which as Pullein-Thompson herself has pointed to in an earlier book as an almost inescapable component of the genre—is sharpened in its significance by the fact that as an individual competitor Noel is ranked higher than either of her male colleagues. With a horse beneath her, Noel's female uncertainties are dissolved into corporate responsibility and the individual desire to excel.

Gender distinctions are never ignored in the relationship between Henry and Noel; rather, they become pointed and stimulating in a sort of childhood version of Beatrice-and-Benedick or Jane-and-Rochester verbal banter. And in the horsey milieu, of course, the potential for physical competitiveness is ever present. In the minor characters, more conventional gender lines are drawn once again with a view to challenging expectations. The accepted prototypes of adult male and female are given childhood expression through the extremes of Eric and Paulina. Eric is stereo-typically masculine, heavy-handed both literally in his horsemanship and metaphorically in social interaction; his intense competitiveness is combined with a bone-headed contempt for the artistic or intellectual and thus similarly for equestrian knowledge. His horses thus suffer, and his riding skills are limited. Paulina by contrast represents the incipient adult woman's vapid sociability and laziness, a girl who instead of applying herself to equestrian problems would, in Noel's words, 'have suggested ennobling causes, smiled sweetly on our tantrums, remained irritatingly clean and done nothing to help'.[19] Neither model, plainly, can compete in the girl reader's imagination either for male attractiveness or for a model of her own potentials.

Development is continued in the childhood mode through *One Day Event*, which provides an amusing and instructive account of the new continental riding methods which were coming into Britain in the post-war years. Here Noel's and Henry's positions in competition are reversed, when he achieves first to her second place in the culminating event. This could be seen as a portent of the inevitably widening gap between male and female achievement as the characters move through adolescence towards adulthood, though Pullein-Thompson carefully modifies this interpretation by portraying Noel's secondary position as due mainly to the fact that she is now riding a young and inexperienced horse. In the final novel, however, the differentiation of gender roles is frankly acknowledged as a tactfully restrained sexuality enters Noel and Henry's relationship.

In *Pony Club Camp* the interest is divided between the usual cast of lively children and their ponies and the burgeoning relationship between Henry and Noel. Henry is now at Sandhurst heading for a cavalry regiment, whereas Noel, with permed hair and lipstick, is consigned to a secretarial course. Horses cannot provide her with a viable career, and thus the early equality of their relationship is lost. The book contains some ironic warnings to the impressionable reader against youthful marriage as an easy happy-ever-after ending (people of Noel and Henry's age, we are told, are 'still romantics. Marriage isn't romantic so you need to become slightly cynical before embarking on it'[20]), and the odd passage of veiled sexual reference which would presumably pass straight over the heads of its intended audience:

'To horse,' said Henry . . . and he added, '"Would it were day".'
'Not very apt,' Noel told him, 'can't you think of anyone wishing for night?'
'Probably,' answered Henry, 'but not in a suitable context.'[21]

The book ends with a hint that Henry and Noel may marry at some unspecified time in the future, followed by a hasty return to the child's world of ponies and future club camps. While a pre-pubertal sexuality can be readily displaced onto love of horses, the genre cannot easily sustain its mature form.

'You've got ice between your legs, Meridon, that's your trouble. All you ever want there is a horse.'[22]

Since horses are no longer an integral part of modern society, they do not, naturally enough, figure largely in the contemporary novel. Certain forms of popular fiction, however, have in recent years used the horse motif in a way which develops the sexual resonances of horses for women both from the nineteenth-century novel and from the children's pony book genre. Probably the writer most immediately associated with horses in popular fiction is Dick Francis, whose adroitly crafted thrillers are normally set either centrally or peripherally in the world of racing. But his works are peculiarly masculine in their appeal, not merely because his tersely-spoken, emotionally repressed heroes face intrigue and violence with a set of characteristics more appealing to male than female readers, but more importantly in this context because of the nature of racing itself. In the world of racing, as Francis's novels acknowledge, horses may be objects of aesthetic beauty and provocations to displays of physical courage and skill in their riders, but they do not on the whole attract much emotional interest. A jockey, after all, is quite likely to have his first encounter with his ride in the parade ring before the race, and may never see it again afterwards. A race horse is an unpromising substitute for emotional or sexual involvement.

Some popular fiction for women, on the other hand, has in recent years returned to the horse motif as a means of expressing images of women's empowerment and sexuality. Two highly successful, though widely differing, practitioners in the field of women's bestsellers are Jilly Cooper and Philippa Gregory, both of whom make horses a focus of interest in some of their work. I will therefore conclude with a comparison of the use of horses in Cooper's *Polo* and Gregory's *Meridon*.

Jilly Cooper's success as a popular novelist is primarily in the broad area of sex-and-shopping, with the emphasis on a cheerful, raunchy promiscuity in a context of upper-middle-class display related in a comic style heavily dependent on Christmas-cracker like puns. In *Polo*, and its equally successful sequel *Riders*, she hit upon the

73

brilliantly appropriate notion of linking these qualities together through a world centred on horses. *Polo* provides women readers with an adult version of the pony book. It contains the same elements of spoilt-brat girls who, through their love of horses and skills in riding, learn to couple values of independence with caring and nurturing, and similarly uses equestrian competition as a means of showing women legitimately shining on equal terms with men. In this grown-up version, of course, sexuality can find proper adult expression, but remains, interestingly, inextricably linked with attitudes towards the horse.

Perdita Macleod, the heroine of *Polo*, has from the age of fourteen 'wanted to be a famous polo player more than anything else in the world'.[23] Hampered by a fiery temper, an unknown paternity, divorced mother and impoverished home, she has little to propel her towards reaching this ambition beyond an undoubted natural ability and an unfeminine aggression essential for the regulated violence of the game. In Cooper's imaginary but aptly named county of Rutshire, characters' thoughts are divided between sex and the saddle, and Perdita is thus able to use her body as a passport into the polo world and its wealth. But, like the nasty little rich girls of the pony books parodied by Pullein-Thompson, Perdita has to learn the values of selflessness and emotion. That she is capable of this is demonstrated intermittently through her relationship with her horses; and her final collapse into abject selfknowledge could come straight from the pages of a twelve-year-old's pony romance:

> 'I deserved it,' said Perdita in a choked voice. 'I deserved everything. I've behaved horribly since the day I was born and now I'm paying for it.'
> 'Your ponies don't think so,' said Rupert gently. 'They absolutely adore you . . .'[24]

A woman's ability to love a horse, therefore, and to link this love to her skills and courage in riding it competitively, is used directly in the adult version of the genre to bring adult rewards. Perdita finds her father, earns his approval by scoring the winning goal in a crucial polo match, and then uses his money to buy a favourite polo-pony for the good but impoverished lover whom she has previously rejected. By the end of the novel she has found father, husband, fame and a nicer nature.

Jilly Cooper's success as a writer of popular fiction for women lies in her skilful combination of the modern lure of independence with well-worn elements of romance. She titillates her reader with the allure of guilt-free sex and material acquisitiveness, while at the same time appealing to the young girl's regard for prepubescent values of physical skill and competitiveness with males. The horse, as I have argued, uniquely allows the latter; the world of polo, according to Cooper, provides ample scope for sex-and-shopping.

Philippa Gregory's novels, while featuring as prominently as Cooper's in the best-selling lists, are an altogether more challenging proposition. I have selected *Meridon* for discussion partly because it has the presumably unique distinction of having simultaneously won the prize for best romance and being nominated for feminist novel of the year, but also for being, in Gregory's own words, 'as much about horses as anything'.[25] It forms the concluding volume to Gregory's *Wideacre* trilogy which follows the fortunes of women from the country-gentry Lacey family through the latter part of the eighteenth and into the early nineteenth centuries.

74

In all three volumes Gregory uses the form of historical romance to explore different models of female behaviour. In the first book Beatrice Lacey learns in early childhood that she will always be debarred by her gender from owning her beloved Wideacre land, and thus reacts to institutionalised injustice by embarking on a programme of progressive personal corruption. Beginning with patricide, she moves on to incest and mutilation, ending with the destruction of the land she has loved and her own murder at the hands of her former lover. She is a portrait, in Peter Ackroyd's words, of 'a certain kind of wildness, of female assertiveness'.[26] In the second novel, *The Favoured Child*, Beatrice's daughter Julia is put through a similar programme of destruction, but this time as victim rather than perpetrator. And in *Meridon* Julia's daughter finally achieves a balance of female independence and secure emotional values.

Meridon the gypsy child is actually the daughter of Julia Lacey, given away in infancy in order to protect the Wideacre land from the corruption inevitably brought by the landowning classes. Hating her vagabond existence, emotionally cold to all human beings except her adopted sister Dandy, Meridon's only hope of escaping a life of brutalised poverty is through her skill with horses. Gregory explicitly rejects the sex as power alternative which Cooper revels in, contrasting the integrity of Meridon's frigid rejection of men with the lazy promiscuity which eventually leads Dandy to her death. Each stage in Meridon's struggle for escape is won through her ability with horses, and it is through her love of a horse that she experiences the first possibility of warmth towards a male creature:

> I found I was whispering endearments, phrases of love, telling him how beautiful he was—quite the most beautiful horse in the world! And that he should be with me for ever and ever . . . that in truth we had found each other and that we would never part again.[27]

Where Cooper draws on the moral fable aspect of the pony book conventions to educate her nasty little rich girl, Gregory produces a more subtle and credible version of the horse as sex-substitute and conveyor of power themes. This is not a children's book, of course, and Meridon does therefore finally achieve a fulfilling sexual relationship with a man. But in producing this ending Gregory also undermines the reader's expectations of the genre by rejecting its rags-to-riches, foundling girl to society wife conventions in favour of political radicalism (Meridon renounces her Wideacre inheritance and makes the estate instead into a workers' collective) and gender equality. Her new-mannish partner takes prime responsibility for children and land, while she earns her keep by breaking and training horses.

Modern romances, therefore, have rediscovered the suggestive power of the horse in providing physical equality, domination and power, and substitute sexuality for women. Where the nineteenth-century novel realistically utilised the actual power and independence uniquely conveyed on women by the horse, the modern bestseller draws heavily on the imaginative pull of ponies for the young girl as embodied in the children's genre. The horse can provide for the female reader an image which may be desired but unobtainable in a man—the possession and control of a creature 'not only . . . more beautiful than any other . . . but willing to respond to [her] every wish'.[28] It is, as the conclusion to a classic of the pony book genre puts it, an image which with horses if not with men, is 'both fact and fantasy'.[29]

NOTES

1. George Eliot, *Daniel Deronda*, 1876, Bk 1, Ch. 13. (For all nineteenth-century texts I have given chapter rather than page references in recognition of the multiplicity of texts available.)
2. *Daniel Deronda*, Bk 1, Ch. 13.
3. M. Cadogen and P Craig, *You're a Brick, Angela!*, London, Gollancz 1976, p. 354.
4. J. Hargreaves, *Sporting Females*, London, Routledge 1994, p. 111.
5. *The Guardian*, 6 August 1994.
6. L. Althusser, *Lenin and Philosophy and Other Essays*, London, New Left Books 1971, p. 139.
7. Cited in Hargreaves, *Sporting Females*, p. 64.
8. Lady Greville (ed.) *Ladies in the Field: Sketches of Sport*, London, Ward & Downey 1894, p. 31.
9. Jane Austen, *Mansfield Park*, 1814, Ch. 7.
10. Thomas Hardy, *Far from the Madding Crowd*, 1874, Ch. 3.
11. C. Harris, *If Wishes Were Horses*, London, Blackie 1961, p. 38.
12. Ibid., p. 38.
13. J. Pullein-Thompson, *I Had Two Ponies*, London, Collins 1947, p. 41.
14. P. Hunt, *An Introduction to Children's Literature*, Oxford, Oxford University Press 1994, p. 175.
15. J. Pullein-Thompson, *The Radney Riding Club*, London, Collins 1951, p. 8.
16. Ibid., p. 9.
17. Ibid., p. 37.
18. Ibid., p. 115.
19. Ibid., p. 138.
20. J. Pullein-Thompson, *Pony Club Camp*, London, Collins 1957, p. 175.
21. Ibid., p. 123
22. P. Gregory, *Meridon*, London, Penguin 1990, p. 82.
23. J. Cooper, *Polo*, London, Corgi 1992, p. 17.
24. Ibid., p. 724.
25. Letter to author, 24 July 1994.
26. Quoted on the back cover of *Wideacre*, London, Penguin 1987.
27. P. Gregory, *Meridon*, p. 120.
28. Harris, *Wishes*, p. 176.
29. Ibid., p. 192.

6 Visible margins: women writers and the English ghost story

Nickianne Moody

Introduction

The ghost story is an interesting hybrid of popular fiction and literature. All too often histories of the genre assert that men are the literary practitioners, whereas women are present only as popular commercial writers. There is a case to be made, however, for putting aside the 'masters of the uncanny' approach, for since the 1840s women have been repeatedly and extensively drawn to this fantasy form. If one concentrates on women writers and considers the ghost story as a gendered tradition of writing and reading, recurrent themes and preoccupations become evident, contrasting with any notion of the ghost story as a male preserve. Moreover, the ghost story can be seen as an experimental as well as formulaic narrative framework for women's writing.

Ghost stories are difficult to define and are usually identified by clear titles or their publishing niche, the anthology or magazine contribution.[1] The variety of ghosts or ghostly experiences appears infinite, but all narratives labelled as ghost stories will at some point address a haunting—a return of the dead or the past in some manner. Ghost stories have shared characteristics with the 'feminine' romance as well as the 'masculine' genre of horror writing, sharing with the latter an interest in the supernatural and the macabre as well as the exploration of repressed sexuality. A non-gendered approach to the genre often obscures the extent to which women as writers explore these themes or are in fact critical of the romantic formula and its celebration of heterosexual love and marriage.

Literary definitions place an emphasis on the artistic achievement of terror. They suggest that the writer should create the frisson of pleasurable fear through an intimate anecdotal style and well-managed economy of atmosphere and suspense, but what is perceived as frightening by the woman writer of ghost stories, and the discourse used to convey it, is sensitive to the changing cultural rather than the literary climate.

In fact, the ghost story emerges as a form which has been used consistently to pursue particular public and private debates concerning women's experience.

Critics see the ghost story as a localised product of nineteenth-century social anxiety which was already in decline after the First World War.[2] The popular advent of the ghost story takes place during a period with an intense interest in spiritualism, as well as a developing cultural interest in psychological phenomena. The supernatural is used as a metaphor for both. However, women's ghost story writing is not solely part of a response to the cultural climate of the Victorian age, but a vital genre, still chosen by contemporary women writers, and which has definite inter- and post-war characteristics.[3]

Ghost stories are particularly concerned with injustice, and the female writer is placed in a position which enables her to redress this and exact retribution by confronting social divisions. In doing so, the writer often actively reverses patriarchally preferred interpretations of events and hierarchies of knowledge. The intimacy of the narrative style, while frequently moral in tone, conveys secrets and confessions. The reader is invested with the responsibility to judge the actions of the past and the outcome of nameless crimes.

Women ghost story writers characteristically choose to set the genre's fantastic elements against a background of everyday life. The principal setting for women's ghost stories is not the haunted castle but the home. The main theme is communication, more frequently between family members than strangers. For these reasons it becomes clear that the ghost story holds a special relevance for women, as the family is foregrounded and women, as the keepers of secrets, are especially empowered—a narrative which questions and establishes mystery around a curious event being ideally suited for the short story form. However, a recognition that the narrative structure of the ghost story is founded upon the consequences of action is crucial to an understanding of how the genre actually works in reviewing past and present experience. The preoccupation with the past found here is not necessarily nostalgic; the stories are more interested in verifying moments of decision or indecision. As with horror writing, nostalgia is often inverted and childhood, previously thought of as a safe haven, is the source of fear and terror. Youth is often re-examined with regret, stories of marriage with hindsight and childhood experience with a dispassionate adult eye.

In women's writing hauntings may be caused by external supernatural agents or by internal psychological states. The form of the haunting is various: visible, physical, extrasensory perception, possession, dreams and the unexplained. The understanding of the ghost as a revenant, a revisitation, is often a vital premise. The return of something or someone known or unknown leads the percipient to understand more about their own present circumstances.

As women's ghost stories focus on the supernatural in the home it may be useful to consider Freud's discussion of *das Unheimliche*, translated as the uncanny, and viewed by Freud as a particular class of frightening things, 'which lead us back to what is known of old and long familiar'.[4] The *unheimlich* tale occurs when the familiar is made strange or, more frequently, the unfamiliar is recognised as familiar. The concept of the *Unheimliche* provides a fictional space which can recover the past. Family histories and secrets have to be faced, desires and fears reconquered.

Nineteenth and early twentieth-century ghost stories detail the instability of status and the oppression of patriarchy visible during the transition into marriage. Later twentieth-century ghost stories have a preoccupation with divorce and the experience of its similarly transitional nature.

Other literary definitions of the uncanny point to the development of ghost stories from an oral tradition, or their place within fantastic fiction. Todorov, for example, sees the uncanny as a type of fantasy where readers make conscious decisions about the fiction that they are reading.[5] They have to make the choice between mimetic or fantastic modes. It is the moment of hesitation before the decision is reached which makes the text pleasurable. Another definition of *Unheimliche* could be unhomely. Freud explores the etymological meaning of *Heimliche* and discovers that its opposite appropriates and distorts the sense of the original: *Heimliche* has connotations of home and comfort which *Unheimliche* retains but also inverts, *Unheimliche* is simultaneously a place free from ghostly influence and one full of ghostly-inspired terror.[6] The home is highly significant: amongst two hundred stories analysed for this survey a common narrative structure is the experience of a woman in her new home which makes her re-evaluate her marriage or family life.

The fears and terrors of the ghost story are not wholly imaginary; they speak of experience:

> In the first place, if psychoanalytic theory is correct in maintaining that every affect belonging to an emotional impulse, whatever its kind, is transformed, if it is repressed into anxiety, then among instances of frightening things there must be one class in which the frightening element can be shown to be something repressed which recurs.[7]

A concluding definition for this recurrence is drawn from Schelling: '*Unheimliche* is the name for everything that ought to have remained secret and hidden but has come to light'.[8]

Antecedents

In *Literary Women*, Ellen Moers argues in relation to Mary Shelley's *Frankenstein* (1818) that fantastic fiction allows women to draw on their own social and personal experience of real and powerful fears engendered by patriarchy.[9] Gothic fiction in the last quarter of the eighteenth century was able to address the frightening and the taboo, the 'socially unspeakable',[10] for the pleasure of the reader, and may be seen as a precursor of Victorian and modern ghost stories. Victorian ghost stories, generally framed by a realist preamble, have a strong sense of place and atmosphere, often focusing on the house and revealing a secret history that confutes the official one. Adherence to social convention is seen to provoke dilemma, even danger, and the stories' heroines learn about past injustice and contemporary social treatment.

By the end of the nineteenth century, the potential for parody is recognised, and the nature of the ghost has become a much more sophisticated mechanism for debating social life:

> 'Oh! I don't mean the usual sort of ghost,' said the Doctor . . . 'The ghost that is common to Scotch castles and English manor houses, and that appears in an orthodox nightgown, screams, rattles chains and bangs doors ad libitum . . . My ghosts are those that move about among us in social intercourse for days, months, sometimes years according to their several missions: ghosts that talk to us, and altogether comport themselves like human beings.' (Corelli, *Ziska* 1897)

The continuity of women's writing in the ghost story tradition

As Briggs has noted, from the 1890s ghost stories foster a sense of transgression which tempers gothic flamboyance with modernist austerity.[11] It is from this period that the ghost story begins to develop into a place for experiment and self-expression, particularly for women's writing. The titles for anthologies begin to change; instead of the Victorian fireside tales ghost stories are found amongst collections of horror and the macabre. Short story collections such as Henrietta Everett's *The Death Mask* (1920), Margery Lawrence's work in *Nights of the Round Table* (1926) and *Terrors of the Night* (1932) as well as the titles given by Phyllis Bottome, *Strange Fruit* (1928) and D.K. Broster *Couching at the Door* (1942), are all indicative of the new mood and tone of the writing.

Ghost stories become the recounting of strange and personal experience without apology, in a cultural climate which positively embraces the supernatural and paranormal. The fascination with ancient Egypt (attested to by Marie Corelli's novel *Ziska: The Problems of a Wicked Soul* (1897), which featured ghosts and reincarnation) became even more extreme after Howard Carter opened Tutankhamen's tomb in 1922. Mystic Egypt, ghosts and the sentimentality of supernatural justice were all suitable backgrounds for Hollywood plots. Cheiro, the society psychic, who acted as 'adviser' to the early film industry, also published accounts of 'true' ghost stories. These included 'Nurse Cavell speaks to me two years after her execution', 'Royal Academy artist and the spirit of a murdered dancing girl' and 'Lost deeds found by a spirit'.[12]

Part of the testimony given by Cheiro in support of his powers notes the interest shown by many eminent professional men. Included in the list of those who had made investigations into psychic phenomena are the criminologist Caesar Lombroso, the astronomer Camille Flammarion and Sir Arthur Conan Doyle. The presence of the supernatural, although debunked by ratiocination, is often found in the work of women detective writers of the period (particularly Georgette Heyer and Margery Allingham), where it is used to explore puzzles, mysteries and crimes against women. Women short story writers who use the supernatural tend to omit the rational or moral ending, using fantasy for exploration rather than atmosphere.

In 1930 M.R. James, one of the masters of English ghost story writing, awarded first and second prize in the *Spectator* ghost story competition to women writers.[13] The first story narrates a curious event, not from the English countryside but the mystic east, while the second records the death of a new housemaid through contact with a ghostly occupant. The traditional role of the ghost was passive, although an encounter was potentially deadly; ghosts were generally apparitions, revenants which performed the ancient task of linking the past to the present. In women's writing in the early twentieth century they become active, hence the movement towards horror writing. Moreover, they have the ability to entice, rather than just represent forbidden desire. They become the ghosts Corelli visualised at large in society and engaged in ordinary intercourse.

Clothilde Graves's story 'The Spirit Elopement' (1915) illustrates the contemporary interest in the supernatural, which encouraged the modification of traditional roles and form. A young bride finds herself 'jealous of a disembodied astral entity' who has been trapped by her husband at a seance prior to their marriage. The presence of the spirit is ruining their honeymoon. Doubt, anxiety and revision of the future are often encountered alongside ghostly experience in a honeymoon setting. In this instance the bride engages a medium to find a spirit suitor for the ghost, and the ghostly pair leave the human couple alone.

Similar difficulties in married life are explored in Daphne du Maurier's ghost stories. Here, a significant theme is comparison between marriage and courtship. The status of wife appears diminished when privileges held at the beginning of a relationship are recalled. Her novels *Rebecca* (1938) and *My Cousin Rachel* (1952) examine women being haunted by the 'ghosts' of their husbands' previous marriages. In 'The Apple Tree' du Maurier locates the spirit of a widower's wife in a tree. The widower recalls his unhappy marriage and reproaches the tree, attempting to destroy it, but is instead killed by it. Ghost stories indeed become a way of re-evaluating memory.

A ghost story more characteristic of twentieth-century writing is du Maurier's 'The Pool'. Again the genius loci is situated in the natural environment but, although the story shares the themes and motives of more straightforward narratives, it is in fact difficult to equate the haunting with an actual ghost:

> Her reflection wavered up at her, and it was not the face she knew, not even the looking-glass face which anyway was false, but a disturbed image, dark-skinned and ghostly.

The adolescent protagonist here is faced with a choice between two worlds: her private childhood and memories of her dead mother, and the practical world after menstruation. If she chooses the latter she will lose the key to the secret world. The unpleasantness of the pond and confusion of the interpretation of emotion are echoed in the later story 'Don't Look Now' (1971) with a grotesque murder at its conclusion. Once more a couple are on a second honeymoon, and discussing spiritualism in the context of the death of their child. Bereavement, grief and guilt are emotional states which the genre increasingly explores.

In the Victorian stories sensational secrets, such as infidelity, revenge and suffering, were ghostly events and therefore distanced from the narrator's life. In the twentieth-century stories, the revelations often concern the narrator's own past.

Selma Robinson's story 'The Departure' (*c.* 1920) introduces a woman who is under medical supervision following the death of her fiancé. At the invitation of the dead man she commits suicide in order to join him. Other protagonists think that they are being adventurous in following up a ghostly mystery but they often find that it is they themselves to whom the secret is directly related. An example of this is 'The Buick Saloon' (Bridge 1939), where a wife newly arrived in Peking hears one side of a love story from a ghostly voice haunting her car. In wanting to learn the full account of the affair she discovers her husband's infidelity.

The new bride's home and honeymoon period are not so prominent within the ghost story of the early twentieth century, but histories of women related to the witness become complex and intricate. As with Edith Wharton's 'Miss Mary Pask' (1925), women have to be dead before they can say what they feel or think:

> Supposing something survived of Mary Pask long enough to cry out to me the unuttered loneliness of a life time, to express at last what the living woman had always to keep dumb and hidden.

Crimes committed against women are still extreme, but they become overt metaphors for contemporary states, with their tales of imprisonment, aphasia and invisibility. The common change in status that women experience in the ghost stories of the early twentieth century is occasioned not necessarily by marriage but more likely by a new job or work situation. The interview becomes an experience of powerlessness, transition and vulnerability. As the Victorian stories retrospectively explored marriage and love affairs, so stories such as Ellen Glasgow's 'The Shadowy Third' (1923) and writers such as Eleanor Scott use their narratives to review a woman's career.

The dominant short story writer of the early twentieth century is the American Edith Wharton. She is frequently anthologised in English collections despite the length of her stories. She examines marital relationships which are often viewed by those who have come to live and work in the strained household—for example 'The Lady's Maid's Bell' (1904). In a later story Wharton affirms the connection between ghosts and houses:

> It was the house itself, of course, that possessed the ghost-seeing faculty that communed visually but secretly with its own past, if one could only get into close communion with the house, one might surprise its secret and acquire the ghost sight on one's own account. ('Afterward' 1909)

The experience of being haunted is not necessarily one of fear for Wharton, but rather the release of previously dormant inner feelings. As in 'Afterward', the ghost is often imperceptible and only recognisable after the event and the revelation of past injustice:

> Afterward I was terribly frightened, but at the time it wasn't fear I felt, but something deeper and quieter. ('The Lady's Maid's Bell')

Like a great many ghost story writers after her, Wharton begins to explore and portray the destructive nature of marriage on patriarchal terms. Two of her stories in this survey visualise marriage as imprisonment within the marital home. In 'Kerfol'

(1916) research on the part of a prospective housebuyer reveals the trial of an early eighteenth-century woman with a desolate married life, who is incarcerated on her husband's death through his jealousy and cruelty. In a later story a woman inherits a house and endeavours to find out its history. She is particularly interested in the story's eponymous and mysterious Mr Jones (1928), who still dominates the household but was originally the jailor of a deaf and dumb heiress whom his master had married for her fortune.

On both these occasions the stories are unconnected with the protagonist other than through the house. Wharton also explores the narrator's more active engagement with memory. In 'The Looking Glass' (1935) a grandmother confesses to her granddaughter that she acted as a medium during the war. She considers her role in contacting the dead lover of 'the rich Mrs Clingsland', and wonders whether she has committed a sin. 'Pomegranate Seed' (1931) is a rather more significant example of how the ghost story is used to explore the past. A wife re-enters the marital home and reviews her marriage. Her husband is being haunted by his domineering first wife. At the story's conclusion the husband is missing and is not expected back.

The openness and inconclusiveness of 'Pomegranate Seed' makes it comparable to the work of those women writers who were more directly interested in psychology. May Sinclair is one of the first writers to use psychoanalytic material in her fiction. 'The Token' (1923) allows a wife to test her husband after her death to see if he loved her. 'Where Their Fire Is Not Quenched' is closely associated with the 'stream of consciousness' technique of which Sinclair is a pioneer. The woman protagonist in this story is brought backwards through time to consider what she has made of life. The conclusion to 'The Victim' is much more surprising. The ghost returns to forgive his murderer, but it is the woman's forgiveness for the real crimes of fear, hatred and jealousy that is more important.

Sinclair's approach to the afterlife has something in common with the work of Margery Lawrence and Mary Butts who were interested in the occult. Lawrence published *Ferry Over Jordan* (1944) which discussed occult philosophy, and Butts was an associate of Aleister Crowley. Their stories such as 'The Haunted Saucepan' (Lawrence 1926) and 'With or Without Buttons' (Butts 1938) balance humour with horror as people are haunted by inanimate objects.

A popular connection was made during this period between the supernatural and psychological states, as seen in Robinson's story. Wharton sees ghosts as the projections of mental obsession (see 'The Eyes' 1910). Doubt, so often voiced in the Victorian ghost story, is now examined in the context of madness and sanity. In 'The Book' (1930) Irwin looks at the altered psychological state of a man possessed by occult knowledge. In 'The Earlier Service' she explores an adolescent girl's *unheimlich* fears of certain places, fear shared by her mother but of which her father is ignorant, hence guiding her into danger.

The hospital and psychiatric ward become a familiar setting for the ghost story. Rebecca West describes illness and fears experienced in a nursing home in 'The Grey Men (An Experience)'. Cynthia Asquith's radio play 'The Follower' (1934) is another tale which involves psychiatric nursing. The introspection of these stories, including Woolf's 'The Haunted House', is replaced after the war by an anti-nostalgic equation of memory with terror. An earlier example is Stella Gibbons's 'The

Roaring Tower' (1937) in which a woman looks back and recalls a period of grief and unhappiness in her youth.

The impetus for this modification of form is found in the work of Elizabeth Bowen and foreshadowed by Gorst's 'The Doll's House' (1933), in which the malevolent haunting of a woman ends in violence. Bowen develops significant techniques for ghost story writing, as in 'The Happy Autumn Fields' (1945) with its parallel narrative where the past and present appear simultaneously, but juxtaposed. 'The Cat Jumps', which is the title story from her 1934 collection, one that is frequently anthologised, is similar to Gorst's story. The Harold Wrights move into a house which was the scene of a brutal murder and are possessed by it. In both cases once again the sense of place is used to explore inner emotions and feelings in the fleeting evocative manner of the ghost story.

In other stories Bowen explores a sense of pursuit and patriarchal oppression, for example 'Hand in Glove'. In this story a deserted wife revenges herself on her thoughtless niece by condemning her to the same fate. 'The Apple Tree' (1934) requires a friend to exorcise the victim of the manifestation so that she can forget the past and face the future. The experience of ghosts is first hand and immediate. 'The Demon Lover' (1966) sees a girl returning to a bombed house. She remembers her escape from a cruel fiancé during the war, only to be carried off in the taxi that he is driving.

Intergenerational narratives and family themes

The popularity of the ghost story continued unabated after the Second World War. Women writers continued to act as editors, but increasingly overlooked magazines in favour of the new genre-specific anthology. The sheer volume of ghost stories appearing in the post-war period can be measured by the regular publishing of anthologies by Pan, Fontana and more recently Headline. The market for magazine fiction began to contract, although the ghost story retained a niche within women's interest periodicals.

A pioneer of anthology editorship was the writer Cynthia Asquith who collected the stories for *The Ghost Book* (1926), *Shudders* (1929) and *When Churchyards Yawn* (1931). She edited her *Second Ghost Book* in 1952 when she was in the position to ask writers to contribute original material. Rosemary Timperley, who edited the Pan series, was also able to publish new work rather than recycling Victorian and Edwardian classics, and her anthologies are characterised by more contemporary work than those of other editors, and feature many women writers.

The predominant themes in these ghost stories can be seen as offshoots of those previously examined, but which have now attuned themselves to the contemporary cultural climate. Not unexpectedly, given social experience since 1974, redundancy appears as a significant theme. It is directly addressed by D.K. Haynes in 'Redundant' (1991) and Penelope Fitzgerald's 'The Axe'. However, the pattern that emerges in terms of women's experience is the coupling of widowhood and redundancy. Widowhood is treated similarly as resulting in the loss of status and role. Such an outlook does not go unchallenged by the ghost stories. The widow in Jean Stubbs's 'A Difficult Man' (1971) re-appraises her marriage. Timperley's 'Lost Pathways' (1983) opens with a familiar scene, that of a widow creating a garden in her new house. More defiantly, Kalpakian's fulfilled but childless and unmarried heroine meets retirement with an outrageous ghostly party in 'A Christmas Cordial' (1988).

In keeping with the publishing opportunities in magazines, these stories feature housework. The telling of tales and family histories is recognisable as an exploration of intergenerational communication and experience, which explains the regularity of ghost stories in women's magazines. The housewife, however, even within marriage is usually a figure alone. Ghost stories in women's interest periodicals return to a sense of the ghostly as homely and comforting rather than frightening. However, two examples of the housewife story reveal an element of subversion. Norah Loft's 'A Curious Experience' (*Woman's Journal* 1971) sees a woman possessed by the house-proud previous occupant of her new home. Fay Weldon, a frequent contributor to *Cosmopolitan*, examines the stress and abuse of power exacted by a houseproud husband:

> Deidre, or some expression of Deidre, went home and churned up the lawn and tore the gate off its hinges. The other Deidre raked and soothed, resuscitated and blamed a perfectly innocent child for the gate. ('Breakages' 1988)

Deidre's unconscious actions force her to the stage where she has to move out and plan a new life. Penelope Lively's story 'Black Dog', published in *Cosmopolitan* in 1986, charts a woman's nervous breakdown within the home. She is haunted by the dog which prevents her from going out and undertaking her role as a housewife. She grows stronger and braver but cannot relate to her husband until he too can sense the dog.

Rather than focusing on difficulties at the onset of marriage, stories in the post-war period look at marital problems such as domestic violence and psychological abuse. Mary Williams is the most prolific British ghost story writer of the period. She published numerous collections throughout the 1970s and her most recent anthology *Ravenscare* was published in 1991. Her ghost stories address various aspects of relationships after marriage. Antagonisms present in her work, and which are found elsewhere, are manifested in the possession of the second wife by the first, a husband's jealousy which results in murder, the wife's leaving a husband because she cannot cope with his obsession, and power struggles over mundane matters such as money. The bizarre 'Falsies' (1978) has a prim librarian making a hasty marriage that she regrets. The marriage finally breaks down when she is haunted by giant breasts which drive her insane.

Mental states within marriage provide many examples of hauntings. In 'Open to the Public' (1989) Muriel Spark charts the breakdown and recovery of a marriage, once the individuals have faced their own private preoccupations. Colvin's story 'Something to Reflect Upon' (1991) finds a woman haunting herself. Her mental collapse after leaving her husband results in her death. Timperley's ghost in 'The Walker Out' returns to her husband after leaving him, but he is only pleased to see her 'corporeal' form because now he can divorce her. The theme of possession recurs in purposeful hauntings which hope to reclaim the husband after death. The divorce stories also develop a sense of non-communication in marriage as in Maggie Ross's 'The Man Across the River' (1982).

The most dramatic and frequently explored theme in the post-war ghost story is divorce. These stories are able to use the fantastic to convey brutal descriptions of possession, revenge and psychological or physical pursuit. Stubbs returns to the motif of the doll's house in 'An Evening with the Cromers', in order to address divorce. Her ghosts are a Victorian family around the dinner table discussing divorce, while the woman who has bought the antique is facing it in reality. Divorce is seen as a more significant change in social position than marriage. In the extreme a 'huis clos' scenario is developed as in Elizabeth Walter's 'Dual Control' (1975), whereas the fear of an ex-husband and the vulnerable status of the divorcée is chillingly detailed by Antonia Fraser in 'Who's Been Sitting in My Car' (1976).

Over a quarter of the stories surveyed feature children, and the loss of a child is a frequent narrative taken up by the divorce stories. Sewell's story 'Prelude' (1991), first published in the second Virago collection, follows a widow's fight with her late husband's ghost for 'custody' of their child. Byatt's 'The July Ghost' (1982) focuses on the grief of a woman who has lost her child in a road accident. Her emotion is so powerful that one character explains the ghost as the visual impression of her memories. Obversely the protagonist of Shelley Smith's 'The Follower' (1982) is haunted by the ghost of a child she has not yet killed. Originally she believes the apparition is a hallucination resulting from her guilt and grief over an abortion.

Ursula Le Guin's 'Crosswords' (1992) provides a complex example of intergenerational conflict and potential resolutions to the traumas of childhood and parenting. A mother starts to work out her problems as a victim of child abuse, and her mother's complicity in this, before communicating with her own daughter. Her mother's ghost follows her, trying to listen. The thought of this need to share experience prompts her to re-establish contact with her own daughter. Examples of writers exploring the relationship between mothers and daughters in ghost stories are strikingly apparent. Barbara Eyre brings three generations of women together in a holiday flat and unites the women through their ability to see ghosts ('Granny's Gift' 1980). A mother loses her daughter in 'Little Girl Lost' because the girl shares psychic ability with her grandmother. In 'The Aunts' (Winifred Wilkinson 1970), an American professor peacefully exorcises Quaker sisters who haunt their nephew and niece. Between them they come to appreciate their spinster aunts' achievements outside marriage, their lifestyle and their concerns for the house.

The status of children in ghost stories is usually that of victim or—as begins to emerge in the post-war period—as representing elusive desire. The childless woman is often seen as redundant, her childlessness leading to her inactivity and sense of loneliness. Apart from Ruth Rendell's 'The Haunting of Shawley Rectory' (1979), where a mother murders her daughter in dispute over their lover, intergeneration narratives are very positive. The Victorian stories and Dorothy Eden's tale 'Madonna Lilies' (1971) record many crimes committed against children due to their illegitimate, unwanted or unsupported birth. Tolerance of the older generation by the younger or vice versa, leading to communication and the end of secrecy in the present, increasingly challenges a formulaic convention which regrets the past.

Conclusion

> But though Miss de Mannering is a gentle ghost, I do not like ghosts, besides, now I know her secret, I could not intrude upon her.

F.M. Mayor, 'Miss de Mannering of Asham' 1935

Over the past twenty-five years the convention of the ghost has been used in a variety of media forms and by other fictional genres. In one of these forms, the television series *So Haunt Me*, the ghost becomes detached from the supernatural and the basis for a situational comedy. In this context what is being scrutinised is the family, changes in values between generations or cultures and the exchange of experience, but though revelation is still a threat the ghost itself is one of the family.

In the introduction to her 1983 collection of ghost stories, Susan Hill reminds us how a ghost story appeals to the reader:

> Its art is the art of omissions of suggestion, not of crude and explicit description . . . It is frightening because it has its roots in the real world.[14]

The ghost story does not allow us to turn away from the apparition and its secret; unlike the horror story, it works in the way Hill describes. The successful structure of the ghost story couples the *Unheimliche* with the sublime, and the horror of ghost story writing is found in obscurity. To describe a part is more terrifying than the whole; readers have to provide their own explanation by comparing the events with their own experience. Ghost stories rarely just recount the event; they address the reader directly. The agenda is very clear: gender roles, new home, new job, the experience of women at all stages in their lives. And ghost stories are traditionally told at Christmas, a period when most strain is put on the family, marriage, budget and homelife.

Debates concerning women's value and status are being popularly articulated; the majority of stories specifically address a change of status rather than a change in life-style. Rather than 'those tragic, wailing, ladies the past specialises in' (Celia Fremlin, 'Don't tell Cissie' 1974), the setting for the ghost story is contemporary and the range of women and their situations extremely broad. In many cases the ordinary women discussed have become outsiders, and there are interstices in ghost story writing which shelter alternative viewpoints. The vital and most recurrent theme is communication; telling and listening become imperative.

All hauntings invite the percipient to share their feelings, and the conventions of the ghost story provide a rhetoric for presenting personal experience. The difficulties in finding popular space for these aspects of everyday living are partially solved by the technical achievements of the ghost story. These stories are purposeful. Pure descriptiveness is not enough for them to succeed; the reader must engage with a chain of consequence. Ghost stories linger rather than shock. They provoke the re-evaluation of the personal history that has been made known. So the ghost story becomes a territory for describing and accounting for powerful emotions such as grief, loneliness, frustration and despair. The available conventions provide a framework for empathy and the subjects of bereavement, loss and the passing of years; the ghost story allows the experience of a lifetime to be contained within the short story:

> The circumstances could hardly be described as beneficial; for in all these incidents I had been involved in a kind of dredging up of the destructive emotions of grief, jealousy or revenge, at considerable sacrifice of my own serenity. (Wade, 'Skimmers Leap' 1986)

Ghost story reading is often seen as ungendered by editors who anthologise it. Its current popularity suggests that the ghost story has not become an antiquated form of fiction and is still relevant for writer and reader. It considers a variety of rites of passage. If these are examined carefully then one finds that where there is a lack of social acknowledgement for life crises—the onset of menstruation, moving house, the death of parents, divorce, widowhood—the ghost story reserves a space for their cultural expression.

As a fantastic narrative the ghost story can be expected to articulate subversive as well as conservative discourse. From the 1890s, its *mise en scène* has been used to impart alternative philosophies regarding life and death. Ideologies of femininity are particularly sensitive to the connotations of language used to value inner emotional and spiritual life. A discourse of percipience and passivity helps perpetuate a mythology of the feminine as intuitive and impractical. The majority of ghost stories take their premise from home and home life. They often set about re-ordering the domestic sphere through tolerance and understanding, the consensual harmony of the romance novel.[15] Nonetheless, these stories are often published alongside those which may advocate abandoning that same home for the sake of self-preservation.

In the 1990s, a period of 'religious crisis', a cultural climate of 'new age' sensibility appears to foster the popularity of the ghost story. 'Trystings' (1991) by Janice Elliott records the reincarnations of 'soul mates'; though it is not strictly a ghost story it is grouped with the genre. The carefully defined collections of the 1960s, 1970s and early 1980s are becoming superseded by women's horror writing, a new mood in detective writing as well as the all-encompassing supernatural tale. Ghost stories are part of a growing genre of self-reflexive writing rather than merely fireside entertainment.

The ghost story continues to fulfil an expressive and commercial purpose. In the 1990s, in accord with the cultural climate, the ghost story is used to disseminate knowledge, not necessarily of occult philosophy, though in the majority of stories narratives detail emotional if not physical afterlife. Stories of abuse, neglect and mental breakdown are made much more palatable through the distancing effect of the supernatural. Stories are told with hindsight, narrators pass on what they have learnt. The stories manipulate their own generic stereotypes, both retaining and subverting the didacticism of the fairy tale. More importantly these stories are circulated and, in the current publishing market, constantly recycled. Popular fiction is viewed as safe and uncritical and left to filter into all kinds of publications.

Any evaluation of the ghost story and women's contribution to it falls victim to the high-versus-low culture debate. Many of its conventions, themes and concerns are present within magical realism and both modes of writing explore the unexpected, supernatural and fantastic within recognisably realist modes. The popular ghost story expects the same mental exertion on a personal scale and covers the same ground. At its core it is attempting to express personal responses to a period of great social change and cultural anxiety.

The visible margins exposed by women's ghost story writing are these anxieties, which remain obscured because they cannot be resolved. Many ghost stories concern crime, violence and injustice where moral retribution is forthcoming. Equally they discuss issues of parenthood, aging, death and family relationships of which there is little sustained and ready public debate. Private support is also absent, a lack paraded in the problem pages of women's magazines. Ghost stories have their place there and have always provided women with an outlet, if not a resolution, for their fears.

NOTES

1. Interestingly, since ghost stories are frequently anthologised, stories from different periods and backgrounds find themselves in the same collection, and writers such as Elizabeth Gaskell (1810–65) are reprinted for a new audience, who will re-interpret nineteenth-century experience.
2. See especially J. Briggs, *Night Visitors: The Rise and Fall of the English Ghost Story*, London, Faber 1977.
3. See, for example, A. Lurie, *Women and Ghosts*, London, Heinemann 1994.
4. Sigmund Freud, *Art and Literature*, ed. Albert Dickson, Vol. 14, London, Pelican 1985, p. 340.
5. T. Todorov, *The Fantastic: A Structural Approach to a Literary Genre*, Ithaca, NY, Cornell University Press 1975.
6. Freud, *Art and Literature*, pp. 346–7.
7. Ibid., p. 363.
8. Ibid., p. 345.
9. Ellen Moers, *Literary Women*, London, The Women's Press 1978.
10. D. Punter, *The Literature of Terror*, London, Longman 1980, p. 417.
11. Briggs, *Night Visitors*.
12. Cheiro was the pseudonym of Count Louis Hamon (1860–1936) who wrote a prolific number of books on various methods of prediction. His work included an undated volume titled *True Ghost Stories* from which these examples have been taken. It seems to have been published just after the First World War.
13. Winifred Galbraith, 'Here He Lies Where He Longed To Be' and Emma Duffin, 'The House Party', reprinted in R. Dalby and Rosemary Pardoe (eds) *Ghosts and Scholars*, London, Crucible Press 1987, an anthology in the tradition of M.R. James.
14. Susan Hill (ed.) *Ghost Stories*, London, Hamish Hamilton 1983, p. 11.
15. This is further discussed in J. Radway, *Reading the Romance*, Chapel Hill, University of North Carolina Press 1984, p 208.

FURTHER READING

Aickman, R., *The Second Fontana Book of Great Ghost Stories*, London, Fontana/Collins 1966. Tenth Impression 1976.
— *The Seventh Fontana Book of Great Ghost Stories*, London, Fontana/Collins 1971. Third Impression 1976.
Allen, W., *The Short Story in English*, Oxford, Clarendon Press 1981.
Asquith, C., *Shudders*, London, Hutchinson and Co 1928.
BBC, *The Man in Black*, London, BBC Publications 1990.
Val Baker, D., *When Churchyards Yawn*, London, William Kimber 1982.
— *Ghosts in Country Villages*, London, William Kimber 1983.

— *Phantom Lovers*, London, William Kimber 1984.

Beer, G., 'Ghosts' in *Essays in Criticism*, 28 July 1978, pp. 259–64,

Campbell, R., *Uncanny Banquet*, London, Little Brown and Co 1992.

Chambers, A., *The Bumper Book of Ghost Stories*, London, Pan 1976. (Previously *The Tenth Ghost Book* 1974 and *The Eleventh Ghost Book* 1975.)

Coghill, H. (ed.) *Autobiography and Letters of Mrs MOW Oliphant*, London, Blackwood 1899.

Corelli, M., *Ziska: The Problems of a Wicked Soul*, 1897.

Cox, M., and Gilbert, R.A., *Victorian Ghost Stories*, Oxford University Press 1991.

Cuddon, J.S., *Roald Dahl's Book of Ghost Stories*, London, Penguin 1984.

Dalby, R., *The Virago Book of Victorian Ghost Stories*, London, Virago 1988.

— *Ghosts For Christmas*, London, Headline 1989.

— *The Virago Book of Ghost Stories*, London, Virago 1990.

— *Horror for Christmas*, London, Headline 1992.

— *The Virago Book of Ghost Stories Vol. II*, London, Virago 1994.

Ellis, S.M., 'The ghost story and its exponents', *Fortnightly Review*, Dec 1923.

Haining, P., *Christmas Spirits*, London, William Kimber 1983.

Hampden, J., *Ghost Stories*, London, Everyman 1963. First published 1939.

Holmes, R., *Macabre Military Stories*, London, Leo Cooper 1979.

Keating, P., *The Haunted Study*, London, Secker and Warburg 1989.

Lamb, H., *Gaslit Nightmares*, London, Macdonald 1988.

— *Gaslit Nightmares Vol. II*, London, Macdonald 1991.

Marcus, D., *The Poolbeg Book of Irish Ghost Stories*, Dublin, Poolbeg Press 1990.

du Maurier, D., *Echoes from the Macabre*, London, Gollancz 1976.

Myers, A., *The Second Book of After Midnight Stories*, London, William Kimber 1986.

Orel, H., *The Victorian Short Story*, Cambridge University Press 1986.

Phillips, R. (ed.) *The Omnibus of Twentieth Century Ghost Stories*, London, Robinson Publishing 1992.

Smith, P., *Haunted Shores*, London, William Kimber 1980.

Sullivan, J., *Elegant Nightmares*, Ohio University Press 1978.

Timperley, R., *The Fifth Ghost Book*, London, Pan 1971.

Terry, R.C., *Victorian Popular Fiction 1860–80*, London, Macmillan 1983.

Turner, J., *The Unlikely Ghosts*, London, Mayflower 1969.

Wharton, E., *The Ghost Stories of Edith Wharton*, London, Constable 1975.

Williams, M., *The Haunted Valley*, London, William Kimber 1978.

7 Nursing an image: the Sue Barton career novels

Julia Hallam

> She had that gift . . . of projecting herself into the interests and feelings of another person. It is a gift also common to good nurses, good friends—and good wives.[1]

The *Sue Barton* career novels were first published in Britain in 1939. By 1960 the series had sold over half a million copies and been reprinted in hardback twelve times. Knight Books brought out their paperback edition in 1967, reprinting it a further eleven times. By the early 1980s, with copies still selling in the bookshops, it was difficult to refute the publishers' claim that the books are the most successful stories about nursing ever printed.[2] At their peak, the books achieved a level of popularity with their young readership that is similar to the popularity of adult genres like mystery and romance. Even now they can still be found sitting on the shelves in many local libraries, although the number of borrowers has declined in recent years.

You're becoming a woman . . .

What interests me in these texts is their ideological role in relation to girls who were on the threshold of 'becoming women'. I can remember that 'becoming a woman' was very much at the forefront of my mind when I was reading these books. My mother's only guidance in this matter was to give me a small pamphlet with a picture inscribed on the front of a young woman holding a baby. It was called, appropriately enough, 'You're Becoming a Woman', and described with the aid of diagrams and drawings the physical processes and changes in bodily appearance that would transform me from adolescent girl to mature woman. But what sort of woman was I to become? In the period before my life became dominated by an overriding interest in young men, I read a large quantity of romantic fiction. For me, these books were landscapes of possibilities, maps to guide me through the unfamiliar terrain of feminine behaviour.

Most analyses of teenage and juvenile fiction tend to focus on romantic novels and magazines and have not included popular career novels. Feminist critics have long argued that romance is a formative ideological influence in creating horizons of expectation in its young readers. Teenage romances tend to focus on issues of female desire, domesticity, sexuality and power. Like all forms of popular literature, teen fictions articulate tensions and contradictions that are present in society. Linda Christian-Smith claims that they present imaginative resolutions to relations between the sexes and are productive of certain subject positions for their readers.[3] The *Sue Barton* books, although they are ostensibly about work, about the material world, use similar tropes and narrative formats to those of teenage romance texts, but their focus is on feminine behaviour rather than heterosexual relations.

Books about nursing and hospital life were usually written by women who worked as nurses themselves.[4] The author of the *Sue Barton* series, Helen Dore Boylston, began her training at the age of eighteen at the Massachusetts General Hospital in Boston in 1913. By the end of the First World War, she was a member of the Harvard medical unit for duty overseas with the British Expeditionary Forces. She later joined the American Red Cross, serving for two years in Poland and the Balkans before returning home to the Massachusetts General Hospital, where she taught nose and throat anaesthesia. It was around this time that a writer friend read her war diary and sent it to the *Atlantic Monthly*, where it was published in serial form. This was the beginning of a new career as a professional writer. The first of the *Sue Barton* series was published in 1939 simultaneously in North America and Britain, the rest following at regular intervals until the early 1950s. Dore Boylston claims that every single incident in the first two books either happened to her or one of her classmates, and that Sue is 'the kind of person and the kind of nurse I wished I were'.[5]

Dore Boylston's stories form a narrative that describes Sue Barton's career in terms of her ongoing romance and marriage to a doctor. The first book in the series, *Student Nurse*, recounts her training and growing romantic interest in the young house officer Dr William Barry. The second book covers her term as a staff nurse at a busy city hospital and her developing romance, the third her engagement whilst working as a district nurse in the city slums. She marries Dr Barry and moves with him to his new post as head of a small country hospital. At the age of twenty-five, after a short spell as a rural district nurse, Sue takes over the supervision and training of the nursing staff, before retiring to have her children. The seven books are filled with detail on how to manage work, romance and family life, with little homilies on how to behave as a good nurse, wife and mother scattered throughout their pages.

Good girls make good wives . . . and nurses

The *Sue Barton* books function in part much as sentimental novels functioned in Victorian times, presenting moral messages of self-abnegation to a young readership on the threshold of womanhood, exposing the reader to ideals of nursing and femininity which in the 1950s nursing recruitment literature are encapsulated by the word 'service'. For Sue Barton, however, nursing is not only a matter of serving but a way of living. An all-encompassing narrative weaves her life into a seamless whole. The books present nursing as an ongoing, developing career that mirrors the development of her romance, marriage and the birth and growth of her children.

Historian Judith Rowbotham stresses the important role played by this kind of didactic fiction in the education of Victorian girls. By the early 1870s, it was becoming increasingly popular to wrap moral messages inside fictional stories, to 'coat the powder of the moral in the jam of a good narrative' in order to make dull lessons about duty seem adventurous and exciting. The authors claimed to write stories that would act as guides and influence children in the ways they would think and act for the rest of their lives. Writers like Charlotte M. Yonge encouraged the development of this new literary style, aiming at the growing juvenile market.[6]

From the 1880s, didactic fiction added another important element to its 'guidebook' aspect, that of careers adviser. For the first time, tales of single women with vocations that take them into professional work outside the home were given narrative resolutions that did not encompass the usual 'happy ending' of marriage and motherhood. Nursing was one of the first careers to be portrayed in this way. Although it had been established as a career for women since Nightingale's efforts in the 1850s had endeavoured to make it a respectable profession, it took a new generation of women writers to begin to reflect a more independent nursing stereotype, albeit one that still encompassed the Victorian middle-class Protestant ideal.

Built on a firm bedrock of Victorian ideals of femininity (as much the legacy of Dore Boylston's childhood experiences as the consequence of the genre she chose to write in), the *Sue Barton* books add a distinctive discourse of 'Nightingalism' to the didactic novel form. They do this at the level of both narrative structure and content. The narrative trajectory of Sue Barton's career parallels the development of Nightingale's own interests in nursing, tracing a path from hospital nursing to the waging of moral warfare against the sick in their own homes. At the level of content Dore Boylston's nurses willingly embrace Nightingale's dictums, promoting a vocational ethos of forbearance and self-sacrifice as well as unquestioning obedience to a hierarchical, military style of authority.

This representation of nurses and nursing depends for its effect on the relationship between content and form that has traditionally shaped women's didactic writing. The *Sue Barton* books, however, add a distinct piquancy to this relationship because the romantic element of narrative pleasure is enhanced through its connection to a medical man. Because Sue marries a doctor, the difference between work in the public sphere as a nurse and work in the private sphere as a wife is subsumed into the discourse of heterosexual relationships. The hospital becomes a metaphor for home life, with doctors as 'fathers', nurses as 'wives' and 'mothers' and patients as 'children'. At an ideological level, the combination of career and personal life in the narratives works to sustain the division of labour in health care, re-enforcing what Gamarnikow identified as the patriarchal familial structures inscribed in the relationship between medicine and nursing.[7] The popularity of these texts in Britain and North America is a testament to how these values could travel across space and time, subsuming cultural differences in an all-encompassing ideal of nursing as a white, middle-class profession.

Fashioning the self

The female 'heroes' of these novels embody a peculiar mix of characteristics which I see as redolent of so much North American writing for girls of the period—a combination of an adventuring, pioneering spirit and a determination to get what they want, yet with a preparedness to serve others and find it a pleasurable, enjoyable task. The *Sue Barton* stories present two versions of this 'ideal type' of femininity embodied in the principal characters, Sue and her best friend Kit.

The novels function structurally on a clear binary opposition which is posed between the public presentation of the private self in mufti and the private presentation of the public self through the wearing of the nurse's uniform. We are given detailed descriptions of the clothes and make-up that Sue and her friends select for every social occasion, whether a walk in the country or a night at the theatre. The books function as manuals on how to present yourself in public, paying close attention to occasional encounters with members of the opposite sex. As well as learning how to dress as a young middle-class single woman, the reader is educated about the lifestyle and attitudes of nurses as a group. In the public sphere of work, individuals' attitudes to their nursing role and work are judged by their personal appearance. Those defined as 'unprofessional' tend to wear their uniform incorrectly, their hair in the wrong style or are described as 'untidy' and 'too casual'. The way these young women look is taken axiomatically to signify their attitude to their work and to their role as nurses. Untidiness indicates a deeper character defect, with connotations of a lack of self-discipline and promiscuity that could erupt and disturb nursing's hard fought for aura of respectability.

Descriptions of clothes in these texts, and of uniforms in particular, are heavily value-laden. They carry within them the codes of a specific set of feminine values, and those values are re-articulated through the transforming process of putting on the uniform, and donning with it an ideal of professional tradition and identity. The student nurses in these stories are measured against this ideal, their success or failure as nurses depending on their ability to become more (or less) like the model nurses Sue and Kit, who are set up as complementary opposites both in terms of their appearance 'types' (red head, brunette) and as working 'types' (practical skills, management skills). The definition of nursing professionalism rests, however, on the personality attributes and character traits of these idealised feminine characters, not on their skills as practical nurses or nurse managers.

Because there is no clear distinction between work and personal life, the public and potentially political space of the hospital is articulated as the shared personal living space of a small tightly knit group of female friends. Admission to the nursing profession involves initiation into this small group or cohort who share the same lowly position at the bottom of a rigid professional hierarchy. Within this hierarchy, the nurses' uniform is a symbol of position and status, representing a yet to be known world of professional etiquette whose complex rules and codes are embodied in its signifying power. The books are littered with detailed, fetishistic descriptions of the 'girls' in their uniforms:

> She was a tall, square shouldered girl, with slim hips, easy swinging walk, and a permanently cheerful expression due to her impertinent nose and high arched brows. A tiny crinoline cap, with a black velvet band around its frilled base, perched at a slight angle on smooth brown hair. White uniform, white shoes, white stockings and Eton collar were immaculate.[8]

The uniform is also presented as a fashion item; the way the hat is worn at a particular angle negotiates the boundary between nursing identity and the wider discourse of femininity as manifest in contemporary ideas about clothes and how to wear them. As Dorothy Smith cogently points out, fashion images are articulated around other meanings of the feminine such as particular virtues and resistances.[9] Femininity is a historically specific phenomenon whose articulations change over time. The nurses' uniform contains within its folds traces of these changing virtues and resistances, inscribing on the bodies of those that wear it both the ghosts of their nursing foremothers and the relationship of those ghosts to contemporary professional ideals.

In the *Sue Barton* books, this foremother is indisputably Florence Nightingale, the British founder of modern nursing. Direct references to Nightingale, as well as veiled hints, refer to a past that is never articulated in historical terms, creating an aura of mythic deification around the Nightingale image. To emphasise the point, in *Student Nurse*, Nightingale's presence is fully evoked through the memories of a very elderly patient who had served as a drummer boy in the Crimea. His memories of Nightingale as a 'lovely slim and gentle young thing' are a clear distortion of the known facts of history, but work at an emotive level in the novel, emphasising self-sacrifice even to the point of death. For young women reading these books, the potency of this martyred image is reinforced by an incident immediately following this encounter, where Sue almost dies in the effort to save a patient's life.

The novels constantly present the reader with little descriptive homilies that remind us of the personal qualities needed to be 'good' women, perfect wives and successful nurses. The following example is from *Sue Barton: Staff Nurse*. This is the sixth book in the series, and was written in 1950. Bored at home with her three small children and feeling that she is wasting her valuable skills, Sue decides to return to work. This causes some consternation amongst the staff on the ward for not only is she the boss's wife, she was also formerly nurse-in-charge of the hospital and had established the training school for student nurses. Sue's best friend Kit, who trained with her and has since been her inseparable companion, is now superintendent of nurses.

Whereas Sue is foregrounded as a practical nurse who excels in her contact with patients, Kit is presented as a skilled manager who is responsible for the training and discipline of junior nursing staff. The medical staff however are totally outside her jurisdiction. One result of this separation of duties and responsibilities is that a young student nurse has to be punished for a doctor's misdemeanour even though she is totally powerless and Kit knows this is unfair. The incident centres on a doctor/nurse romantic entanglement between a soon-to-be-qualified student nurse and her doctor boyfriend. Messing about in the hospital dining room, he picks her up and carries her off. Although the powerlessness of her situation is obvious (we already know Frank to be considerably bigger and taller than she is), nursing management (Kit) feels bound to seriously punish the nurse with suspension because she has set a bad example to other students. Not to do so might lead to a breakdown of hospital discipline amongst 'irresponsible students', who would see this as a green light for misdemeanours with the medical staff. Placed in the position of having to treat a student nurse unfairly, our resourceful 'girls' Kit and Sue decide to solve the problem by playing a trick on the doctor. His 'violently masterful' response to their challenge and subsequent proposal of marriage to the student is exactly the response Kit and Sue expect. An institutional problem, the disciplining of doctors to respect their nursing colleagues as equals in the public sphere, is resolved by emotional manipulation. Kit knows that she cannot 'punish' the doctor, she has no power to do so, and to complain to the medical hierarchy about such a display of boyish high spirits would only demean her. She uses subterfuge (her feminine wiles!) to get what she wants, rather than any kind of public, political action that would disturb the existing power relations. Nursing's subordination to the medical profession is naturalised in the narrative, accepted and circumvented, leaving the structural relationship between doctors and nurses unquestioned and intact.

This lack of separation between the private and public world reinforces an unproblematic and apparently fixed identity against whom all women are judged as deviant or 'other' if they do not meet the white heterosexual middle-class criteria. Race is an almost invisible absence in the books, only presented as the peculiar characteristics of certain working-class patients from the slums. In all the stories, patients are treated much in the way that Sue treats her children, emphasising the 'innate' motherliness of nursing work. These 'career' novels subject girls to an image of work against which they can measure themselves not in terms of intellect or ability, but in terms of how they look, what colour they are, what class they come from, and how they conform to nursing's feminine ideal.

'Excitement, romance and adventure make my career thrilling and my books thrilling too'[10]

Re-reading these stories provoked the same feelings of frustration I remember experiencing when I read them the first time round more than twenty-five years ago. Sue Barton was not my favourite fictional nursing character, she was much too much of a 'goody goody' for my juvenile taste, someone who always conformed to authority and never broke the rules. I much preferred the more outgoing and adventurous protagonist of another popular nursing series, Cherry Ames. Unlike the *Sue Barton* books, however, the *Cherry Ames* series has been less enduring; I found no trace of the books on the shelves of local public libraries, only the odd tatty copy in charity shops. The last edition was printed in hard back in 1960; there is no evidence to suggest a paper-back edition was ever produced. My curiosity was aroused. Why had one series been so enduring, while the other was rapidly disappearing, leaving barely a trace?

Whereas the *Sue Barton* stories use heterosexual romance and marriage to structure their serial narratives, the *Cherry Ames* books are primarily mysteries with 'investigative thriller' narrative structures. Cherry Ames is a nurse who helps her patients back to health by solving the problems surrounding their illnesses. These are social rather than medical problems and are often rather fantastic, such as tracing long lost relatives (*Flight Nurse*), or revealing the motives of a greedy fortune hunter (*Superintendent Nurse*). The titles of the books indicate how the series is structured around the central character working as a nurse in a range of situations *Cherry Ames—Cruise Nurse*, *Cherry Ames—Chief Nurse*, *Cherry Ames—Mountaineer Nurse*. Rather than mapping out a progressive career path in different fields of nursing work as the *Sue Barton* books do, the *Cherry Ames* books present nursing as a series of exciting job possibilities in different locations. Nursing becomes associated with travel, adventure and excitement rather than duty, discipline and sacrifice.

The use of an investigative narrative structure articulates a rather different relationship between nursing and femininity than that of the Barton books. Cherry Ames wears both powder and nail varnish on duty, a sign of lower-class immorality and a promiscuous personality to Sue and her friends, but in these books a mark of Cherry Ames's middle-class glamour, sophistication and confidence. There is less detailed description of clothes and uniform, and much more about the actual work that Cherry is doing. In the Barton books, the emphasis is on the social and professional status of nursing; in these books, nursing work itself sounds interesting and challenging. In *Flight Nurse*, for example, we are told in considerable detail how Cherry copes with arresting haemorrhages, dressing wounds, adjusting splints, administering plasma and giving shock treatment whilst flying injured patients home from the battlefield without a doctor present. There seems to be more reason in these texts for professional discipline and self-sacrifice, because nursing work amounts to more than administrating tender loving care through soothing words and gestures. As well as possessing, like Sue, this 'innate' ability to care for others, Cherry demonstrates her knowledge of a range of practical nursing skills accompanied by a courageous, outgoing personality and strength of mind. Although descriptions of the work do lapse into a Nightingalish sentimentality at times, the investigative format of the narratives effectively presents her as an intelligent, independent young woman who can act on her own initiative.

In other ways, though, the image of femininity Cherry represents is still that of the good girl, someone who wants to please because pleasing others is the key to popularity, and therefore to happiness. Although she is resourceful and uses her own initiative, Cherry unquestioningly obeys doctors' orders and treats patients like naughty children when they break hospital rules. Nursing is a less powerful profession than in the Barton books, perhaps because its contextual relations are described in more detail. In the situations where Cherry works, doctors have the power to hire and fire the nursing staff. In *Cherry Ames—Night Supervisor*, for example, although Cherry is in charge of the nursing staff it is clear that she is employed by the chief medical officer who runs the hospital. Nursing seems to be more of a job than a profession, a worthwhile and satisfying job, but one which is clearly limited by the power of male doctors. The opportunities nurse training appears to offer a young woman in these texts are occasions for travel and adventure, rather than a vocational life of service to professional ideals and values embodied in the trope of marriage to a medical man.

The *Cherry Ames* stories provide a model of nursing as a career that was perhaps far more dynamic at the time than appears to be the case now. Cherry was certainly the epitome of my young dreams of ideal femininity—beautiful, intelligent and adventurous, living a life where she was footloose and fancy free, much sought after by young men, but not in need of a husband even in the closing pages of the book. The image of nursing presented here is much less didactic and more glamorous, in the sense that there is less emphasis on professional ideals and middle-class feminine etiquette and more on a range of opportunities for travel and personal development. Nursing is a demanding and interesting job that has a varied social life but is less a way of life in itself.

These books are not as visible now as the *Sue Barton* series and there is less information available about the writers, Helen Wells and Julie Tatham, who produced the series between the early 1940s and the late 1950s. Nonetheless, the books were undoubtedly popular—*Cherry Ames—Flight Nurse* was reprinted five times in Britain between 1956 and 1963.

The enduring quality of the *Sue Barton* books, compared to the virtual disappearance of the *Cherry Ames* series, poses interesting questions about popular fiction's ideological relationship to images of femininity. The *Cherry Ames* books are more entertaining, less pedantic in tone and contain more information about doing nursing work, but they were nonetheless quickly discarded, a less valued cultural product. There are practical reasons why the *Sue Barton* series has remained more visible: its reprint history, its popularity, for example, amongst librarians with purchasing power. The didactic form of the *Barton* books, with their moral messages wrapped in sacrificial narratives of tender loving care, obviously appealed to those adults with access to the institutional power to keep them in circulation. In a guide to children's literature written in the early 1970s, librarian Sheila Ray singles out the *Sue Barton* series as an exemplar of the kind of text popular with juvenile readers, making a link between reading these books and 'the light romances which may well be read by the same girls in their late teens and on into middle age',[11] a path that numerous commentators have referred to as 'the female reading career'.[12]

Nursing aspirations and medical fascinations

The popularity of both these nursing career series coincides in Britain with the development of medical romances as a bestselling adult genre. As in teenage romance fiction, analyses of the adult genre tend to privilege the romantic elements of the story as the key ingredient. Typically, the woman is fascinated by a mysterious man with an unknown past who is seen as dangerously threatening and sexually attractive.

In medical romances, however, the man is adored not because he is a tall dark stranger, but because he is a doctor with the ability to save life. The nurse is accustomed to meeting this man in the course of her daily work; her fascination is with his medical knowledge, his power to heal. Her desire for the man is portrayed as a desire to serve; in this sense, it is a quasi-religious fascination, based in part on a doctor's licence to heal through touch, to cure by a laying on of hands. The nurse can sexually desire this man without contaminating her vocational moral purity, providing she undertakes to serve and obey him.

In the post-war years, Lucilla Andrews, who had spent the war years 'in service' as a nurse, began to produce romantic fictions featuring doctors and nurses based in a hospital setting. Her bestselling novels place her at the forefront of the development of the subgenre of medical romance, which publishers Mills and Boon claim really 'took off' when they started publishing the books in paperback form. Perhaps a diet of nursing career novels amongst juvenile readers did feed an appetite for adult stories of a similar type, but that appetite was itself a symptom of a rising level of public interest and awareness in the new discourses of scientific medicine.

Throughout the 1950s and 1960s, the medical establishment was at the peak of a pinnacle of popular belief in its power to cure and heal. In the newly nationalised health system, doctors took on the vocational mantle of serving the patient. Doctors were fighting for the right of all patients to have equality of access to medical care, irrespective of their ability to pay. Doctors were fighting the former killer diseases of poverty with new and powerful drugs. Doctors were inventing new surgical procedures that could save and prolong lives. In this social climate a new kind of 'folk hero' developed, replacing the brave wartime soldier with a peaceful social warrior, waging the war for progress on the home front.

This change in the public imagination is apparent throughout all forms of popular representation of medicine, nursing and hospital life. Karpf notes a change in the BBC's health programming from a 'look after yourself' approach focused on diet and exercise, to 'the medical approach', which sees the history of medicine as 'a soaring graph of progress, with successive scientific discoveries and breakthroughs extending human knowledge and curative powers, and replacing primitive nostrums and folk remedies'.[13] The infant medium of television exploited new video technology to bring live pictures from hospital operating theatres into people's front rooms. In programmes like *Your Life in Their Hands*, doctors performed centre stage with the eyes of the newly enfranchised viewing public watching in fascination. *Emergency Ward 10*, now regarded as a hospital soap but seen at the time as a dramatised documentary of hospital life, featured doctors saving lives by applying modern medical knowledge.

In all these representations, nurses appear as secondary characters. Pushed to the margins of the screen, their only lines are to repeat doctors' orders, their only actions to pass them their instruments and clear up their mess. No longer are they self-sacrificing 'angels of mercy', tending sick patients and nursing them through the crisis; displaced by modern drug therapies, they become servants to modern medicine and handmaidens to doctors. Their patients become merely the physical bodies around whom the romance with medicine is played out. In films like *The Feminine Touch* (GB 1956), ostensibly about nurse training and nursing life, nurses no longer spend time at the bedside, but in ward kitchens preparing food for doctors at the bedside.

99

Across the spectrum of medical representations, doctors display a new masculine ethos of care and concern played out across the body of the patient. Nurses lose their monopoly of the feminine image of caring to a new masculine iconography of care and concern. Nursing's claim to professional autonomy rested on a 'separate spheres' philosophy that 1950s imagery erodes; nurses no longer care for patients but serve doctors and the new dictates of medical science.

'Helping and encouraging a man in his work is the finest work a woman can do'[14]

There was little change in this image throughout the 1960s. In the work situation, across all popular fictional forms, nurses were either portrayed as 'sexy playmates' or doctors' handmaidens where, like all good women, they served their men. In adult medical romances, they combined a public life of institutional service to medicine with a private life of domestic service to doctor husbands. The narrative resolution to this commitment to work is posed in terms of a 1950s notion of middle-class marriage which promoted separate but equal spheres of responsibility. The nurse and her doctor husband will be 'one person doing one job'.[15] Nurses in these stories always marry doctors who support their own ethical values, so that in giving up their public role to support their husbands, they are nonetheless continuing to support the ideals and beliefs that have informed them as nurses. Their power as women becomes the power of social influence, and it is here that part of the attraction lies for the reader.

The aspiration to marry medical men cannot be wholly separated from the other strong appeal doctor/nurse romances exerted on their readers, a fascination with medical knowledge and power. In some books, this knowledge and power is encapsulated in the figure of the brilliant surgeon whose new surgical procedures will save people from death. In these books, the doctor tends to remain a distant, unknown figure whose 'truth' is discovered by the heroine, once she decides to trust him. In other texts, however, the doctor heroes are much more human characters. The mysteries of medicine are revealed to them and the nursing heroines through the narrative, involving the reader in solving medical mysteries and health problems. In initiate stories in particular, readers learn with the new nursing recruits the language of medicine, including the terminology for describing parts of the body and its functions and the shorthand or slang of hospital communication. Although the frequent references to Florence Nightingale and the descriptions of nursing work tend towards a notion of nursing work as 'housewifeliness', the reader can learn from these stories something about medical scientific discourse, as well as the power relations that are built into the discourse itself. The books offer to many readers the pleasure of 'insider' knowledge of medicine and hospital life, without having to be actively involved in the hard and dirty work of nursing.

The doctor/nurse romances of the late 1950s and early 1960s can be seen as amalgamating fantasies of feminine aspiration and fascinations with medical knowledge and power into a single generic form, satisfying a demand for stories in which female characters gain access to social status, power and knowledge through their sexuality and femininity. Nurses' sexual desires, often described as actively seeking satisfaction through pleasure in kissing and touching, become sublimated through relationships with 'good' doctors into a quasi-religious ecstasy centred on the male because he will do good in the world.

The *Sue Barton* books exist comfortably within this milieu of representations of nursing and hospital life. Although they can now seem to present a reactionary, old-fashioned view of what it means to be a working woman, within the melding of their discourses of the public sphere of work and private domestic life there is some space for recuperation. In the 1940s and 1950s, giving up work on marriage was virtually mandatory for most middle-class wives. The nursing profession took a dim view of women who married; marriage effectively terminated their careers, although it was possible to get jobs in non-hospital posts. Sue Barton manages to combine marriage and a career; through this juggling act, she symbolises the possibility of institutional change for those becoming nurses in the future. By comparison, Cherry Ames, the problem-solving individualist, becomes something of an anachronism, somewhat outside the enclosing orders of 1950s nursing femininity. There seems to be no place within the reconstituted vocationalism of the 'medical family' for the single woman seeking adventure and excitement. Cherry Ames became increasingly out of tune with the schoolgirl fictions of the times, whilst Sue Barton struck just the right narrative chord.

NOTES

1. Helen Dore Boylston, *Sue Barton, Superintendent Nurse*, London, Hodder and Stoughton 1968, p. 54.
2. Knight Books, Hodder and Stoughton 1981.
3. Linda K. Christian-Smith, 'Romancing the girl: adolescent romance novels and the construction of femininity', in Leslie Roman *et al.* (eds) *Becoming Feminine*, London, Falmer Press 1988.
4. Three of the most popular 1950s writers of adult doctor/nurse romances were Lucilla Andrews, Kate Norway and Valerie Nelson, all of whom trained and worked as nurses.
5. Helen Dore Boylston, *Sue Barton, Student Nurse*, London, Hodder and Stoughton 1971, endnote.
6. Judith Rowbotham, *Good Girls Make Good Wives: Guidance for Girls in Victorian Fiction*, Oxford, Basil Blackwell 1989, p. 5.
7. E. Gamarnikow, 'Sexual division of labour: the case of nursing', in A. Kuhn and A. Wolpe (eds) *Feminism and Materialism: Women and Modes of Production*, London, Routledge and Kegan Paul 1978.
8. Dore Boylston, *Sue Barton, Superintendent Nurse*, p. 8.
9. Dorothy Smith, 'Femininity as discourse', in Roman *et al* (eds) *Becoming Feminine*, pp. 37–60.
10. Back cover, *Cherry Ames* dust jacket, 1958.
11. Sheila Ray, *Children's Fiction: A Handbook for Librarians*, Leicester, Brockhampton Press 1974, p. 90.
12. See, for example, A. McRobbie, *Feminism and Youth Culture: From Jackie to Just Seventeen*, London, Macmillian 1991, and Janice Radway, *Reading the Romance*, Chapel Hill, University of North Carolina Press 1984.
13. A. Karpf, *Doctoring the Media*, London, Routledge 1988, p. 11.
14. Valerie Nelson, *Staff Nurse*, London, Mills and Boon 1957, p. 127.
15. Kate Norway, *The Lambs*, London, Mills and Boon 1965, p. 157.

FURTHER READING

Baker, Niamh, *Happily Ever After? Women's Fiction in Postwar Britain 1945–60*, London, Macmillan 1989.

Cadogan, M. and Craig, P., *You're a Brick, Angela! A New Look at Girls' Fiction from 1839 to 1975*, London, Gollancz 1976.

Klein, Viola and Myrdale, Alva, *Women's Two Roles: Home and Work*, London, Routledge and Kegan Paul 1956, 1968.

Modleski, T., *Loving with a Vengeance: Mass Produced Fantasies for Women*, London, Methuen 1984.

Pawling, C., *Popular Fiction and Social Change*, London, Macmillan 1984.

Snitow, A., 'Mass market romance: Pornography for women is different', in A. Snitow, C. Stansell and S. Thompson (eds) *Desire*, London, Virago 1984, pp. 253–75.

Wilson, Elizabeth, *Only Halfway to Paradise: Women in Postwar Britain 1945–1968*, London and New York, Tavistock Publications 1980.

8 Stories of love and death: reading and writing the fairy tale romance

Stephen Benson

> You had the sense to see you were caught in a story, and the sense to see that you could change it to another . . . for many things may and do happen, stories change themselves, and these stories are not histories and have not happened.
>
> A.S. Byatt, 'The Story of the Eldest Princess'[1]

In Janice Radway's influential survey of a community of romance fiction readers, participants were asked to identify the three most important ingredients necessary for a good read: the second most popular answer, after the prerequisite happy ending, was 'a slowly but consistently developing love between hero and heroine'.[2] Placing this within her theoretical model of the ideal fictional romance, Radway stresses the need for the representation of a gradually developing but focused relationship, without excessive digression. The pleasure this model gives is indicative of the narrative purity of formulaic fiction, the desire for an uncluttered, smooth path from beginning to end—in other words the desire for a love *story*, a narrativised representation of a relationship that fixes the flux of human relations into the primordial structure of a tale. The desire which is built up between the protagonists is matched by the desire of the reader to be fully satisfied by the ordered fulfilment of an already known outline of events.

This pleasure is especially prominent in genre fiction, at least in its popular manifestations, where plot is drained of excess to the point where it pivots and draws upon the motor of narrative itself: the desire to know, to uncover, to understand. The curiosity of the reader is analogous with the curiosity of the detective or the curiosity of the folkloric heroine, both of whom follow a path from confusion to enlightenment. Because of this priority, genre fiction draws on a store of relatively easily identifiable representations which can be slotted into a preordained story structure without the need to halt its inexorable flow. Generic characterisation is thus undertaken with broad strokes, producing characters which can be read speedily, and it is for this reason that genre fiction gives a revealing insight into the cultural context out of which it grows and back into which it feeds its distilled prototypes. The interplay between text and context is particularly prominent here; individual texts are read with reference to prior generic norms, yet these norms are only granted meaning in their individual manifestations. Genre itself is an abstract which is only knowable in an historical and cultural context. To follow the history of a genre is to follow the history and status of a set of shifting representations.

Genre is thus similar to gender, in the sense that both are abstract categories that need to be read contextually. Etymologically, the two are linked (gender is, after all, a biological genre) and individual genres—romance fiction, detective fiction, fantasy fiction—are usually written for a particular group of readers, thus allowing us to speak of 'the gendering of popular genres'.[3] Generic characterisations often stem from the allocation of roles according to gender, and the exploration of these roles and the norms by which they function is particularly fruitful. The study of a particular genre reveals the manner in which norms and expectations function within a textual world, one which works by rules and not by nature. It is the intersection of the biology of gender and the textuality of genre that provides a window on the construction of roles within society, where the allocation of roles according to historically defined rules is often carried out under the cloak of a putative nature.

My purpose here is to provide a reading of the popular romance genre, with particular reference to the activities of reading and writing, a selective reading of the lineage of the genre and the forms in which elements of this lineage have been re-read by contemporary writers. As my introduction suggests, this is a self-consciously literary approach which draws on the self-conscious manipulation of generic expectations in certain strains of recent fiction; as such, this can be placed alongside the sociological approach found in Bridget Fowler's *The Alienated Reader* and the ethnographical investigation carried out in Radway's *Reading the Romance*. The process of teasing out the strands that make up each particular genre provides an insight into the manner in which certain aspects of the narrative are given prominence at certain times. It is in this way that Fredric Jameson, attempting to break away from the holistic continuities of Northrop Frye's generic models, refers to the intertextuality of genre—the historical process by which certain representations or aspects of character are incorporated as part of the generic narrative—and the tensions in the positioning of these aspects at different historical moments. The interest lies in the 'substitutions, adaptions, and appropriations' that result, the individual text as 'a synchronic unity of structurally contradictory or heterogeneous elements, generic patterns and discourses'; 'properly used, genre theory must always in one way or another project a model of the coexistence or tension between several generic modes or strands'.[4] It is the resulting 'generic discontinuities' that provide a means of disrupting the inexorable drive for order in the formulaic narrative.

Traditionally, the lineage of the popular romance (including the gothic subgenre) is traced back, by various routes, via Charlotte Brontë, Jane Austen, and the sensation novel in the nineteenth century, to the sentimental novel of the eighteenth century and, in particular, Richardson's *Pamela*. Bridget Fowler traces the 'literary preconditions' of the popular domestic romance 'through the lines of lower-class descent', from the fairy tale and peasant novella through the popular domestic fiction of the eighteenth and nineteenth centuries. She allies this to an analysis of the social and ideological contexts within which the form took shape, from 'the dependence, propertylessness and vassalage of women vis-à-vis men in feudalism', to the increasing stress on the private sphere as constituting the female environment as capitalism developed from the seventeenth century, 'conditioned by the double exclusion of women, both from the contractual rights of bourgeois (male) individuals and the arena of production entered via wage labour'.[5] This latter overview is particularly important as a background to any predominantly literary approach, such as that taken here.

The intertextual strand upon which I wish to focus is that suggested by the responses to Radway's survey, where narrative itself and the curiosity it both engenders and feeds on is paramount. There is obviously a link between the romance as it exists today and the medieval chivalric romances, in which the hero's life was narrativised into a quest—what Northrop Frye refers to as 'a sequential and processional form'.[6] These wish-fulfilment tales, with their strongly fantastical vein, are powerfully masculine narratives, and provide a sequential model of an idealised masculine life. Yet the romance in its more modern form is very much a female *Bildungsroman*, and while it is possible to chart a process of the 'feminisation' of romance from these masculine origins, it is equally possible to locate a parallel tradition of female quest tale, namely that exemplified by the myth of 'Cupid and Psyche'.[7] Here we find three dominant motifs: the curiosity of the heroine, which is the pivot of the prohibition-violation motif; the subsequent series of ordeals which function as the quest element; and the resulting marriage of the original protagonists, which serves as the heroine's reward and the endpoint of the narrative. Marina Warner reads this tale as 'a founding myth of sexual difference', in which 'Psyche remains in the foreground as the protagonist who functions as the chivalrous questor'.[8] The structure of this tale—the role of male and female characters, the movement from the unknown to the known, and the resultant social harmony—has been particularly potent throughout history, and is perhaps best known in its later form as the underlying pattern in the animal-groom cycle of fairy tales.

Before we move on to focus on this tale type and its function as an intertextual strand in romance fiction, it is worth digressing to introduce the fairy tale as it figures in this area. The formulaic romance and the fairy tale are comparable on a number of levels. Both are popular forms; indeed the status of the romance as a representative of popular culture is vindicated by its association with the communal, peasant tradition of the fairy tale. In the same way that the romance (depending on which strand you wish to unravel) underwent a process of feminisation and secularisation, so the fairy tale shifted from being a particular type of folk tale (a wonder folk tale) into the realms of European literary culture via the salons of late seventeenth-century Paris and the brothers Grimm, to eventually stand as a timeless representative of a type of fiction specifically for children, a prime element in a child's socialisation. The formulaic nature of the popular romance—the generic stamp of Mills and Boon or Harlequin—could be said to have grown out of the structured, repetitive form of the folk tale, in which what Jameson refers to as the 'social contract' between teller and listener was indicative of their communal status. This contract is, of course, prominent in genre fiction, where the bond between writer and reader centres on the repetition of already known expectations and fulfilments.[9]

One of the problems for recent criticism of the genre has been the search for a way of reading the romance which avoids condescension, both from the point of view of mainstream literary culture and feminism. The consensus view, as expressed by Radway, Fowler and Modleski, draws on the underlying contradiction implicit within the romance narrative, which we can see as a direct result of the intertextuality of genre—the persistence of archaic elements in modern manifestations. Fittingly, it is Jameson who is used once again: all the above critics refer to his suggestion of the possibility of locating a critical voice within the products of mass culture, stemming from

> within the unity of a single mechanism . . . which strategically arouses fantasy content within carefully symbolic containment structures which defuse it, gratifying intolerable, unrealizable, properly imperishable desires only to the degree to which they can be laid to rest.[10]

This notion of a fundamentally conservative text which nevertheless contains—literally and metaphorically—disruptive elements, is directly comparable to the common conception of the function of folklore, as described in William Bascom's influential essay:

> the basic paradox of folklore [is], that while it plays a vital role in transmitting and maintaining the institutions of a culture and in forcing the individual to conform to them, at the same time it provides socially approved outlets for the repressions which these same institutions impose upon them.[11]

It is thus possible to conceive of both the romance narrative and one of its primary antecedents as essentially contradictory—a contradictoriness that is closely related to the intertextual nature of genre fiction.

For the purposes of this essay I am using the two most famous animal-groom fairy tales, 'Beauty and the Beast' and 'Bluebeard', as indicative of the conflicting strands within the popular romance narrative.[12] This type of tale is characterised by the transformation of the male protagonist, brought about by the action of the heroine. In 'Beauty and the Beast', the change is literal—from beast to man—and results in marriage; in 'Bluebeard' the change is metaphorical—from man to murderous beast—and the result is the death of the male protagonist. In this sense, the former is the paradigm of a successful romance narrative, in which the gradual uncovering of the secret held by the central male character parallels the gradual movement of the narrative; while the latter is a failed romance, in which the overpowering curiosity of the heroine—her desire to know Bluebeard's secret—is the cause of the failure of the narrative to bring together (or at least keep together) the original protagonists. It is thus not surprising that 'Beauty and the Beast' is a fundamentally linear story while 'Bluebeard' is primarily static; nor is it surprising that the former has had a history as one of the canonical fairy tales, particularly in the form of the didactic children's story adapted in the mid-eighteenth century by Madame Leprince de Beaumont specifically for the education of young ladies. 'Bluebeard', on the other hand, is very much the dark offspring of the literary fairy-tale tradition. While it appears in Perrault's *Histoires ou contes du temps passé*, it was only included in the first edition of the Grimms' tales and has been ignored, or deemed unsuitable, in the sub-sequent shift towards the childhood morality tale.

'Beauty and the Beast' is the story of the uncovering of a man's true identity by the patient action of a woman. This taming motif functions as the pivotal moment in Radway's assessment of the ideal fictional romance. The ideal narrative structure she distils from readers' responses is one in which the romantic heroine 'simply brings to the surface traits and propensities that are part of the hero's most basic nature', for which her reward is true love and marriage; the initial doubts about the male charac-ter are retrospectively explained and understood by both reader and heroine.[13] The didactic nature of the fairy tale as a model for female behaviour is persuasive: it teaches patience, perseverance, and sacrifice as the means of achieving a place in the existing social order. As Bruno Bettelheim says of 'Cupid and Psyche':

[n]otwithstanding all the hardships woman has to suffer to be reborn to full consciousness and humanity, the stories leave no doubt that this is what she must do. Otherwise there would be no story: no fairy story worth telling, no worthwhile story to her life.[14]

This fairy tale romance is thus a carefully coded utopian vision, and it is the utopian aspect that has persisted into the modern romance narrative while the fantastical ele-ments have been subsumed under the shift to realism.

The traits that 'Bluebeard' secretes into the romance narrative are far more equiv-ocal. As well as an atmosphere of gothic menace that has been particularly influential in the subgenre of the gothic romance, this tale draws out the pivotal action of female curiosity that is present in 'Cupid and Psyche'. The portrayal of an initially strong, inquisitive female heroine is carried over into the ideal fictional romance, where she is differentiated by her 'unusual intelligence or by an extraordinarily fiery disposition'.[15] The allocation of male and female spheres is particularly pronounced, indeed is used as a plot device when Bluebeard apparently leaves to attend to press-ing but unspecified business while his new wife is given the conditional freedom of the house. The secret that the man holds is here objectified in the form of the bloody chamber, while the menace exuded by the hero is more pervasive and cannot be given a benign retrospective interpretation that cancels out the energies the initial uncertainty produces. Therefore, the 'Bluebeard' tale-type fits far less comfortably as an intertextual strand in the ideal fictional romance: while the motifs of the independent heroine, the rich but mysterious hero, and the setting of the tale are present, the *dénouement* casts a disturbing shadow across the narrative, as does the silent presence of the female bodies that form the unspeakable background to the story. Oddly enough, the tale has traditionally been read from the point of view of the culpable heroine, and her justifiable *cognitive* curiosity is taken by many commen-tators as the sign of sexual infidelity—an over-active *sexual* curiosity that is read as indicative of a corrupt nature and of the biological tie between this heroine and Eve. The blame is thus shifted away from the male who is at worst guilty of administering an unnecessarily extreme punishment.[16]

The problematic, marginal status of this tale is a potentially disruptive presence in the romance narrative, suggesting a failed marriage and a genuinely beastly male nature—a murderous rather than benign secret. Its gothic atmosphere and setting, along with its threat of female confinement, suggest links with the alternative tradition of the female gothic romance, as characterised by Ellen Moers, Dale Spender and Rosemary Jackson.[17] It is thus not surprising that 'Bluebeard' is a strong presence in *Jane Eyre*, a primary text in an alternative tradition of romance in which the norms of the genre are, to varying degrees, open to manipulation.[18] The popularity of this novel as a gothic romance is exemplified by its influence on Daphne du Maurier's bestseller, *Rebecca*, and more recently by the success of Susan Hill's sequel, *Mrs de Winter*.

It is within this alternative female romance tradition that I wish to read Angela Carter and Margaret Atwood, both of whom draw on *Jane Eyre* as a source text for its self-conscious yoking together of the romance and the fairy tale as a means of suggesting the darker undercurrents of the utopian narrative. Like Brontë, both Atwood and Carter display a keen interest in folk tale that goes beyond the standard reading of specific stories as childhood morality tales. This stems from an awareness of the fairy tale as a form that arrives with us via the mediation of generations of strongly ideologically-motivated readings and interpretations, along with an awareness of the field of wonder tales that lies beyond the rigidly defined boundaries of the standard, classic canon. Carter edited two volumes of fairy tales which specifically focus on redefining notions of the folk-tale heroine and 'the richness and diversity with which femininity, in practice, is represented in "unofficial" culture: its strategies, its plots, its hard work'; while Atwood talks of the Grimms' collection as 'the most influential book I ever read': 'the unexpurgated *Grimms' Fairy Tales* contains a number of fairy tales in which women are not only the central characters but win by using their own intelligence'.[19] More specifically, both writers show a keen interest in the 'Bluebeard' tale-type. The title story in Carter's collection of rewritten fairy tales, *The Bloody Chamber*, is an elaborate retelling of the 'Bluebeard' story, and references to it occur in a number of her works, most noticeably in *The Magic Toyshop*. Atwood singles out the Grimms' 'Fitcher's Fowl', a close narrative cousin of 'Bluebeard', as one of her favourite tales, and her work is littered with allusions to and adaptations of the theme, in novels such as *Lady Oracle* and *The Robber Bride* (which draws on the Grimms' 'The Robber Bridegroom', another relative of 'Bluebeard'), in the short stories 'Bluebeard's Egg' and 'Alien Territory', and in poems such as 'Hesitations Outside the Door'. The extent to which both writers are drawing on a whole tradition rather than the canonised and bowdlerised products of a historical selection process is important. By drawing on the intimately related 'Robber Bridegroom' and 'Fitcher's Fowl' as well as the more famous 'Bluebeard', Atwood is able to highlight the motif of female cunning which is quietly present in the latter but celebrated in the former, thus implicitly questioning orthodox interpretations that seek to read the heroine as a folkloric Eve, the subject of the tale's critical moral. Similarly, Carter's use of a female rather than a male means of escape in 'The Bloody Chamber' is not so much a feminist swipe at the portrayal of female reliance as an historically justified questioning of the dominance of Perrault's version; as Stith Thompson comments, 'the "Bluebeard" tale with the brother as rescuer has had no wide distribution and does not seem ever to have gained popularity . . . in most countries . . . the rescue is done by the youngest sister'.[20]

This interest in variants and alternative tale-traditions is indicative of an awareness of the multiplicity of the folk narrative tradition and the implicit instability of any particular narrative in the shifting web of closely related tale types. Carter has commented that '[t]he fairy tale, as narrative, has far less in common with the modern bourgeois forms of the novel and the feature film than it does with contemporary demotic forms, especially those "female" forms of romance', and it is thus not surprising to find the director of publishing at Harlequin (globally the most successful publisher of formulaic popular romances) advising aspiring writers that 'the fantasy must have the same appeal that all of us discovered when we were first exposed to fairy tales as children'.[21] Yet the generic fairy tale evoked here is actually highly specific, based on gender relations as they figure in 'Cinderella', 'Sleeping Beauty' and above all, as we have seen, 'Beauty and the Beast'—tales especially conducive to being made to function as ciphers for a particular description of proper female behaviour. When Karen Rowe comments that 'what is on trial in *Jane Eyre* is . . . the validity of an entire concept of romance derived from fairy tale', this again refers to a narrow strand of tales that have become representative of a putatively universal tradition of children's literature.[22] In fact, what we have in the ideal fictional romance is a tendentious reading of the 'Beauty and the Beast' narrative—in its more recent, didactic manifestation—that dominates, subordinating the other intertextual strands to its utopian vision. To an extent, narrative itself is always a remembering or a retelling, yet when generic norms become static the repetition is passive. It is only by drawing out other submerged, partially silent narrative voices that we can seek to hear the conflict and tension that lie beneath the surface, to repeat actively rather than passively, and thus generate change.

The self-consciousness of the alternative romance tradition is signalled to varying degrees by the intertextual figure of the reading protagonist, who lies at the centre of a chain of reading and interpretation. The ideal fictional romance pivots on the activity of reading; Modleski refers to the 'necessity of "reading" people, especially men' in Harlequins and Gothics, and Radway comments that the romance 'thematizes the activity of interpretation and reinterpretation', centring on the process of 'learning how to read male behaviour'.[23] Yet this reading is carefully coded into a binary structure whereby initially confusing, threatening behaviour is retrospectively understood and justified in the light of the hero's transformation, as it is in 'Beauty and the Beast' (thus drawing on the fundamental structure of narrative itself). Critics have referred to the dangers of the inculcation of this reading structure, seeking as it does to justify a certain type of masculinity and suggesting patience and submission as suitable, indeed necessary, reactions. At stake here are 'the specific implications of internalised romantic patterns', and, to modify the title of one such study in this area, the implications of female acculturation through the fairy tale.[24]

In Carter's 'The Bloody Chamber', the heroine reveals that she longs 'to lose [herself] in a cheap novel', while Melanie in *The Magic Toyshop* is reading *Lorna Doone* and presumably, in the light of references to herself as 'Jane Eyre' and Victoria as 'Mrs Rochester', has read Brontë's novel.[25] In Atwood's *Lady Oracle*, Joan comments that she 'always found other people's versions of reality very influential', but it is the 'trashy books' she first reads in her youth that structure her expectations.[26] Late on in the spiralling narrative, we witness her in the bathroom, 'my refuge', where she submerges herself in one of Mavis Quilp's 'nurse novels' (the subgenre of the doctor and nurse romance): 'I longed for the simplicity of that world, where happiness was possible and wounds were only ritual ones. Why had I been closed out from that impossible white paradise where love was as final as death . .?'. Joan is a self-confessed 'sentimentalist . . . of the sloppiest kind', 'an optimist, with a lust for happy endings'; on arriving in London she reveals the influence of a childhood reading of Tennyson's 'The Lady of Shalott': 'I wanted castles and princesses, the lady of Shalott floating down a winding river in a boat . . . I was a romantic despite myself'.[27]

In these metafictional texts we follow the process of reading as it passes over into the external world, and we see the characters read their lives through the norms of the genre. We first encounter Joan, suitably enough for this inveterate Juliet, on a balcony: 'I felt that if I could only manage to stand on one long enough . . . something would happen, a shape would appear below, sinuous and dark, and climb towards me'; it is thus not surprising that on meeting a potential partner, she proceeds, with relief, to slot herself into the preordained role: 'I myself was bliss-filled and limpid-eyed: the right man had come along, complete with a cause I could devote myself to. My life had significance.'[28] Yet the figure of 'Bluebeard' is never far away in these narratives. Melanie in *The Magic Toyshop* repeatedly refers to walking 'past all the closed doors of Bluebeard's castle', deducing that the presence (so she imagines) of a 'freshly severed hand' in a kitchen drawer signals that 'Bluebeard was here'. She also casts herself in the role of the threatened heroine, wanting to 'find out what lay behind all the doors' and prey to the lure of curiosity in her night-time escapades.[29] In *Lady Oracle*, Joan describes herself in terms drawn from 'Fitcher's Fowl', Atwood's favoured 'Bluebeard' variant: '[i]n a fairy tale I would be one of the two stupid sisters who open the forbidden door and are shocked by the murdered wives, not the third, clever one who keeps to the essentials'.[30]

As we have seen, this presence threatens the stability of the standard romance narrative, and it is the portrayal of gender relations in this folk tale that pervades the atmosphere of *The Magic Toyshop*. Carter reads the motifs of male secrecy and female subordination not as a necessary stop on the path to utopian relations, but as indicative of traditional gender relations themselves. Thus Uncle Philip is the towering patriarch whose word of law is unchallengeable—as is Bluebeard's—and who evokes a series of idealised romance narratives from history as enactments of a seemingly natural state. Similarly, in 'The Bloody Chamber', fictional romance is depicted as an inherently sado-masochistic structure (with Bluebeard as a connoisseur of esoteric pornography), thus echoing critiques of the genre: 'The desire that romance structures . . . is exclusively heterosexual, patriarchal, sado-masochistic . . . in which pleasure is the result of masculine activity and feminine dependence and passivity'.[31] This is sexuality as the articulation of power, and Bluebeard's bloody chamber can thus be momentarily misread as an extension of the norm, 'a little museum of perversity . . . installed . . . only for contemplation'.[32]

It is a mark of the rather schematic nature of this account that both Radway and Modleski seek to shift attention towards an understanding of the construction of female masochism in the romance narrative as a symptom of discontent, an adaptation that seeks, once again, to benignly reinterpret events in order to retrospectively defuse the situation. Carter signals this in 'The Bloody Chamber' by allowing the narrative to suggest a female desire that is not contained within the existing relations:

the heroine's 'dark, newborn curiosity', both cognitive and sexual, is an energy that lies at least partly outside the drama, uncontained by the narrative, at least in the sense that she is manifestly unsatisfied as well as self-consciously aware of the one-sided struggle that characterises her sexual relations.

In *Lady Oracle*, Atwood signals the characteristic interplay of generic text and historical context by the gradual seeping in of Louisa's (Joan's pseudonym) current gothic romance, the ominously titled 'Stalked by Love', into Joan's actual life. As Atwood's writer-protagonist becomes increasingly disillusioned with the consistently unordered, non-generic path of her life, so her usually precisely formulaic, bestselling retellings of the romance are disrupted. It is the obstinate persistence of Joan's disillusionments that precipitates a shift away from the formula, as initially it is disillusionment itself that is both engendered by romance reading and creates the need to repeatedly return to its certainties. What emerges in herself (albeit tentatively) is the manipulative, plotting side of her character, previously in the service of an orthodox plot which she was attempting to repeatedly simulate, with real life as the bad copy of an ever-imminent ideal. The fictional narrative under construction begins to suggest sympathy for the female foil, whose strong sexuality is traditionally denigrated in the ideal romance, and who is thus related to the heroine of 'Bluebeard', as she is traditionally read—a woman of immoderate sexual curiosity.

Finally, in a setting referred to as 'the central plot', 'Bluebeard' itself is revealed as the central plot of the romance: the hero/secret of 'Stalked by Love', ultimately revealed as death, stands in the doorway, 'the only way out', while the ghosts of the heroine return in the form of the repressed lives of Joan herself, those that she deleted as unsuitable for her desired role as real-life heroine.[33] As this plot is 'Bluebeard' and not 'Beauty and the Beast', the *dénouement* involves death and not marriage, or marriage as the death of the story and thus of the heroine, as she finishes her quest and is rewarded with the prescribed utopian ending of her role. It is interesting to note in the midst of this tendentious melodrama that 'Bluebeard' has been read as covertly encoding the genuine fears of death in childbirth that were prevalent in the communities—both peasant and, later, aristocratic—in which the tale originally circulated. Thus one of the covert meanings of the tale is that marriage may well be the cause of the heroine's death.[34] Again, fictional and real-life stories intertwine.

'Bluebeard' figures in these narratives as the submerged intertextual strand that is drawn out to provide an alternative to the culturally sanctioned utopian vision of the ideal fictional romance. As we have seen, this is produced by a selective reading of the sedimented layers of tradition, layers that shift at different stages in the history of the genre, producing the continuities and discontinuities referred to by Jameson. By rewriting the romance in this way, Atwood and Carter provide a critique in the form of an alternative story, thus allowing for the continued satisfaction of the desire for narrative that is central to genre fiction. The folk-tale tradition itself problematises any attempt at narrative fixity by offering multiple alternatives to any standardised, official version, such as that exemplified by the orthodox reading of the 'Bluebeard' tale-type. This is not a process of uncovering a hidden meaning—text as palimpsest, substituting one orthodoxy for another—but rather a challenge to narrative orthodoxy itself. It is out of such orthodoxies that normative roles and rules are produced, suggesting certain story patterns—life stories—as natural, and it is through an

[handwritten margin notes: analysis regardless a problem requiring a solution]

awareness of the intertextuality of genre that these can be critiqued as merely constructions, readings that can be rewritten.

NOTES

1. Included in Christine Park and Caroline Heaton (eds) *Caught in a Story: Contemporary Fairy Tales and Fables*, London, Vintage 1992, pp. 12–28.
2. Janice A. Radway, *Reading the Romance: Woman, Patriarchy and Popular Literature*, London, Verso 1987, p. 66.
3. Janet Batsleer, Tony Davies, Rebecca O'Rourke and Chris Weedon, *Rewriting English: Cultural Politics of Gender and Class*, London, Methuen 1985, p. 73.
4. Fredric Jameson, *The Political Unconscious: Narrative as a Socially Symbolic Act*, London, Routledge 1989, pp. 103–50 (p. 141).
5. Bridget Fowler, *The Alienated Reader: Women and Popular Romantic Literature in the Twentieth Century*, Hemel Hempstead, Harvester Wheatsheaf 1991, pp. 7–19. See also Tania Modleski, *Loving with a Vengeance: Mass-Produced Fantasies for Women*, London, Methuen 1984, pp. 11–35.
6. Northrop Frye, *Anatomy of Criticism*, London, Penguin 1990, p. 186.
7. Lucius Apuleius, *The Golden Ass*, translated Robert Graves, Harmondsworth, Penguin 1988. The 'feminisation' of romance is referred to in Batsleer *et al. Rewriting English* p. 71.
8. Marina Warner, *From the Beast to the Blonde: On Fairy Tales and their Tellers*, London, Chatto and Windus 1994, p. 275.
9. See also Radway, *Reading the Romance*, p. 198.
10. Fredric Jameson, 'Reification and utopia in mass culture', *Social Text* 1, 1979, p. 141.
11. William Bascom, 'Four functions of folklore', in Alan Dundes (ed.) *The Study of Folklore*, New Jersey, Prentice-Hall 1965, p. 298.
12. Both of these tales are included, in their 'classic' forms (adapted by Madame Leprince de Beaumont and Charles Perrault respectively), in Iona and Peter Opie's *The Classic Fairy Tales*, Oxford, Oxford University Press 1974, pp. 179–95 and 133–41.
13. Radway, *Reading the Romance*, p. 129.
14. Bruno Bettelheim, *The Uses of Enchantment: The Meaning and Importance of Fairy Tales*, Harmondsworth, Penguin 1991, p. 295.
15. Radway, *Reading the Romance*, p. 123.
16. The distinction between cognitive and sexual curiosity occurs in Maria Tatar, *The Hard Facts of the Grimms' Fairy Tales*, New Jersey, Princeton University Press 1987, pp. 156–79; and 'Beauties vs Beasts in the Grimms' Nursery and Household Tales', in James M. McGlathery (ed.) *The Brothers Grimm and Folktale*, Urbana and Chicago, University of Illinois Press, 1988, pp. 133–45. She also provides an overview of the history of interpretations of 'Bluebeard', in both fiction and criticism.
17. Ellen Moers, *Literary Women*, London, The Women's Press 1978, pp. 90–110; Dale Spender, *Mothers of the Novel*, London, Pandora 1986, pp. 230–45; Rosemary Jackson, *Fantasy: The Literature of Subversion*, London, Routledge 1988, pp. 95–140.
18. Angela Carter signals the equivocal status of this text in characteristically frank terms: 'of all the great novels in the world, *Jane Eyre* veers the closest towards pure trash', *Expletives Deleted: Selected Writings*, London, Chatto and Windus 1992, p. 162.
19. Angela Carter (ed.) *The Virago Book of Fairy Tales*, London, Virago 1991, p. xii; Margaret Atwood, *Conversations*, ed. Earl G. Ingersoll, London, Virago 1992, pp. 46 and 115.
20. Stith Thompson, *The Folktale*, New York, Holt Rinehart and Watson 1946, pp. 35–6.
21. Carter (ed.) *Virago Book of Fairy Tales*, p. xx, quoting Ann Barr Snitow, 'Mass Market Romance: Pornography for Women is Different' in Mary Eagleton (ed.), *Feminist Literary Theory: A Reader*, Oxford, Basil Blackwell 1986, p. 138.
22. Karen E. Rowe, '"Fairy-born and human-bred": Jane Eyre's education in romance', in Elizabeth Abel, Marianne Hirsch and Elizabeth Langland (eds) *The Voyage In: Fictions of Female Development*, Hanover, University Press of New England 1983, p. 82.
23. Modleski, *Loving with a Vengeance*, p. 34; Radway, *Reading the Romance*, p. 151.
24. Rowe '"Fairy-born and human-bred"', p. 69; Marcia K. Lieberman, '"Someday my prince will

come": female acculturation through the fairy tale', in Jack Zipes (ed.) *Don't Bet on the Prince: Contemporary Feminist Fairy Tales in North America and England*, Hampshire, Scolar Press 1993, pp. 185–200.

25. Angela Carter, *The Bloody Chamber and Other Stories*, Harmondsworth, Penguin 1981, p. 16; *The Magic Toyshop*, London, Virago 1981.
26. Margaret Atwood, *Lady Oracle*, London, Virago 1982, pp. 160 and 150.
27. Ibid., pp. 284, 15, 210, 143.
28. Ibid., pp. 7, 171.
29. Carter, *The Magic Toyshop*, pp. 146, 118, 58.
30. Atwood, *Lady Oracle*, p. 152.
31. Batsleer *et al. Rewriting English*, p. 99.
32. Carter, *The Bloody Chamber*, p. 28.
33. Atwood, *Lady Oracle*, pp. 341–3.
34. See Warner, *From the Beast*, pp. 263–5.

3 Private power

9 Eating the evidence: women, power and food

Sarah Sceats

If psychology has not made of [the] conjuring power of food as much as it might, literature on the other hand has been its diligent observer.

Kim Chernin, *The Hungry Self*[1]

Because of the close cultural association between women and food, or because of feminism's politicisation of the domestic, or because of the advance of a material culture, the work of women writers in the latter half of the twentieth century is particularly fruitful for an examination of the relations between power and food. Not only are covert struggles within families and between friends, colleagues and lovers exposed and explored, but a whole gamut of hierarchical relations is called into question, through eating interactions, appetites and primal desires. Sometimes, though not always, the conflicts depicted are to do with gender, but the lines are rarely simply drawn; as with sex—or maybe even more so—the activities, motivations, interactions and ramifications are complex, and the boundary between enslavement and empowerment is sometimes difficult to establish.

Power relations in their broadest sense can be seen to operate, and fluctuate, in all activities associated with food and eating, encompassing cooks, carers and consumers. The ideas of Michel Foucault, with their emphasis on both the instability and positive potential of power, are illuminating in this respect. Power is exercised, Foucault maintains, in a complex network of 'micro-powers', through discourses and discursive practices that manifest themselves in every aspect of social life. Just as we occupy different positions in different discourses, so power is not monolithic, something to be acquired or overthrown, but is multiple and ubiquitous, every struggle being both localised and part of an interconnecting network.[2] Power is not merely oppressive, but positive, he claims, since 'it produces reality; it produces domains of objects and rituals of truth', and is inseparable from knowledge.[3] Power and knowledge are thus mutually necessary, not only for the wielder of power or dominant party, but for whoever subverts power (and thus claims it).

If the exercise and experience of power, and the desire for it, are manifested through interactions lending themselves to Foucauldian analysis, much of the underlying motivation of eating behaviour relates to psychoanalytic theory. The giving and receiving of nourishment lies at the core of human bonding and, according to Freud, underpins adult sexuality.[4] Melanie Klein places still greater emphasis on the early oedipal 'oral stage', when the process of nourishment is inseparable from the love relationship with the mother, and the infant is said to take everything it experiences, including the breast, to be an extension of itself. Thus subject (the infant) and object (food, mother, love) are perceived as one and the world is whole, complete, undifferentiated. When the infant discovers the difference, she or he learns ambivalence, experiencing conflicts of love, fear and aggression towards the love object, newly perceived as external and unfamiliar.[5] Klein suggests that, as a defence against anxiety, the object becomes split into 'good' and 'bad' according to whether it gratifies or frustrates—the 'good breast' gratifying desire, the 'bad breast' causing frustration by its withdrawal. The infant projects both loving and destructive instincts onto the love object, through, for example, the desire to incorporate it.

This may, on the face of it, seem remote from adult power and social and political reality. Yet striving for power, figured in wanting to 'eat the world', has its roots in such yearnings for incorporation. As Freud suggests, consumption is a model for desire: 'The original pleasure-ego wants to introject into itself everything that is good and to eject from itself everything that is bad'.[6] What connects so well with Foucault and this chapter is that feeding is established psychologically as the locus of love, aggression, pleasure, anxiety, frustration and desire for control. Precisely, in other words, the ingredients of power relations.

Viewed from a slightly different angle, these ingredients may be seen as the stuff of fiction and drama. Food and eating are pervasive throughout literature; indeed, it is difficult to find novels in which they do not appear in some guise. And since, as I have sketched, food and eating are inseparable from both physical and psychic appetites and power relations, it is clear that writers use feeding, feasting, cooking and starving for more than simple mimetic effect.

For women writers in particular, the provision of food is problematic. You have only to think of battles between parents and children over food to recognise eating as a major source of conflict and power struggle. The ostensible power of a nurturing mother is considerable, if not absolute. But the resolutely closed mouth of a toddler may speak otherwise, and, as anyone who has cooked for a family will know, nurturing may be experienced rather as an enslavement than as a power. Literature, like life, is full of mothers faced with relentless demands for food, the cost of which may be an engrossment in her domestic role that leaves the mother without a self. Claudia, in Alice Thomas Ellis's *The Other Side of the Fire*, is just such a denuded woman, whose loss leads her to a wholly inappropriate passion (see chapter 12). Angela Carter's *The Magic Toyshop* takes maternal disempowerment and domestic enslavement to an extreme in the figure of Aunt Margaret, who is deprived even of the power of having her own children, and rendered mute and practically anorexic by her husband.

Some of the dangers, difficulties and mistakes of mothering are worked through in the course of Doris Lessing's five 'Children of Violence' novels. Maternal control is established when a child is young and helpless, and in *A Proper Marriage* the young Martha Quest is appalled by the power she perceives as inherent in her role as mother. Martha deliberately abandons her daughter when she quits her immature and unawakened husband, believing that she thereby frees her from the oppression of maternal nurturing. Tormented by the prospect of repetition—both because it spells the stranglehold of colonial politics and social custom, and because she feels herself to be a victim of her own mother's intrusive caring—Martha wishes to spare her child such an experience. Significantly, there are detailed descriptions of huge and messy feeding battles between Martha and her daughter, only surmounted once Martha becomes able to pretend that she doesn't care.[7]

May Quest, Martha's mother, is incapable of engaging in any such pretence, and is unable to separate psychically from her independent daughter until, quite old, she has a breakdown on a visit to Martha in London. When, in *Martha Quest*, the young Martha first moves to town, living in digs with full board, Mrs Quest nevertheless sends food parcels from the farm. Much later, when the divorced and hectically busy Martha briefly visits her parents, her mother criticises her thinness (and by implication her sexuality) and, though Martha leaves quickly, orders enough supper for two, even cooking some jam tart:

> Martha is so fond of it, she had thought. Though she knew quite well Martha never ate sweets of any kind. Imagining the scene, where she put a slice of tart, with its trickles of sweet cream, before Martha, but she shook her head, Mrs Quest's eyes filled with rejected tears.[8]

Mrs Quest's mothering, with its mechanism of overfeeding and withholding, is both deluded and self-serving, characteristics which go some little way to explaining why Martha finds it so peculiarly oppressive.

But the relationship of nurturer and nurtured (cook and consumer) is more complicated than mere maternal oppression, and the nurtured are not necessarily as helpless as a baby at the breast. This is amply illustrated in a number of Lessing's novels, such as *The Memoirs of a Survivor*, in which a young girl is left with the narrator, who cares for but does not control her, or the poignant *Diaries of Jane Somers* in which the eponymous protagonist becomes involved with a fiercely proud and needy old woman and has also to negotiate the needs and expectations of two nieces, one of them desperately and anarchically hungry.

In *The Good Terrorist*, Lessing features apparently very different feeding relations from the built-in power hierarchy of parent and child. Here the central character, Alice Mellings, uses her practical and nurturing skills to try to draw together a disparate group of misfits in a squat to form the family she craves. Her personal dysfunctions—inability to relate to or separate from her parents, repression of her sexuality and unreciprocated devotion to the damaged and homosexual Jasper—are representative of the group as a whole, and provide the motivation for her overriding desire for a family. Her efforts are complicated by the expressed political convictions of most of the comrades, herself included, which reject anything perceived as 'bourgeois', including families, household requirements and domestic comfort of any sort, not to mention home-cooked meals. Alice has something of a struggle to convince them that they could eat more cheaply by combining forces and cooking instead of eating out or buying take-aways—a resistance that gives the lie to their professed communality. Notwithstanding this resistance, however, 'her' soups become something of a point of reference for the comrades, pervading the house with their smell, focusing the group around the kitchen table and expanding to accommodate a seemingly infinite number of consumers. She calculates who is hungry and when they will have eaten, makes coffee for people when they come into the kitchen, gets up to eat breakfast with an early worker and even feeds a helpless-looking stray cat who comes to the window.

Does Lessing represent Alice's caring and cooking as a currency with which to buy affection, or a means of exerting some influence and exercising power? Her cooking and catering reflect her character: torn between the motherly and the childlike, a conflict evident in her youthful 'management' of her mother's kitchen, a place where she felt safe and where she could exert some control over the world. In recollection she realises that she usurped the place of her mother, who had loved cooking. The centrality of her role as cook, maker of coffee and general fixer in the squat leads her to be regarded as an authority figure, so that the bringing-in of take-aways or going to Fred's Caff for breakfast become acts of rebellion, expressions of autonomy, of resistance to Alice's control, and to what she represents.[9] Alice is certainly aware of the force of her practical and caring abilities, and is at her most powerful when exercising these unhindered. Yet her childish inability to give up expectations of nurturing from her own parents, her lack of any real engagement with the political issues the comrades' lives are supposedly devoted to and the suppression of her sexuality render her powerless; as her mother comments, she really achieves no more than to replicate the maternal pattern of caring and cooking.

Part of Alice's incapacitating outrage stems from misplaced childhood feelings of rejection and neglect. Indeed, neglect may be as powerful a means of control as overprotection, and parental indifference engenders long-term consequences, both personally and in political terms. Neglect and stifling are interwoven in Molly Keane's Anglo-Irish novel of manners, *Good Behaviour*.[10] Here the large, unattractive daughter of the house, Aroon St Charles, is both confined by the unspoken restrictions of her class and milieu (in which, it appears, emotional repression, double standards and neglect are unremarkable), and isolated by her parents' sporadically exclusive relationship and her mother's absorption in gardening and painting, and withdrawn, careless distance. As a child Aroon is portrayed as highly conscious of the potential of food to dismay or comfort, though she learns frighteningly young the 'good behaviour' of ignoring the misery of bad food's disgustingness. Her coping strategy is effectively one of withdrawal. Later, she takes comfort in her disempowerment by eating, by dancing exuberantly with her brother and in a fantasised and half believed-in romance with her brother's illicit lover, whose covert homosexuality she innocently misunderstands. The two young men, for whom she unwittingly provides a useful cover, call her 'Pig', and make a great joke of her capacity for food, which she plays up to for the reward of their approval. After her brother's death and his friend's flight, however, and particularly once her beloved father falls ill, she becomes increasingly cold and hungry, but her always critical and now punitively economising mother only responds as though her appetite and need for warmth are an affront. Ultimately, following her father's death and her surprise inheritance, Aroon takes a carer's revenge on her ailing mother, promising in a voice 'humid with kindness' that she will always look after her. Her final, wonderfully ambiguous act of ostensible caring is to cook a perfect dish of rabbit quenelles in a cream sauce for her mother, who cannot stand rabbit.

The mother's cool disregard for her children's physical or emotional nourishment exerts a powerful, negative force which, we may infer, contributes significantly to ensuing events. Her carelessness about what they eat in the nursery and her subsequent discomfort with their presence in the dining room are neatly inverted in the 'looking after' of Aroon's revenge, which renders her mother helpless and subject to the absolute control of being cared for, in contrast to Aroon's own youthful domination by want and neglect. Keane's structure skilfully emphasises the irony of revenge-by-looking-after: at the beginning of the novel, which features the mother's death, Aroon seems a monster of bullying insensitivity, but by the end it is impossible not to relish her bitter-sweet victory as she assumes control, casting off her passivity and hunger.

Power and influence are, of course, more easily and rapidly exerted positively than by omission, and the nurturing aspect of cooking may be wilfully, even wickedly abused. The cook is, after all, in command of the ingredients, and may use this dominion either to reinforce or sabotage the status quo. Angela Carter exploits this possibility to considerable comic effect, producing figures who disavow the archetype of woman as nurturing and caring cook and feeder, emphasising instead her power over those within the sphere of her catering. *Wise Children* features an unreservedly malignant manipulative cook in Saskia, a pantomime bitch who begins her career when still a child with such delights as putting frogspawn in the porridge, and dragging the carcass of a roast swan out to eat in the undergrowth while her mother's house burns down.[11] She wields not the power of the maternal but that of the professional cook and schemer, manipulating people, witch-like, through her cooking and sexuality. She is not at all averse to putting a little something in people's food: holiday aperients for the girlfriend of her half-brother, Tristram; possibly aphrodisiacs for Tristram himself, whom she repeatedly seduces; poison (twice) for her father.

Saskia's exertion of power is not directly visible; it is almost lethally effective, but well disguised within the food. But her power is sexual also, her particular combination of control, seductiveness and cruelty being vividly conveyed by a television food programme in which she jugs a hare. This she dismembers 'voluptuously', talking 'huskily' to the viewers about the sharpness of the blade, 'lovingly' preparing its bath of wine and vegetables, and eventually 'moaning' how delicious it tastes. Her control is twofold, functioning through a compelling sexuality and by means of the food itself. Motivated primarily by revenge, her cooking activities are essentially subversive; she attempts to manipulate all situations to place herself alone in the position of power. Saskia's cooking paradoxically manifests appetite, connoting revenge, libido, power. Appetite, in other words, is powerful.

Of all contemporary writers, Angela Carter portrays appetites and their satisfaction with the greatest gusto, power being most evident where the appetite is both huge and predatory, exhibiting the 'omnivorous egocentricity' Carter identifies as symptomatic of the modern condition.[12] Such appetite has political as well as psychological overtones, as demonstrated by the tyrannous puppet-maker, Uncle Philip, in *The Magic Toyshop*. A domestic tyrant who controls the family budget not just meanly but in order to be in control, he dominates the household—and the table—in every respect, demonstrating an impressive capacity for food both in his eating and his size. His presence at meals dims the family's appetites, despite the wonderful food through which Aunt Margaret, oppressed and speechless since marriage, finds eloquent means of expression.[13] The pleasure he takes from food is not just from eating, however. He draws a peculiar satisfaction from Aunt Margaret's *inability* to eat at Sunday tea, imprisoned as she is by the silver choker he made for her wedding present, whereas he eats his way through a 'pink battalion' of shrimps, a whole loaf of bread with half a pound of butter and most of a large cake. Significantly, his sexual appetite is also routinely exercised following this meal.

Here is a profoundly greedy man, a bully with an omnivorous appetite. His power is primarily economic, though implemented through degradation and brutality—those useful tools in the service of tyranny. This and his resemblance to a Victorian pit-owner suggest him as a figure for patriarchy. He sets up all interactions to reinforce his dominance, allowing little scope for the shifting instability in power relations that I have invoked. But his yearning for absolute control, tantamount to wanting to devour the world, might in psychoanalytic terms be said to indicate a lack.[14] Fuelled by a sense of loss, the lust for control, heir to the imperious desire of the oral stage infant, is in fact out of control, an obsession. The apparently unassailable puppetmaster has no centre; not only is his power sabotaged by the incest, music and community of his wife and her brothers, it rests on the shaky foundation of a hollow and compulsive greed. And ultimately Uncle Philip is a loser, destroyed by his inflexible rage at the satisfied desires of the marginalised and contingent.

I am suggesting a disjunction here between the external manifestations of power and control, and the internal dynamic of ravenous—and pathetic—insatiability. Perhaps it is this very contradiction, and the subversion of apparently inexorable force by its own interior, that makes cannibalism such an attractive trope for Carter (and particularly, maybe, when it is sketched as a figure for patriarchy).[15]

The libertine Count, in *The Infernal Desire Machines of Doctor Hoffman*, is probably her most extravagant creation in this respect. A figure of monstrous egocentricity, greed and voracious sexual appetite, the Count both dreads and is most drawn to his dark counterpart, the Cannibal Chief. With his fantasies of omnipotence and desires for negation, he responds to the world as though it were 'good breast' and 'bad breast'. His anguish in captivity, the nemesis of a disempowered monster, is also the infant's fantasy that the love object that he desires to incorporate and destroy will, in fact, eat him. Like Uncle Philip the Count craves wholeness, but the union he seeks is entirely solipsistic. The Cannibal Chief, as his alter ego, voices the narcissistic desire: 'I want to learn the savour of my flesh. I wish to taste myself.'[16] So, the Cannibal Chief-cum-Count acts out the early or pre-oedipal infant's conflict: the loved object (in this case himself) is both desired and feared, for its power to complete and to destroy. The Count triumphs when he is cooked; as he comes to the boil he learns, finally, to feel ordinary pain, to be unified with himself, as both subject and object. An appetite of some sort is satisfied. It is an ambiguous triumph though: the moment of wholeness and completion is the moment of death.

Cannibalism is an extreme example of dehumanisation, and, with its qualities of rampant power and insatiability, suggests the absolute supremacy of the consumer. The victim cannot be taken account of in any real sense; the eaten is hardly equal with the eater, and consuming is an act of absolute control. Yet even here, power relations are not monolithic, and some satisfactions or even authority may be wrested from the subjection. In *Doctor Hoffman*, cannibalistic desire is seen as belonging to the victim, and its masochistic aspect is emphasised. In one incident the hero, Desiderio, longs to become part of a tribe of river people who have taken him in; they, however, have more literal ideas about his incorporation, planning him as the central dish at his own wedding feast. At a 'realist' level the narrative draws on tribal beliefs: Desiderio possesses an ability to read which the people want; the way to obtain this is by literally incorporating it, so that by eating pieces of him they will effortlessly receive his knowledge. For Desiderio, the incorporation, in all but the literal culmination (that he escapes), suggests engulfment and regression, and Carter weaves psychic stages into his sojourn so that it becomes a revisiting of the maternal, utterly different, but comparable to those depicted by Michèle Roberts (discussed at the end of this chapter). But the mismatch between Desiderio's agenda and that of the tribe is a reminder that wholeness is transient and the act of eating destroys what is eaten. There is no possible stasis, and neither the Count nor Desiderio is able to achieve his longed-for condition of completion, for it is an illusion.[17]

Does the unfulfilability of desire undermine the view I offered earlier of appetite as powerful? Only, I think, where the desired satisfaction is stasis. The point about the model of unstable power relations is that dominant and subordinate positions are not fixed; why this is so relevant to food and eating is that hunger is continually renewed, and appetite is neither constant nor more than temporarily to be satisfied. Both eater and eaten in cannibalistic scenarios are subject to an inner void or insatiability.[18] The emptiness of the orally obsessed does manifest a depressive force of its own, of course, whether figured in the deathly hunger of the tyrant or the yearning of the disempowered. Ravenous megalomania propels Carter's characters to confuse food with sex, self with other, empowerment with oppression; appetite, like power, is for Carter both slippery and creative of truths.

But what of the relation of power to *lack* of appetite, or more accurately to the supposed empowerment of not eating, in the disorders of anorexia nervosa and bulimia? On one hand, the refusal of food may constitute an autonomous determination not to submit to intrusion by the outside world (intrusion often taking the form of parental domination, maternal rivalry or sexual abuse); the subject's own body, and specifically its size and outlines, become the only piece of the world over which she or he can manifest influence. On the other hand, anorexia may belie a slavish devotion to a culturally constructed slim body ideal that has more to do with the products of the diet industry than the health or beauty of the individual, though even here a rejection of the curvaceous body shapes associated with femininity and maternity may connect with assertions of autonomy. What eating disorders represent is difficult to disentangle from what causes them, however, and the considerable volume of writing about them suggests a combination of cultural and personal factors.[19] Two, in particular, relate to my argument here: the psychological; and those cultural or environmental pressures that may be considered to represent an exercise of societal power over the individual. The market economy's simultaneous exhortations to consume and to be slim, for example, are vividly reflected in the bingeing and vomiting cycles of bulimia.

In her novel *Life-Size* Jenefer Shute offers a complex portrait of an angry, self-hating and disturbingly unpleasant anorectic. Josie embodies both multiple causation (Shute includes a glossary, which suggests that she knows her stuff) and 'positive' and 'negative' interpretations of the relation between self-starvation and power outlined above. Josie has framed her condition to herself in positive terms; what emerges through the narrative is her disempowerment, as her rage is played out in a struggle to deny herself which must logically end in death. Defensively convinced of her invincible control over her body, Josie takes a daily inventory of bones and sinews, driving herself to ever more punishing exercise routines, while obsessively regulating her intake of tiny pieces of non-fattening food. She perceives her treatment in hospital, and the food and care she receives there, as invasive, even rapine, and resists it energetically. Gradually, however, as she uncovers her history, her deep fears are revealed and a terrible underlying hunger becomes apparent. Her self-control is a response to *being* controlled, but it runs nightmarishly *out* of control until she can do nothing but abstain.[20] Her not eating, construed by her as empowerment, is in fact an enslavement, a means of evading the hungry cry within that occasions episodes of bulimia. It is only when she finds herself asking the nurse to feed her, acknowledging her need for both food and maternal care, that Josie really begins to recover.

The mechanisms shown to be at work in Josie's condition and recovery suggest a general pattern of interactions in which power may be seen to shift according to a number of factors. These include institutions, social and family structures and traditions, pressures created by late twentieth century capitalism, politics and—importantly—physical and psychological influences. This is not to say Josie is only a victim; she may be sick, tortured, frail, but at times she is an extremely powerful figure. It is such a combination of vulnerability and power that crops up again and again in women's writing on food, whether endorsed, explored or rejected.

Michèle Roberts makes a direct connection between women, empowerment and insatiable hunger, particularly in her earlier novels, which focus on individuation and self-development where there are difficulties of separation from the mother—difficulties, it is interesting to note, that are cited as causal or predisposing factors in much of the writing about eating disorders. Bulimia, and particularly anorexia, appear incidentally throughout Roberts's fiction, which suggests that these are a constant in women's lives.

Roberts's first two novels address the problem of a young woman's insatiable hunger, and offer an imaginative or emotional revisiting of the pre-oedipal as a means to resolution. In *A Piece of the Night*, for example, the heroine, Julie Fanchot, is filled with memories and fantasies of the reciprocal needs and pleasures of breastfeeding and the concomitant pains of adolescent individuation. Julie is outwardly contained but avidly needy, 'sucking at love she will never exhaust' as she kneels in the school chapel, 'stuffing her anger down with slices of bread and peanut butter' when her husband withdraws from lovemaking, floundering in support, love and jealousies with her women friends and especially her lover, Jenny.[21] She remembers sleepwalking in inconsolable need of her mother, and recalls herself, externally, as a baby crying with rage and abandonment, battling with a mother who dutifully feeds her by the clock, unaware of her devouring, single-minded, ecstatic hunger. When they go to Mass, the priest speaks of the voraciousness of women. The hunger, we are given to understand, is not patriarchally sanctioned, and Roberts's male characters (such as Julie's husband) are repelled by its uncontrollable depth.

Roberts's drift is specifically feminist. Her women are hungry with grief and desire, replaying birth, nurturing and separation as a means to reconciliation and autonomy, and learning along the way to give voice to their hungers. Her second novel, *The Visitation*, features another desperate baby, who must share her mother with a twin. She experiences only dissatisfaction and frustration, an unsatisfied appetite sharpened by rivalry. The twin is, incidentally, a brother, her shadow and counterpart. The frozen adult Helen is released when she finally makes herself express her needs to a lover by whom she feels fed and nourished, but not until she has rediscovered the 'paradise' of 'fatherlessness, the time before language . . . not-separation and not-speech'.[22] The image is of baby at the breast, in blissful undifferentiated consciousness of itself-mother. We are back to the all-powerful nurturing mother, but here as part of a larger female power, and not an oppressive one. In *The Wild Girl*, for example, the narrator, Mary Magdalene, insists not only upon the physicality of Christ, but on the palpable, spiritual power of the mother.

Like her empowered characters, Roberts has moved on from hunger for a sense of wholeness with the mother to more complex ground. In *Daughters of the House*, she weaves an intricate web of maternal deprivation, personal and communal ghosts, spiritual and emotional hunger, French cookery and the intense and bitter rivalry of the two girls, Thérèse and Léonie, who are cousins and may be sisters. The balance of power in their relationship shifts and slides throughout the novel, as they play and strive for supremacy in the kitchen, in the affections of their parents, servants and neighbours, in holiness. The plot is complex and the atmosphere highly charged. The need for satisfaction of various hungers—physical, emotional, spiritual—is no light matter and gives rise to almost mortal intensity, so that the adult Léonie is pleased to pretend for twenty years that Thérèse is dead. Even when they meet again, a battle for supremacy is played out over the meal Léonie provides in an attempt to control Thérèse through leek and potato soup and roast veal, in a kitchen thick with remembered feelings and textures. Near the end of the novel, rivalry, hunger, memory, joy and loss all come together, briefly, in Léonie's fleeting vision of Rose Taillé, 'foster-mother, mother-in-law, second mother, fostering mother', who had been wet nurse and superstitious protector to both girls.[23]

Michèle Roberts's writing about food is so sensuous as to suggest pleasure in food as a power in itself. It is hard to resist the notion of gustatory satisfactions as a force for good, and food itself might just be neutral.[24] There is no shortage of pleasurable eating in fiction, least of all in the writers I have discussed, who describe mouth-watering meals and the pleasures of taste, smell, cooking, sharing, dining, feasting and saturnalia. The problem is that such pleasure cannot exist in a vacuum. Every meal incorporates political, cultural, personal and psychological ingredients before even a bite is taken. Any appetite may masquerade as another, or none. Power is a slippery commodity, and its practitioners may be skilled and subtle dissemblers. So, fictional cooks and consumers wrestle publicly or surreptitiously for domination: of themselves, of each other, of the food. And the wise reader watches for revelation.

NOTES

1. Kim Chernin, *The Hungry Self: Women, Eating and Identity*, London, Virago 1986, p. 144.
2. In relation to food, for example, we might be on the receiving end of power within discourses of varying degrees of disciplinary force (recipes, mother's advice on cooking, advertising and marketing, reports on diet and health, religious and cultural customs), or we might find ourselves laying down rules and meanings (forbidding children to eat sweets, telling them carrots will make them see in the dark, offering chicken soup to an invalid, extolling the virtues of vegetarianism). Mostly, it seems, we are in neither extreme position, but struggling for our own voice within the dominant discourse (amending recipes, eating just a little butter, allowing a few sweets *after* meals, counting fish as vegetarian or creating birthday party rituals).
3. Michel Foucault, *Discipline and Punish*, London, Penguin 1977, p. 194. For a lucid and detailed account of Foucault's thinking, see also Alan Sheridan, *Michel Foucault: the Will to Truth*, London, Tavistock 1980.
4. Encapsulated in the much-quoted passage: 'No one who has seen a baby sinking back satiated from the breast and falling asleep with flushed cheeks and a blissful smile can escape the reflection that this picture persists as a prototype of the expression of sexual satisfaction in later life', Sigmund Freud, *The Standard Edition of the Complete Psychological Works of Sigmund Freud*, translated James Strachey, London, Hogarth 1953–74, Vol. 7, p. 182.
5. The 'object' in this context, stated baldly, is the person, part person or thing (e.g. breast) upon which the ego is focused.
6. Freud, *Standard Edition*, Vol. 19, p. 237.
7. Doris Lessing, *A Proper Marriage*, London, Michael Joseph 1954, Part III, Ch. 2. In *The Four-Gated City* (London, MacGibbon and Kee 1969), the final volume of the series, Martha recognises that while she might have freed her child, she also starved her (of herself), thereby repeating the pattern set by her mother, who had unwittingly starved the infant Martha through mixing her milk feed at half strength.
8. Doris Lessing, *Landlocked*, London, Paladin 1990, p. 97 (MacGibbon and Kee 1965). See also *Martha Quest*, London, Michael Joseph 1952.
9. In part, what she represents—despite herself—is her own middle-class upbringing and expectations. She can't help but deplore excess sugar in tea, fried breakfasts and fish and chips, and opts whenever possible for the virtuously wholefood, vegetarian, thrifty alternative. *The Good Terrorist*, London, Paladin 1990 (Jonathan Cape 1985).
10. Molly Keane, *Good Behaviour*, London, Abacus 1982.
11. Angela Carter, *Wise Children*, London, Vintage 1992.
12. In *The Sadeian Woman* (London, Virago 1979). Carter says it is Sade, via the Romantics, who is responsible for 'shaping aspects of the modern sensibility; its paranoia, its despair, its sexual terrors, its *omnivorous egocentricity*, its tolerance of massacre, holocaust, annihilation' (p. 32, my emphasis).
13. As suggested earlier, Aunt Margaret is a disempowered provider; though the savour of her cooking is directed towards her brothers (especially Francie, whom she loves incestuously), she is unable to exert much influence through her cooking; in Carter's writing the power is with the consumers, and it is significant that Aunt Margaret barely eats. *The Magic Toyshop*, London, Virago 1981.
14. Lack or loss here suggests a yearning for the undifferentiated wholeness of infantile bonding with the mother.
15. The enormous size Uncle Philip has attained since his sister's wedding, and the crushing of Aunt Margaret and her brothers, suggest he is in some sense feeding off them, that his appetite is in effect cannibalistic.
16. Angela Carter, *The Infernal Desire Machines of Doctor Hoffman*, London, Penguin 1982, p. 162.
17. The satisfactions of cannibalism curiously parallel the fantasised satisfactions of the oral stage: eating a loved one as an ultimate act of possession (penetration of the self by the love object through its incorporation); eating to obliterate someone (destruction of the love object by its absorption); or eating a brave enemy to become courageous (keeping the love object within to appropriate its qualities).
18. Just to confuse matters, Carter does also figure cannibalism, or the cannibalistic, as benign, in the ebullient figure of the winged aerialiste, Fevvers, in *Nights at the Circus* (London, Chatto and Windus 1984). Though she twice overtly dissociates herself from cannibalism in conversation, Fevvers has an appetite to match her size, an appetite that figuratively incorporates the journalist, Walser. Fevvers is

not immune to helpless longings and nostalgia—as her substitute mother Lizzie suggests, all wise children want to stay in the womb, to remain whole and undifferentiated—but her relationship with Walser ultimately suggests a mutual devouring, always with 'the most voluptuous lack of harm' (p. 204).

19. See especially Joan Jacobs Brumberg, *Fasting Girls: The Emergence of Anorexia Nervosa as a Modern Disease* (Cambridge, Mass., Harvard University Press 1988), for a model of causation that suggests a web of interaction between biological, psychological and cultural factors.

20. Josie's emptiness and the feared insatiability of her hunger are strongly reminiscent of Carter's cannibalistic characters; the difference between their externally-directed despotism and Josie's *self*-control, however, is that she damages only herself. *Life-Size*, London, Mandarin 1993.

21. Michèle Roberts, *A Piece of the Night*, London, The Women's Press 1978, pp. 49, 83.

22. Michèle Roberts, *The Visitation*, London, The Women's Press 1983, p. 172.

23. Michèle Roberts, *Daughters of the House*, London, Virago 1992, p. 169.

24. Hillel Schwartz projects a utopian fantasy of a 'fat society' in which dinners would be delicious and sociable, children would be well fed when hungry, fat people would dress expressively and be forthright about the body and women especially would 'wear their weight with new conviction'. Needless to say, such a society would be comforting, caring, less 'harshly competitive, less devouring', and consuming would be satisfying only in relation to its social function. Nice to think so. See *Never Satisfied: A Cultural History of Diets, Fantasies, and Fat*, London, Collier Macmillan 1986.

FURTHER READING

Ellmann, Maud, *The Hunger Artists: Starving, Writing and Imprisonment*, London, Virago Press 1993.

Kilgour, Maggie, *From Communion to Cannibalism: An Anatomy of Metaphors of Incorporation*, New Jersey, Princeton University Press 1990.

Lawrence, Marylin (ed.) *Fed Up and Hungry: Women, Oppression and Food*, London, The Women's Press 1987.

Mitchell, Juliet (ed.) *The Selected Melanie Klein*, London, Peregrine Books 1986.

Orbach, Susie, *Hunger Strike: The Anorexic's Struggle as a Metaphor for our Age*, New York and London, Norton 1986.

Schofield, Mary Anne (ed.) *Cooking by the Book: Food in Literature and Culture*, Bowling Green, Ohio, Bowling Green State University Popular Press 1989.

10 Battling with the Angel: May Sinclair's powerful mothers

Terry Phillips

May Sinclair has an important place in the number of novelists who have something significant to say about woman's story. In her day she was one of England's best known novelists, but after her death in 1946 her reputation became almost totally eclipsed until the re-publication of three of her novels in the early 1980s, although one of them has sadly since been allowed to go out of print.[1] These novels represent interesting experimentation in fictional techniques but their chief interest for the modern woman reader is in their representation of the lives of middle-class women in Victorian and Edwardian England.

Sinclair's interests extended well beyond novel writing or even literary criticism. She was a philosopher of no mean order, a member of The Women Writers' Suffrage League, and, most interestingly for the present subject, a founder member of the Medico-Psychological Clinic of London.[2] She retained throughout her active life an interest in both Freud and Jung, publishing several articles on their work. Her interest was thus directed towards the psychological development of women in families and the conflict between their ascribed family roles and the development of their individual consciousnesses.

Mothering is of course crucial to these interests, and is of particular importance to women. Most women, like most men, experience being mothered, but their experience of the relationship is inevitably closer, and furthermore and crucially, almost all women in our society are prepared for a mothering role, whether or not they eventually undertake it. Many of Sinclair's novels deal with women's experience as mothers, and rather fewer, but among them some of the most significant, with their experience as daughters. Meaningful critical debate about Sinclair is inevitably restricted by the lack of availability of most of her novels, and while the two novels I intend to discuss focus primarily on the experience of daughters and include rather unsympathetic portrayals of mothers, it is important to note that elsewhere she deals sympathetically with the plight of women as mothers.

Sinclair has no romantic illusions about motherhood, and seems to consciously reject male idealisations of the subject, remarking acerbically of one of her early characters:

> It seems a simple thing to believe in the divinity of motherhood, when you have only seen it in the paintings of one or two old masters . . . But sometimes the divine thing chooses some morsel of humanity like Mrs Nevill Tyson, struggles with and overpowers it, rending the small body, spoiling the delicate beauty.[3]

Sinclair's novels often expose, rather in the manner of the example just cited, the cultural inscription of women within art and literature. Equally their inscription within the discourses of science and medicine is often challenged, in texts such as *The Combined Maze* and *The Creators*.

The latter novel includes Sinclair's most important and most detailed early study of motherhood in her portrayal of the novelist, Jane Holland. When Jane marries and becomes a mother, she finds the roles of writer and mother almost irreconcilable. Indeed they are only sustainable at a cost to her own integrity and she leads her life in fragmented fashion, fulfilling alternately one role and then the other, so that one of her friends describes her thus:

> She seemed to have suffered some spiritual disintegration that was pain. She gave herself to them no longer whole, but piecemeal . . . There was, she seemed to say, no more left of her.[4]

The sense of there being 'no more left of her' in fact reflects the lived experience of motherhood for many women, and is a far cry from its various idealisations by male writers, painters and doctors. It is important to remember that Sinclair's texts reflect this lived experience, as it applies to the mothers of small children, in order to place in context her full-length portraits of motherhood, the most important and detailed of which are to be found in *Mary Olivier: A Life* and *Life and Death of Harriett Frean*. Both these novels are written from the point of view of the daughter, and narrate the experience of being mothered as crippling and destructive.

I wish to suggest that the texts' representation of these daughters' unhappy experiences, like the earlier characters' unhappy experiences of mothering, can be traced to the gap between idealisations of motherhood and the lived experiences of women. Although the novels were published in 1919 and 1922, they portray their heroines as roughly contemporary with Sinclair herself, growing up in late Victorian England, an age which Virginia Woolf has identified as the age of 'the Angel in the House'. Woolf's description of the attributes of the Angel itself acknowledges a male literary origin in Coventry Patmore's poem. The behaviour of the mother characters in the two novels I wish to discuss can be seen as attempts to live up to the ideal of the Angel. Woolf describes her succinctly, highlighting several characteristics:

> She was intensely sympathetic. She was immensely charming. She was utterly unselfish. She excelled in the difficult arts of family life. She sacrificed herself daily . . . Above all—I need not say it—she was pure.[5]

The representation of Mrs Olivier, the mother in *Mary Olivier: A Life*, from the perspective of her daughter, may be considered in the context of the ideal of the Angel.

Her complex relationship to her daughter is intimately connected with her idea of motherhood and her attempts to live it out.

Mary Olivier: A Life traces the life up to middle age of Mary, the only girl in a family of three sons: Mark, her mother's favourite, Dan and Roddy. The novel, focalised entirely through Mary, centres on her struggle for the affection of her mother who loves her sons more than either daughter or husband, and the conflicting impulse of her fight for independence against repressive social and religious influences which seek to turn her into a dutiful daughter.

One early scene, occurring in the second volume, 'Childhood', is of particular importance in illustrating the central issues of Mrs Olivier's relationship to her daughter. It begins with Mary's anxiously pleading with her mother, almost in the manner of a lover, for a confession of love, a confession which Mamma deliberately withholds, reprimanding her daughter in words which underline the similarity of the situation to that between two lovers: 'You're going to be like your father, tease, tease, tease, all day long, till I'm worn out'.[6] Mrs Olivier's answer to Mary, refused in words, takes another form when she invites her to look in her sewing basket, which Mary does reluctantly, being uninterested in her mother's needlework:

> The basket was full of tiny garments made of the white stuff, petticoats, drawers and nightgown, sewn with minute tucks and edged with lace. (*MO* 69)

The sight of the clothes 'for your new dolly' produces in the young girl an ecstasy of delight and, after one last effort to persuade her mother to offer the desired confession, compliance:

> And Mary would bring the long sheet that dragged on her wrist, and the needle that pricked her fingers, and sit at Mamma's knee and sew, making a thin trail of blood all along the hem.
> 'Why do you look at me so kindly when I'm sewing?'
> 'Because I like to see you behaving like a little girl, instead of tearing about and trying to do what boys do.' (*MO* 70)

This scene is central to an understanding of the relationship between Mrs Olivier and her daughter. It demonstrates explicitly that Mary can win approval only if she takes up occupations which conform to the conventional gender stereotype. Mrs Olivier is moulding her daughter in the pattern of the Angel, a pattern which she herself has so faithfully followed, teaching her daughter 'the difficult arts of family life'. The values which underlie Mrs Olivier's concern with domestic tasks are clearly those of the gendered division of the public and private spheres. When her daughter is fourteen, Mrs Olivier becomes embroiled with her in a dispute about Mark's Greek books which Mary wants to read after Mark has left home, complaining angrily that studying has distracted her daughter from occupations such as darning. It is Mrs Olivier herself who makes explicit the opposition between household tasks on the one hand and learning Greek on the other. Her daughter records: 'Her mother's face shivered with repugnance. It was incredible that anybody should hate a poor dead language so' (*MO* 126).

The arbitrary division between male and female activities is one which will haunt Mary well into adulthood. It is not just that Mary is required to spend her time on activities such as hemming sheets, but that a binary splitting of gender roles appears to mean that she cannot therefore undertake any serious reading, and particularly that she cannot enter that exclusively male preserve of the study of classical languages which, at this time, would still largely control entry into the universities, and therefore into positions of power.

In displaying opposition to Mary's activities, Mrs Olivier is behaving exactly as her society has taught her to behave. One of the many sources for Woolf's model of the Angel is to be found in the exhortatory works of Sarah Ellis who deals with this very issue of classical learning, remarking confidently: 'What man is there in existence who would not rather his wife should be free from selfishness, than be able to read Virgil without the use of a dictionary?'.[7]

The root of Mrs Olivier's revulsion against the notion of her daughter's learning Greek is to be found in her own unsuitability for the role of Angel. Mrs Olivier is undoubtedly a powerful woman and on such women sympathy and unselfishness, which Woolf defines as some of the properties of the Angel, do not sit easily. Mrs Olivier's answer is to have achieved dominance in her household, in the carefully defined sphere of the management of servants, the carrying out of household tasks, the education of her daughter. She is a strong-minded woman who finds the exercise of her power threatened by her daughter who wishes to transgress the boundaries of private and public spheres. Her response is to seek to mould her daughter in her own likeness, on the surface to be the passive and self-sacrificing woman, a living example of a nineteenth-century construct of femininity.

Lacking in any substantial power, with her power even in her own house circumscribed by that of her husband, and with her conduct and manners of necessity conforming to those of the Angel, Mrs Olivier is adept at manipulation, often employing the surface charm of the Angel. When Mary has reached maturity, and the family have moved to Morfe, a conversation between Mrs Olivier and her daughter has been concluded by Mary agreeing not to speak of her lack of religious belief, in order to preserve her mother's respectability. The final paragraph reads: 'Mamma held her face up, like a child, to be kissed' (*MO* 171). The brief phrase, 'like a child', highlighted by its placing in the final line, suggests that she simulates likeness to a child, thus projecting the gentle unassuming image of the Angel, but is in fact a subtle manipulator.

In her own circumscribed world, Mrs Olivier exhibits the very vices which she seems so anxious to extirpate from her daughter: wilfulness and selfishness. Recognition of this is eventually forced on Mary herself, but not until after she has grown up:

> Mamma had married for her own pleasure, for her passion. She had brought you into the world, without asking your leave, for her own pleasure. (*MO* 229)

What Mary pinpoints here, however, is not only her mother's selfishness, but her unacknowledged sexuality, which exposes the other great contradiction that lies at the heart of the relationship between Mrs Olivier and her daughter. It must be remembered that the Angel was above all, pure, and yet her primary function in the house, the production of children, cannot be severed entirely from sexual passion.

In order to explore this contradiction more fully, it will be helpful to return to the incident with which I began, which culminates in Mary's discovery of the doll's clothes. The incident demonstrates very clearly both the source and the exercise of Mrs Olivier's power: the child's intense desire for her mother, and her mother's insistence that she undertake activities suitable for the domestic role chosen for her. However it also demonstrates the ultimate goal of Mary's education. She is to be educated for the marriage market, to be the object of desire of a future suitor, while herself exhibiting and experiencing no desire. The importance of dolls in the daughter's education is that they demonstrate the acting out by the daughter of the mother's role model but in a curiously sexless way. The clothes in this scene are, significantly, white and highly decorative. The Victorian doll is clearly to be as well protected by underclothing as the Victorian woman.

Mrs Olivier's situation is fraught with contradictions which are beyond her control. Compelled to live out the pure role of the Angel in a household where her very presence is testimony to her sexual function, her attitude to the most determined of her daughter's suitors, Maurice Jourdain, is ambivalent. On the one hand her remark about the proposed marriage, 'I'd rather see you in your coffin' (*MO* 210) suggests unease with the idea of her daughter's sexuality, and yet her attitude to the engagement does not entirely convey disapproval: 'She hated Maurice Jourdain, yet you felt that in some queer way she loved you because of him' (*MO* 214). The contradiction in Mrs Olivier's attitude has its roots in the same fundamental contradiction at the heart of Victorian expectations of women. For all that she dislikes the thought of her daughter's relationship to Jourdain, Mary has pleased her because she is about to fulfil her function in life.

Indeed, while Mary's sexuality is repressed, that which society has constructed as its opposite and which might prevent its ultimate manifestation, the pursuit of learning, is also to be repressed. Thus Mrs Olivier tells her daughter after Maurice breaks off his engagement: 'I can tell you *one* thing . . . It was those books you read. That everlasting philosophy. He said it was answerable for the whole thing'(*MO* 224). Thus the artificial splitting of gender roles along a binary divide which was discussed above recurs, but this time the issue is more complicated. For Mrs Olivier to tell her daughter that while mending sheets is acceptable, learning Greek is reprehensible, is one thing, but what she does here is effectively to tell her that while a sexual relationship with a man is acceptable, discussing philosophy with him is not. However, Mary's whole upbringing has in many ways implied that a sexual relationship with a man is not acceptable. In totality, Mary is thus taught that she must abstain from one action in order to perform another which she must abstain from. The implications of this both for Mary and her mother are devastating.

For Mrs Olivier, despite her denial of sexuality in keeping with the role of the Angel, is, as Mary herself recognises in the passage quoted earlier, a woman of passion, although her passion has become displaced from her husband on to her son, Mark, whom she regards with jealous possessiveness. Mrs Olivier's sexuality is thus directly present in the text, and is divined by her daughter Mary. Nevertheless it cannot be spoken and she remains trapped in the same double bind as her daughter, condemned to abstain from one set of activities, the intellectual function and its concomitant occupation of the public sphere, in order to embrace another, the domestic and maternal function including, necessarily, a sexuality which is forbidden her. The sexuality of both women is necessary to the patriarchal society of which they are a part, and yet it represents at the same time a threat. Kristeva and Irigaray, among others, have pinpointed the way in which the sexuality of women is detached from male experience and denied expression.[8] Mrs Olivier, accepting such a role, the role of the vehicle of desire who has no effective speech and therefore no means of expressing such desire, merely carries out her function and complies with the repression of the speaking of her sexuality which is exacted as the price of its acceptance. The necessary consequence of this is that she will educate her daughter to do the same.

Although Mrs Olivier is a very strong, determined and passionate woman, her power is circumscribed. In accepting confinement to the private domain of the 'Angel in the House', she loses her son Mark who leaves home to join the army, and loses control over her husband and her son Dan, whose drinking drives the one to an early grave and the other to disgrace, and indirectly to emigration. Nevertheless, in spite of their striking similarity as strong women, Mrs Olivier and her daughter are destined to fight. Ultimately a woman's power, if she accepts the dominant, gendered ideology of her society, can only be over other women, in Mrs Olivier's case only over Mary.

It remains to consider the peculiar source of this power, the power which apparently enabled so many women to reproduce the figure of the Angel in the lives of their daughters. For, although her daughter succeeds in maintaining her own independent way of thinking, she does it at the price of a great struggle, and it can be argued, as Jean Radford for one argues, that ultimately she sacrifices her chance of marriage rather than desert her mother.[9] A reading of the scene with which I began, in which Mary begs her mother to say she loves her, is shown the dolls' clothes, and is commanded to hem sheets, strongly suggests that Mary's relationship with her mother always remains at some level pre-oedipal.

The family relationships of the Olivier family are complex. Mrs Olivier has transferred her affections from her husband to her son Mark, and the consequence for her daughter is that she never sees her father as an object of desire. Desire is therefore turned in on her mother, as the scene with the dolls' clothes illustrates. Indeed sexual elements in the desire for the mother may be suggested by the trail of blood on the hem of the sheet. The immediate cause of the little girl's willingness to drag the heavy sheet and to prick her fingers is the reward of the dolls' tiny clothes. Dolls have a special significance in the mother-daughter relationship. Often given as a mark of affection by mother to daughter, they might as a gift be seen as parallel to a new-born child, the gift in one sense of man to woman, and implying a pre-oedipal affinity between mother and daughter.

There are of course grounds in the novel for claiming that the Olivier family, as it is represented, is in some way pathological, and that the break-down in the relationship between Mary's parents accounts for an abnormally strong pre-oedipal tie with her mother. However, to analyse characters in a novel as though they are patients in a case study is an unproductive way of proceeding and it seems to me that, in its treatment of the relationship between Mrs Olivier and her daughter, the novel represents something common to the mothering and 'daughtering' experience of many women. Nancy Chodorow, in her sociological and psychoanalytical study *The Reproduction of*

Mothering, attests to the significance of the strength of the once-neglected pre-oedipal mother-daughter relationship in perpetuating the mothering function, arguing that psychoanalytical accounts make clear that 'a girl develops important oedipal attachments to her mother *as well as* to her father'.[10]

The text suggests that the unique mother-daughter relationship is a key influence in the life of Mary Olivier. What it does in her case is not to reproduce mothering but, because her mother accepts the ideology of patriarchy and uses all her considerable power to persuade her daughter to accept it, perpetuates in her a sense of the separation of the sexual/maternal function from the intellectual function, thus paradoxically ensuring that she rejects motherhood. Such a rejection is made all the more likely by her mother's refusal to speak her sexuality, referred to above.

The consequence of the daughtering experience for Mary is that her desire for intellectual activity, her fear of her own sexuality, and her acceptance of the gendered split between the intellectual and the domestic lead her to reject the marriage proposal of Richard Nicholson and ultimately to end her sexual relationship with him. The text, in the form of Mary's narrative, offers other explanations for her abandoning of the relationship with Nicholson, notably her neo-Platonic pursuit of the Ideal, but it remains Mary's narrative and Mary remains, however indirectly, the product of her mother's rearing.

Mother-daughter relationships are the site of powerful and complex negotiation. A very different version of the relationship is explored in *Life and Death of Harriett Frean*. It is a remarkable novel, noteworthy for its economy of style and suggestion, focused by the viewpoint of the central character, Harriett, the only child of Hilton Frean, a dilettante and unsuccessful business man. Mrs Frean is on the surface a much less dominating woman than Mrs Olivier, more naturally suited for the role of Angel, but she nevertheless achieves a total success in the domination of her only daughter. The consequence is that Harriett not only shows no desire to do anything which her mother would not approve of, but is so stunted by the formative years of her early life that she fails even to achieve her mother's limited satisfaction in the role of wife and mother.

Mrs Frean shows the self-sacrificing qualities of the Angel almost to a fault, reacting to her husband with a generosity which, in the case of his announcement of his bankruptcy, the reader suspects goes beyond his deserts, declaring that 'We shall be no worse off ... than we were when we began. We were very happy then.'[11] Nevertheless her generosity is double-edged and what the reader encounters in Mrs Frean is a much more successful adaptation to the ultimately manipulative role of Angel, since what she does by her generosity is to win her husband back from the dangerous sphere beyond the home, offering the comforts of an attractive private world.

In relation to her daughter, Mrs Frean's angelic methods of control are demonstrated in a crucial scene which has a significance beyond the merely representative. It is a childhood incident in which Harriett makes almost her only attempt at rebellion against parental authority, by walking in Black's Lane, where she has been forbidden to walk:

> It had come all of a sudden, the thought that she *must* do it, that she *must* go out into the lane ... She was forbidden to go into Black's Lane ...

> She kept on saying to herself: 'I'm in the lane. I'm in the lane. I'm disobeying Mamma.' (*HF* 16–17)

Her mother's angelic response ensures that she never disobeys again. On Harriett's return from the lane where she has been frightened by the man who lives there, she meets her mother:

> Her mother was coming down the garden walk, tall and beautiful in her silver-gray gown with the bands of black velvet on the flounces and the sleeves; her wide, hooped skirts swung, brushing the flower borders. (*HF* 19)

In this description of Mrs Frean, attention is drawn predominantly to her dress, rather than herself, in this way enacting the cultural repression which makes Mrs Frean what she is. Her dress is highly decorative, as Victorian woman was encouraged to be, but significantly part of the decoration is in the form of black bands, and the hoops of the skirt brush the flower borders. Thus images of encirclement predominate over the flowers, which represent natural growth.

Mrs Frean represents in her very person the supremacy of the cultural over the natural order. She manifests, much more effectively than Mrs Olivier does, yet another characteristic which Woolf ascribes to the Angel. She is charming. She conceals her first reaction to Harriett's disobedience, although clearly upset both by the disobedience itself and by the sexual connotations of a visit to the lane, where Harriett later learns 'something had happened to a little girl' (*HF* 24). She focuses on the red campion flowers, wild flowers representative of natural forces. The text unarguably represents them as sexual symbols: 'On each side a long trail of white froth with the red tops of the campion pricking through' (*HF* 18). Mrs Frean's response is different: 'Look, Hatty, how *beautiful* they are. Run away and put the poor things in water' (*HF* 20). Her reaction to the flowers preserves the Angel's purity and is a re-enactment of Victorian patriarchy's response to women. The flowers, already cut from their roots by Harriett, are seen as beautiful and decorative, to be placed in a vase which parallels woman's pedestal. Mrs Frean's education of her daughter reflects this construct of woman. The one predominant principle of behaviour which is instilled into the child Harriett is that of 'behaving beautifully', again recalling the charm of the Angel. The conclusion to the Black's Lane incident sees Hilton Frean tell Harriett that she must behave beautifully. Her parents refuse to punish her, thus binding her even more effectively to themselves, and from this moment she takes 'behaving beautifully' as her watchword. The plot of the novel is coextensive with Harriett's life and its only major incident is her refusal of the offer of marriage, made by Robin Lethbridge, the fiancé of her best friend, which results in much unhappiness for Robin and his two wives. Yet when Harriett thinks about the incident, 'she felt a thrill of pleasure in her beautiful behaviour' (*HF* 67). Thus she learns from her mother a code of conduct based on mere surface appearance.

Harriett's desire for maternity is the only form which her repressed sexuality is allowed to take. The source of her desire for motherhood is clearly her relationship to her own mother, for whom likewise maternity is the only acceptable expression of sexuality. The relationship is evoked very clearly at the end of another early childhood incident. Mrs Frean's actions at the school-treat, prompted by her fear that her daughter may have been greedy, have resulted in Harriett having nothing to eat at all. The consequence, however is not resentment but a disturbing closeness:

> Her mother had brought her a piece of seed-cake and a cup of milk with the cream on it. Mamma's soft eyes kissed her as they watched her eating her cake with short crumbly bites, like a little cat. Mamma's eyes made her feel so good, so good . . .
> Sitting up there and being good felt delicious. And the smooth cream with the milk running under it, thin and cold, was delicious too. (*HF* 14–15)

The account, with its emphasis on the sensuous experience of the milk, is strongly suggestive of suckling, and of Harriett's inability to move beyond a pre-oedipal relationship. Such an idea is confirmed when she talks to her mother about babies. She has visited a neighbour who has given birth to a baby boy, and talks excitedly about the baby she will have when she grows up:

> 'Which would you rather have, a little girl or a little boy?'
> 'Well—what do you think -?'
> 'I think—perhaps I'd rather have a little girl.' She would be like Mamma, and her little girl would be like herself. She couldn't think of it any other way. (*HF* 11)

Harriett, unlike Mary, is quite willing to model her behaviour on that of her mother, but there is a sense in which, in her own terms, Mrs Frean has been too successful, since Harriett evinces not so much a willingness to imitate her mother, but an inability to think of herself as separate from her. This notion of a daughter unable to progress beyond the pre-oedipal bond can be supported from elsewhere in the novel. There is Harriett's rejection of Emily, the doll given to her by her father as a birthday gift, and the second scene of the novel in which Harriett's mother puts her to bed, kissing her with the 'kiss-me-to-sleep kiss', to be followed by her father who kisses her with a 'kiss-me-awake kiss', suggesting an Oedipal resolution which one might argue Harriett never achieves (*HF* 3). However, rather than suggest an arbitrary distinction between desire for the father and desire for the mother, it seems more appropriate, as in the case of Mary Olivier's relationship to her mother, to see the text as suggesting the enduring quality of the pre-oedipal bond.

Chodorow's observations support such a view. An inextricably close bond which produces conflict in the case of Mrs Olivier and her strong-minded daughter, produces a smothering closeness in the case of Mrs Frean and the compliant Harriett. Harriett's gradual loss of identity after her mother's death may be linked with Chodorow's observations of the frequency of cases of daughters who 'act as *extensions* of their mothers', quoting one psychoanalyst, who, without being aware of the full implications of the finding, comments that 'being empty of oneself is found more often in women'.[12]

This accords with the adult Harriett's experience after her mother's death. In a passage which employs the vocabulary of the central character she seems to acknowledge this: 'But she was not there. Through her absorption in her mother, some large, essential part of herself had gone' (*HF* 108). From here on, the adult Harriett's progress is a slow regression to babyhood which reaches its climax in the final scene of the novel: 'The white curtain walls of the cubicle contracted, closed in on her. She was lying at the bottom of her white-curtained nursery cot. She felt weak and diminished, small, like a very little child' (*HF* 184).

The representation of motherhood in *Life and Death of Harriett Frean* has certain similarities to its representation in *Mary Olivier: A Life*. Both women take upon themselves the duty of bringing up their daughters in the mould which Virginia Woolf has described as that of the 'Angel in the House'. In Harriett's case this manifests itself mainly as 'behaving beautifully' and in the denial of sexuality, although by implication she apparently takes on the home-making role of the Angel. Unselfishness and self-sacrifice are manifested by a host of small actions, but ultimately by her rejection of Robin. All this is learnt from her mother. Both women, in spite of their self-projection as charming and unselfish, may therefore be seen as very powerful women within their limited domestic sphere, who use manipulative means in their attempt to dominate their daughters.

It might be argued that women like Harriett and her mother, where they exist, are highly suited to the angelic role. Nevertheless, Mrs Frean is sufficiently concerned with her own needs to ensure herself complete dominance over her daughter, and some domination over her husband. Both women, having accepted the role which society has given them, are whole-hearted in their attempts to ensure their daughters follow suit. The contradictions of the role, the masking of both sexuality and the desire for power, account for some of its strains. The denial of sexuality by the mothers appears to result in its complete repression by their daughters.

For modern women, many of the social conditions and cultural assumptions which colour these versions of mothering have changed or are in the process of changing. They serve as records of the lived experience of middle-class women of the time. What is less likely to have changed is the strength of the pre-oedipal bond between mother and daughter. Chodorow argues with some plausibility that the strength of such a bond, which often has debilitating effects of one sort or another, will remain as long as one parent is encouraged to enter into such an exclusive relationship with her baby, commenting that 'those very capacities and needs which create women as mothers create potential contradictions in mothering'.[13] Others, such as Irigaray, seem to argue for the centrality of such a bond but regard it as somehow distorted by its role within a phallocentric culture. Without doubt, phallocentrism has ignored the importance of the mother-daughter relationship, which is only now receiving long overdue attention. The two novels discussed in this essay, taken with several other of Sinclair's novels, bear testimony to the centrality of the demands of mothering, and particularly of the mother-daughter relationship to the experience of women, whether or not they themselves mother.

NOTES

1. May Sinclair, *The Three Sisters*, London, Virago 1982.
2. For these and other details of Sinclair's life, see Theophilus E.M. Boll, *Miss May Sinclair: Novelist*, Rutherford, New Jersey, Associated University Presses 1973.
3. May Sinclair, *Mr and Mrs Nevill Tyson*, London, Blackwood 1898, p. 77.
4. May Sinclair, *The Creators*, London, Constable 1910, p. 347.
5. Virginia Woolf, 'Professions for women', *The Death of the Moth and Other Essays*, London, Hogarth Press 1942, p. 150.
6. May Sinclair, *Mary Olivier: A Life*, London, Virago 1980, p. 69. All further references will be given in the text with the abbreviation *MO*.

7. Sarah Ellis, *The Women of England: Their Social Duties and Domestic Habits*, London, Fisher, nd, p. 71.
8. See Julia Kristeva, 'About Chinese women', in Toril Moi (ed.) *The Kristeva Reader*, Oxford, Blackwell 1986, translated Sean Hand; and Luce Irigaray, 'This sex which is not one', in Elaine Marks and Isabelle de Courtivron (eds) *New French Feminisms*, Brighton, Harvester 1981.
9. Jean Radford, Introduction to *Mary Olivier*, Virago 1980.
10. Nancy Chodorow, *The Reproduction of Mothering*, Berkeley, University of California Press 1978, p. 127.
11. May Sinclair, *Life and Death of Harriett Frean*, London, Virago 1980, p. 84. Further references will be given in the text, with the abbreviation *HF*.
12. Chodorow, *The Reproduction of Mothering*, p. 104.
13. Ibid., p. 211.

11 Love hurts

Philippa Gregory

More than two hundred years and innumerable shifts in popular culture separate the modern commercial novel from eighteenth-century stories, but one feature has survived: the victimisation of women. The restrictions and pains suffered by women two hundred years ago in the real world were reflected and exaggerated in the fictional world. Surprisingly, these agonies have been prolonged and replicated by modern novels.

The modern novels are the true heirs of the eighteenth century novel which was created from a combination of other narrative forms. By the end of the eighteenth century the most popular form was a linear narrative told in the third or first person. The favoured material of the stories also evolved. The older tales had been of adventure and miraculous escapes; today we would think of them as fairy tales. But by the end of the eighteenth century the preferred theme was the growth of an individual, spiritually, emotionally and materially, in a realistic domestic setting.

These literary conventions were virtually unchanged in the popular novels of the nineteenth and twentieth centuries. Postmodernist experiment with novel form and material has scarcely touched the form of the popular commercial novel which remains stubbornly linear and realist. And the survival of the literary conventions has been matched, astoundingly, by the survival of moral conventions. Despite dramatic progress made by women in the changing real world over the last two hundred years, the status and safety of heroines is little improved.

What are these thriving moral conventions? The most striking is the double sexual standard. The hero of the eighteenth-century novel is modelled on the hero of the picaro tales. He is brave and adventurous, he travels in the wider world, he takes charge of his own destiny and he is powerful. He earns his own living and often makes an enormous fortune, returning home a wealthy and successful man to claim the woman of his choice. He is sexually active; before marriage he is adventurous and aggressive in his sexual behaviour. He can be promiscuous without attracting criticism, he can seduce, he can assault, he can even rape. After his marriage he can be adulterous and this is regarded not as a problem for him, but as a problem for his wife to resolve (as in Richardson's *Pamela in Her Exalted Condition*). We see such heroes in the classic eighteenth-century novels of Henry Fielding, or Tobias Smollett, or the early novels of Eliza Haywood.

In this acceptance of rampant and uncontrollable male sexuality the novels merely reflected the views of the real world. As Dr Johnson explicitly states, husbands cannot be expected to demonstrate sexual fidelity, and a wife should tolerate this:

> if for instance, from mere wantonness of appetite, he steals privately to her chamber maid. Sir, a wife ought not greatly to resent this. I would not receive home a daughter who had run away from her husband on that account.[1]

The heroine meanwhile is virtually confined to the home. Anxious to preserve her virginity which is a prerequisite of the only career open to her—marriage—she dares not wander too far from safety. She is dependent on men politically and financially: first on her father or guardian, and then on her husband. There is no work available to her and travel is terrifyingly hazardous. Her constant difficulty is the ill nature and malicious gossip of other women which could destroy her reputation and thus her marriageability.

Some unfortunate heroines are inadequately protected and suffer violence, are often abducted and very occasionally raped. The heroine's relationship to violence is peculiarly interesting in that her suffering seems to demonstrate her virtue, and often redeems the hero from his bad ways. For instance the suffering, bravely borne, of the heroine in *Pamela: or Virtue Rewarded* convinces her would-be seducer and torturer to love and marry her. The emotional agony of the heroine of Fielding's *Amelia* persuades her husband to give up adultery and gambling. In my doctoral research on popular eighteenth century novels, I found that 57 per cent of the heroines suffer severe physical pain, while almost all of them endure a period of intense distress before achieving their reward of marriage.[2]

The heroines let their pain speak for them since words of complaint would give offence:

> To expostulate I feared might estrange his affection, and I hoped *that* melancholy which I could not disguise, and that tender behaviour which my heart prompted, would awaken his reflection, and enable his duty to gain the victory.[3]

The heroines of the eighteenth-century stories are pain specialists; they endure more assault, imprisonment, and abuse than any other character—even more than the villain who deserves punishment. Some authors relish the vulnerability of the heroines, and this is betrayed in the masochistic tone they give them. In *Sir Charles Grandison* the heroine is sensuously attentive to the injuries incurred while begging her chaperones to stay with her:

> I begg'd, pray'd, besought them not to go, and when they did, would have thrust myself out with them. But the wretch, in shutting them out, squeezed me dreadfully, as I was half in, half out; and my nose gushed out with blood.
> I screamed: He seemed frighted: But instantly recovering myself—So, so, you

have done your worst!—You have killed me, I hope. I was out of breath; my stomach was very much pressed, and one of my arms was bruised. I have the marks still.[4]

The eighteenth-century novels tell a powerful story of male adventure and female suffering, of male freedom and female restrictions. They were written at a time when women had no political or financial rights and they dramatise and glamorise female dependency. But between then and now women have demanded and won political equality, the right to own and keep their property, have been promised financial equality in the labour market and equality of opportunity. Women can control their own fertility, they can be sexually active outside marriage, they can choose to marry, to co-habit or to live alone. One might therefore expect that the modern novels would reflect, perhaps even celebrate, the liberated heroine.

In some ways they do. Heroines of modern bestsellers tend to be educated women with jobs. They are shown to be earning their living, they are free to travel. They work mostly as freelances in glamorous and interesting jobs in the creative arts, fashion and entertainment industries. They are active in their adventures and they improve their positions, becoming more wealthy and ascending the social scale during the course of the story. Apparently, these heroines are successfully running their own lives. Indeed, in the sex-and-shopping genre which dominated the 1980s, heroines are often corporate executives and directors.

The sex-and-shopping story is a female version of the male fortune novels such as those by Jeffrey Archer. In his *Kane and Abel* the privileged young American boy and the illegitimate Polish immigrant both seek to win their fortunes in America. The drama of the novel is the world of business: trading, loans, stocks and shares, and the rise of a luxury hotel group. The two men's business ambitions conflict with their family and emotional commitments, but there is no suggestion that they are ever betraying their true nature. They are born competitive. They are born winners.

In contrast to this positive view of ambition and achievement are the stories of businesswomen. One of the best known, *A Woman of Substance*, shows a working-class girl surviving seduction, unwanted pregnancy, abandonment and rejection, to seek her revenge through wealth. She establishes a small shop and then a massive retail chain. But even this apparent success story hints that women lose their desirable feminine vulnerability when they battle it out with men. Emma is ambitious because her true destiny, love and marriage, has been denied to her. The consequences are unhappy. Her children conspire to destroy her and her company, and have to be bribed into acquiescence. She has only one close friend and her husband and lovers are dead:

... there were those who had dealt with Emma as a formidable adversary, who considered her to be cynical, rapacious, cunning and ruthless. On the other hand Gaye knew that she was generous of her time and money and understanding of heart. As she was being understanding now. Perhaps Emma *was* wilful and imperious and even power-ridden. But surely life had made her so. Gaye had always said to Emma's critics, and with the utmost veracity, that above all the other tycoons of her calibre and stature, Emma Harte had compassion, and was just and charitable and infinitely kind.[5]

It is interesting that Bradford—the most confident of all the sex-and-shopping authors—undermines her own message of female power. The story would work perfectly well if Emma were a completely self-made woman; but in fact the bulk of her fortune is inherited from her lover. The apparent theme of the book is female struggle and triumph; but the major source of Emma's wealth is her lover's estate, and she pays for her success in emotional deprivation. Again and again Emma's worldly success and determination are shown to cause an automatic loss of tenderness and vulnerability. She wants to be a success *because* her heart was broken and her nature twisted when she was a young woman. The corruption of her early gentle nature makes her desire success, and makes her hard-hearted enough to achieve it. The woman tycoon is a woman who has been unsexed. In contrast to the tough old lady, the most attractive female character is Emma's granddaughter, who is as efficient as her grandmother but completely lacks her ruthless nature. She falls in love and marries the man of her choice in a completely conventional love story.

An even more dramatic example of commercial success corrupting a woman's true nature is in *Oliver's Story*—the sequel to *Love Story*—when the successful hard-bitten female executive is contrasted with the beautiful, tender and caring wife who has tragically died. The female executive is a stereotypical rich bitch character, and her relationship with Oliver collapses when he finds that she runs her company at a profit by exploiting child labourers in Far East sweatshops.[6]

Other self-made working women of the modern bestsellers are not what they seem. They are not self-made nor are they shown at work. One typical heroine of the 1980s sex-and-shopping novel has inherited her position from her father. In *Old Sins*, it is the father who is shown building up the company from nothing. It is the father who is the entrepreneur who launches the cosmetics company from his garage and makes it into an international multi-million business. When the daughter inherits, there is no expansion, consolidation, or even problem solving. Her task is to secure her inheritance by personal struggle in which she must destroy her rivals: his mistress and an illegitimate son. It is a drama of personalities, not of business. She is shown arriving or making lunch appointments in her office, but the emphasis is on the decor, not on the work. The day-to-day business of running a commercial company is completely ignored.[7]

There is no female-oriented equivalent to the novels of Arthur Hailey which feature a business in crisis and the men who solve the problems. Hailey's novels are fine examples of well-researched, infinitely detailed stories about the internal workings of commercial and industrial enterprises. The men who make them work, and solve the operating problems, have no effective female colleagues. Women in these novels are in support—as secretaries, wives, mothers, or lovers—or they are victims when the industries go wrong. They are not powerful problem-solving workers.

Many women executives are simply unsuccessful, like the heroine of *Out of Africa* who is bankrupted and loses her farm and has to hope that the new owners will fulfil her promises to her workers.[8] Few heroines are employers; in about half of my survey of modern novels women are specifically shown to be unsuccessful in directing others: they cannot even organise their own lives or achieve their ambitions.

Most women workers are junior or inferior members of teams led by men. They are rarely shown at work at all, and their adventures generally take place outside their work, during holiday time or sick leave, emphasising the peripheral nature of their work. The heroine of *Palomino* is a campaign manager for an important advertising company, at the peak of her career. Her husband's betrayal triggers a deep depression which her employers reward with limitless sick leave. During her holiday she visits a ranch and meets the cowboy hero, and the main issue of the story is whether she can recover from her disappointment to love and trust again. Her work is virtually forgotten.[9]

The vast majority of heroines in the modern novels are casual, part-time or freelance employees, illustrating yet again their tenuous connection with the world of work. Most of them work as sexual objects. The heroine of *Lace* is a pornographic actress, the heroine of *Hollywood Husbands* is a model, as are the heroines of *Mistral's Daughter* and *Princess Daisy*. As a structural device this choice of work benefits the plot by exposing the heroines to exploitation and abuse, and injects the glamour of the fashion and entertainment industry. However it also means that modern heroines are shown as having made no gains from improvements in education and opportunity in the real world.[10]

As the name of the sex-and-shopping genre makes explicit, the business of heroines is not to produce, but to consume commodities, and enjoy or endure sexual intercourse. The heroines' travelling, working, achieving, is nothing more than consumption on a wider scale. Men make money, achieve ambitions, plan, plot, scheme, and triumph. Heroines consume and are consumed.

The most striking difference between the heroines of modern novels and their eighteenth-century predecessors is their sexual freedom. Heroines of the modern novels are almost all sexually active, and all of them acknowledge their sexuality. They consciously seek and choose their partners. They have sexual intercourse with the man of their choice before marriage, and some of them have more than one sexual partner. However, in more than half of the books of my survey the emotional response of the man is a disappointment. There seems to be a reproduction of the double sexual standard of the eighteenth century in that men are still less emotionally committed than their female partners. Although heroines are sexually free and can make the sexual running—courting, demanding and seducing—this does not make the men of their choice particularly responsive. In more than half the novels the heroine wins the man of her choice but without a ringing authorial endorsement. His response is not the equal of hers. Although couples may be equally sexually active, heroines are still more emotionally vulnerable than men, they are more tender, and they have more at stake. Their love is requited uncertainly, without guarantees. With little else of interest in their lives, the love affair is their prime concern. But for men who are struggling with work, with danger, and with moral issues, the love affair is a final reward, not the driving desire of their lives. Unlike their eighteenth-century predecessors, the modern novels do not conclude with a triumphant marriage and the certainty of happy-ever-after.

In one sense this is realism. The continual liberation of the divorce laws has meant that in the real world more and more marriages end in divorce and authors are not complacent about marital happiness. But on reading the novels a greater uncertainty becomes apparent. The authors seem to suggest that the very nature of men is less emotionally serious and less emotionally committed than that of women. Women

143

simply seem to love men more than men can love them back. Samantha, the heroine of *Palomino*, has just discovered her husband's infidelity, and in her disappointment she recalls that her first and enduring feeling for him was worship:

> They had become lovers at nineteen. He had been the first man she had ever slept with, when they were both at Yale. He had been so big and blond and beautiful, a football hero, a big man on campus, the golden boy everybody loved, including Sam, who worshipped him from the first moment they met. 'You know what I thought, you son of a bitch? I thought you were faithful to me. That's what I thought. I thought you gave a damn, I thought'—her voice quavered for the first time since he'd said the awful words—'I thought you loved me.'[11]

The sexual freedom of modern heroines is not always to their benefit. They often engage in deviant practices with men who hurt or abuse them. A number of heroines are infatuated with their fathers, such as the heroine of *Once is Not Enough*, or have sex with their brothers as in *The Seeds of Yesterday*, or with near relations such as a foster brother in *The Kissing Gate*, or a brother-in-law in *The Moth*. In *The Little Drummer Girl* the heroine sleeps with the man she has been hired to betray to his death, and her sense of corruption nearly destroys her.[12] The heroine of *Destiny* has her clitoris stapled with a diamond earring, and Shirley Conran suggests this variant to the usual sexual conventions:

> Abdullah, murmuring soothing words of flattery and love, encouraged most women to behave in a more voluptuously agile manner than they had ever thought possible as he led them swiftly through an erotic crash course which culminated in his sensuous pièce de résistance. With silken cords he would bind the wrists of the more adventurous ones to the bedhead and then he would dip one golden hand— his skin wasn't very dark, just a permanent sun-bronzed tone—into the bowl of golden fish that always seemed to be at his bedside. Abdullah would quickly scoop out one little fish and swiftly push the wriggling creature into the girl. At this point, she generally stiffened and shrieked with surprise, but Abdullah threw his body on top of hers and held her hard against the mattress until she relaxed and was able to enjoy the strange erotic sensations as she felt the little fish move inside her warm body. As soon as the girl started to groan, with pleasure, Abdullah would slide down her body and—with great dexterity—he would languorously suck out the goldfish.[13]

This scene makes clear that adventurous women respond delightedly to having dying fish stuffed up their vaginas; indeed, an unfortunate 43 per cent of abused women in my survey of modern popular fiction are willing accomplices of their own sexual abuse. Altogether 29 per cent of the heroines are savagely assaulted, and 71 per cent are physically or emotionally hurt. This is a powerful message about the suitability of women victims for pain and sexual abuse, and the high proportion of willing and enthusiastic victims is a ringing authorial endorsement of the popular myth that women permit or even welcome sexual abuse. The most nauseating catalo-guist of female pain is undoubtedly Wilbur Smith, whose immensely popular novels draw on both racism and sexism for their power. Most of his novels feature a rape, almost all his white heroines are threatened with rape by black men. In this scene, which is by no means exceptional, two black women are threatened by two black men:

> The constable guarding Imbali strained for a glimpse of what was happening. His lips were open and he licked them. He could make out blurred movement through the leafless branches and then there was the sound of a body falling heavily to earth and the breath being driven violently from Ruth's lungs by a crushing weight.
>
> 'Hold still kitten,' the *kanka* panted. 'You make me angry. Lie still,' and abruptly Ruth screamed. It was the shrill ringing cry of an animal in mortal agony, repeated again and again, and the *kanka* grunted. 'Yes. There, yes,' and then snuffled like a boar at the trough, and there was a soft rhythmic slapping sound and Ruth kept screaming . . .
>
> . . . Imbali was fifty paces down the hillside, flying like a gazelle over the rough ground, driven by her terror. The man thumbed back the hammer of his Winchester, flung the butt to his shoulder and fired wildly, without aiming. It was a fluke shot. It caught the girl in the small of the back and the big soft lead slug tore out through her belly. She collapsed and rolled down the steep pathway, her limbs tumbling about loosely.
>
> The constable lowered the rifle. His expression was shocked and unbelieving. Slowly, hesitantly, he went down to where the girl lay. She was on her back. Her eyes were open and the exit wound in her flat young stomach gaped hideously, her torn entrails bulged from it. The girl's eyes switched to his face, the terror in them flared up for an instant, and then slowly faded into utter blankness.[14]

The explicit sexual detail of rape and abuse scenes in modern commercial fiction might surprise critics who dismiss all women's fiction as light romantic nonsense. It is a secret known only to the readership that behind the soft-focus covers and the gold lettering there are scenes which are powerfully erotic, perverse and violent. In *If Tomorrow Comes* the heroine, who has been a privileged beloved fiancée of a wealthy young man, finds herself wrongly imprisoned and vulnerable to the lesbian fellow-prisoners.

> She was awakened by a hand clamped across her mouth and two hands grabbing at her breasts. She tried to sit up and scream, and she felt her night-gown and underpants being ripped away. Hands slid between her thighs, forcing her legs apart. Tracy fought savagely, struggling to rise.
>
> 'Take it easy,' a voice in the dark whispered, 'and you won't get hurt. . . .'
>
> Tracy broke loose for an instant, but one of the women grabbed her and slammed her head against the bars. She felt the blood spurt from her nose. She was thrown to the concrete floor, and her hands and legs were pinned down. Tracy fought like a mad-woman but she was no match for the three of them. She felt cold hands and hot tongues caressing her body. Her legs were spread apart and a hard, cold object was shoved inside her.[15]

In a disturbing echo of the eighteenth-century belief of female pain redeeming men from their sins, and recalling them to the paths of virtue, nearly 60 per cent of the heroines of my survey manage to win their men to good behaviour by the excess of their distress. In *Firefly Summer* the heroine Kate's crippling accident makes her husband take seriously his responsibilities, and is the first step in making the rich newcomer respect the community. The structure of the story may indeed require another accident—although one might think that there are plenty of female victims already—but the excessive pain suffered by Kate seems to exist only to sharpen the reader's sensibilities, and to locate Kate as a saint:

> She saw Brian Doyle waving at her frantically as she approached the site. He had both hands in the air and was shouting something. But she hadn't heard what it was by the time she felt the terrifying sharp pain. It was so sudden and worse than anything she had ever known, like the terror in a dream or a nightmare. And it only lasted seconds because that was all it took for Kate Ryan to be hit sideways by the huge digger, flung up in the air and crashed to the ground. It only took a few seconds to break her spine.[16]

Whatever these stories of pain, abuse and perversion are telling, it is not a tale of empowerment and liberation. This is the eighteenth-century morality tale of threat and danger to any adventurous woman, and saintlike suffering for any good woman, transferred entire to the present day. The modern trappings of independence—the careers, the travel, the expenditure—are nothing more than a gloss on the traditional cautionary tale. Eighteenth-century heroines were warned that any foray into the outside world would cost them their reputation, their physical safety, or even their life. Modern heroines roam greater distances but they too are in jeopardy until they find and secure the protection of the hero. Their sexual activity is not an empowering and enjoyable exercise: it exposes them to unwanted pregnancy, to sexual abuse, and to emotional distress.

At one level this hardly matters. These books are not taught in schools, they are not hailed as role models, they are neglected by critics. They are read for entertainment and then discarded. But the attitudes and conventions of the fictional world have a relationship to the real world.

The eighteenth-century novel produced fictional heroines whose behaviour reinforced the conventions and morals of the real world. Young ladies, whose mothers were doing their best to protect and guide them, read novels in which female virginity was an essential prerequisite for survival. The exaggeration of the dangers of the outside world, peopled by rakes, rapists, and all sorts of villains, reinforced the conventions of the real world: that young women should stay inside their homes. In several novels, for instance, the heroine is kidnapped from a masked ball, where the confusion of disguises and the admittance of the general public makes her abduction possible. These fictional cautionary tales repeated and emphasised the real-life warnings in magazines and journals which demanded a continual narrowing of the boundaries for young ladies. They warned that young ladies should not attend masked balls, and that all entertainments for young ladies should be exclusive and limited to guests with invitations.

Even the rise of the marriage of choice, which is sometimes regarded as a triumph for women who were thus able to suit themselves in their choice of partner, was not wholly happy. Instead of being paired with a man on the basis of financial convenience and parental preference, women were chosen on the basis of a suitor's tastes.

The surplus of marriageable women to marrying men, and the absence of any other form of employment, made this a difficult experience for many individual women. The development of the Season in London and Bath and then in the provincial towns was a response to the need for young women to be seen and selected for marriage. A situation in which a woman parades herself and competes with others can hardly be seen as a liberating experience. Women became commodities, chosen by the consumer on the basis of their looks, their reputation, their connections, and their dowries.

Such a system puts a premium on attractive looks and attractive behaviour, and, in the case of eighteenth century England, attractive behaviour for young women became more and more restricted. Likewise, in *Pride and Prejudice* Elizabeth Bennet's muddy petticoat, incurred while walking cross-country to see her desperately ill sister, was worthy of critical comment. The rules of conduct became increasingly limiting as the century wore on, and in time women internalised these rules into a whole range of beliefs about the nature of femininity: docile, unsexual, obedient, clinging, fearful. Heroines of the fictional world and real women in the real world shared and indeed celebrated these disabling characteristics. What is perhaps surprising is that along with the structure, length, voice and style of the eighteenth-century novel, the convention of female powerlessness has survived also.

The modern novel, like its eighteenth-century predecessor, celebrates female vulnerability and female pain. When women act in the wider world they expose themselves to abuse and exploitation. When they act in business or industry they make mistakes, they abuse others, and they lose touch with their own true nature. More often they do not attempt to compete with men at all in the world of work, but only consume. When they dare to be sexually and emotionally active they find themselves exposed to abuse and danger, and even when they are successful, their advances are only partly requited. They are still the more vulnerable gender, they seldom meet with a satisfactory response. Heroines are still the reward for the hero at the end of his struggles and his exciting adventures. Their fidelity earns his return, their pain still prompts his reform. Two hundred years of real-life change and literary experimentation has made little difference to the women of popular fiction: they are still the specialists in suffering.

NOTES

1. James Boswell, *Boswell's Life of Johnson*, ed. G.B. Hill and L.K. Powell, Oxford 1934–50, pp. 55–6.
2. Philippa Gregory, 'The popular fiction of the eighteenth-century commercial circulating libraries', unpublished PhD thesis, University of Edinburgh 1984.
3. Anon, *The School for Wives*, 1763, p. 175.
4. Samuel Richardson, *The History of Sir Charles Grandison*, 1754, Vol. 1, p. 158.
5. Barbara Taylor Bradford, *A Woman of Substance*, London, Granada 1981, p. 35.
6. Erich Segal, *Oliver's Story*, London, Panther 1978; *Love Story*, London, Panther 1976.
7. Penny Vincenzi, *Old Sins*, London, Arrow 1990.
8. Karen Blixen, *Out of Africa*, London, Penguin 1986.
9. Danielle Steel, *Palomino*, London, Sphere 1982.
10. Shirley Conran, *Lace*, London, Penguin 1983; Jackie Collins, *Hollywood Husbands*, London, Pan 1987; Judith Kranz, *Mistral's Daughter*, London, Corgi 1984, and *Princess Daisy*, London, Corgi 1981.
11. Steel, *Palomino*, p. 4.

12. Jacqueline Susan, *Once is Not Enough*, London, Corgi 1974; Virginia Andrews, *The Seeds of Yesterday*, London, Fontana 1984; Pamela Haines, *The Kissing Gate*, London, Fontana 1982; Catherine Cookson, *The Moth*, London, Corgi 1987; John le Carré, *The Little Drummer Girl*, London, Pan 1984.
13. Conran, *Lace*, p. 292; Sally Beauman, *Destiny*, London, Bantam 1988.
14. Wilbur Smith, *The Angels Weep*, London, Pan 1982, p. 126.
15. Sidney Sheldon, *If Tomorrow Comes*, London, Pan 1985, pp. 63–4.
16. Maeve Binchy, *Firefly Summer*, London, Coronet 1987, p. 264.

12 Alice Thomas Ellis: Kinder, Kirche und Küche

Peter Conradi

Yet it is the masculine values that prevail . . . This is an important book, the critic assumes, because it deals with war. This is an insignificant book because it deals with the feelings of women in a drawing-room . . .

Virginia Woolf, *A Room of One's Own*[1]

. . . [Claudia] had realised with astonishment that the perfect couple consisted of a mother and child and not, as she had always supposed, a man and a woman.

Alice Thomas Ellis: *The Other Side of the Fire*[2]

As Erasmus showed in *Moriae Encomium* ('In Praise of Folly'), an *apparent* or *assumed* foolishness can be a deadly effective stance from which to satirise and wage war upon the real follies and vanities of the world. This was the Czech anti-hero Schweik's discovery, too. If you belong to an oppressed group, to pretend to be powerless can render you safe from attack, and at the same time secure you a privileged viewing-post from which to watch and comment on historical change and struggle. The oppressor must needs perceive the oppressed as foolish, and the strategy here is accordingly to 'play foolish', but with so suitable an irony that, in the end, your oppressor may be exasperated and rendered powerless to respond. In Ellis's case, a dippy 'feminine' *faux-naiveté* has proved a very effective hiding-place from which some of the idiocies of the contemporary world and thought can be exposed. The intelligence involved has its own fierce, clear-sighted passion.

It is a passion that does not turn its back on 'Kinder, Kirche and Küche', the traditional realms, but encompasses them.[3] Earlier women writers were often childless (Austen, the Brontës, George Eliot, Woolf). Today's are as likely to have reared a family, and Alice Thomas Ellis's children were nearly grown-up before she found the time to write fiction. Before that she had, under her own name (Anna Haycraft), written two cookery books, one of them entitled *Natural Baby Food*, the other, co-written with Caroline Blackwood, *Darling, You Shouldn't Have Gone to so Much Trouble*.

A.T. Ellis admires those who have a strong sense of irony, parody, self-mockery. The theme runs through her novels. The possession of such a sense distinguishes those smart and always self-sufficient ladies who act to some extent as her spokespersons—not that they ever remain immune from criticism—from the others, who lack their special self-consciousness about themselves, or wit about their world. Rose, Sylvie, Aunt Irene, Lydia and Lili seem a new kind of heroine, or perhaps a new version of an old kind, where the ability to cook, house-keep or bring up children does not *preclude* wit and satire, but, on the contrary, is their essential condition. Of these five, only Rose and Sylvie have children, and only Lydia has a career—as a journalist. But all show some skill in looking after others. Even if motherhood is not a biological necessity, it appears to be an epistemological privilege.

It is a privilege from which men are excluded. Few writers insult men so systematically, so wittily, or to such deadly effect. Men, throughout her work, seem falsely convinced that women think of nothing but *them* (*CW* 93). A.T. Ellis creates in each novel a gallery of interesting women, but men who are mainly notable for their alienness and stupidity. The general, and satiric, note is given by one woman character who ruminates to deadly effect that 'in the unremitting dissension between the sexes, despite the current mood of passionate sympathy for the poor down-trodden female, it was the male who really summoned forth the tears—albeit tears of mirth' (*OSF* 45).

The Summerhouse Trilogy contains one man who murders a woman, probably because she laughed at him. Men 'take offense at the slightest thing' (*FO* 36). Another has interfered with his daughter when she was a small child. The plot concerns the attempt to prevent a marriage and, incidentally, humble the prospective groom who is an odious and spoilt fool. This is not the only place in her work where a happy ending, unlike that of a traditional novel, depends upon the *prevention*, through scandal, of marriage or of sexual love. *Unexplained Laughter* has a comparable shape. In that book Lydia, who is admittedly angry with an ex-lover, has a catalogue of witty complaint. She asserts that she has never known a woman behave as weirdly as a man, by which she means as moodily or tyrannically, since men childishly insist that their moods be taken note of (*UL* 126).

All this might suggest some species of feminist, but Ellis is too maverick for that, apart from having an innate and a '*contrary*' horror of belonging, and therefore of resembling others. 'That's the trouble with the *bien pensant*—rather than resemble them in any degree one rushes to the other extreme . . . ' (*HL3* 37). She reports herself 'confused by human feminism, because if you disapprove of [men] so much why wash off the make-up, crop the hair and slap on the boiler-suit in order to resemble the rotters?' (*HL* 38), and also reports herself 'increasingly bored with the pretence that Western woman has been hideously oppressed until now while her menfolk enjoyed lives of blissful freedom and exercised their powers to keep the females in their place'.[4] Gabriele Annan recently pointed out that Ellis's central theme 'links up with what looks like a branch of feminism', but perhaps is in reality more of 'a protest against the importance given to sex in the modern world'.[5]

Her work, perhaps for this latter reason, celebrates throughout an antithetical and largely self-sufficient woman's realm, in the articulation of which she has a large investment. The rest of this essay thus falls into two main sections. In the first, and drawing on her non-fiction writing, including occasional journalism, I sketch some qualities inherent in Ellis's definition of this self-sufficiency. These qualities include materialism, a tension between dandyism and drudgery, and a continuing baffled attempt to enclose a space both outside and safe from the horrors of modernity, particularly *English* modernity, a realm her books are always eloquent and informative about. In the second section I trace how these themes resonate within her first five novels, and also how her cult of self-sufficiency is attended by at least two dangers: a sterile view of sexual love; and, underneath all the incidental comedy, a related pessimism if not despair about life itself. I reserve the question of Ellis's pessimism to the end.

The drudge and the dandy

A dogged and sensible materialism is visible throughout her work, despite many flights of fancy. Indeed what stimulates these flights is the material world itself. Many quite normal women spend a great deal of time 'talking to and feeding people whom they would not, themselves, have chosen to entertain' (*UL* 25). Thus the kitchen is one of the most important rooms in every house and likely to continue to matter in every culture because, to put it at its most positive, 'Once you'd fed people you had admitted responsibility, like saving a life' (*27K* 53) and 'a companion is literally one with whom one breaks bread' (*UL* 8). On the negative side, it is inadvisable to be rude to that most important person, the cook, since she has the ability to poison you or make you decidedly unwell (see *27K* 104–5). Aunt Irene in *The 27th Kingdom*, who is not the first or last Ellis heroine to be preoccupied with and very witty about food, feels that her first question to the risen Christ would have been: 'What did you have to eat?' (103). Irene's kitchen is described as having 'the innocent importance of an essential place . . . kitchens, being necessary, were as holy as bread and water' (25). The parallel between kitchen and Church recurs throughout the novels, and takes its force from an appreciation of food and its central place in culture which, for all that her heroines are often Catholic, and sometimes other-worldly, is in itself wholly pragmatic.[6]

Those who feed their world exercise both their power and also their other-centredness. In this they share the moral and artistic qualities necessary, for example, and pertinently, to novelists. Aunt Irene is just such an artist, her artistic skills described as lying in cooking and housekeeping: 'People weren't merely her audience but in a sense her raw materials to be disposed and manipulated as the fancy took her' (14). Like the novelist, the matriarch has the problem of trying to see others intrinsically, as ends not means, a danger not always escaped by some of these heroines. Wickedness, indeed, is defined by Aunt Irene as an inability to see the truth of a different person (132).

This is a danger attending equally on the wit of the heroines and of the novelist who creates them, and the fact that she can play a willing 'drudge' gives interest to her provocative stance; she accounts, for example, the happiest days of her life the

151

'playing house' in Wales where, with back-breaking work, she brought up her big family—making jam, 'washing nappies, making dinner, and advising the current baby not to put his fingers in the sheepdog's eyes' (*WC* 94).

But she is also a dangerous secret 'dandy'-wit. Dandies have traditionally adopted an aristocratic stance in everything except their background. They are 'both the embodiment of the aristocratic principle and also an insolent threat to it' since they are often democrats also and classless, like bohemians who dress down at the same time as they dress up.[7] So Wilde, Saki, Waugh and Spark, those dandy-writers, seem her forebears. In any case it is one part of her dandyism and bohemianism that she is, though 'smart', somehow unsnobbish, on easier terms with the unlettered than with the stupider and more conventional bourgeoisie. In *Home Life* it is not surprising to find that lawyers are 'detestable, judges . . . distinguished by asinine arrogance . . . architects are arrogant too . . . ' (*HL3* 36), while the lower classes are commended as much better mannered than the upper (*HL1* 80). If you judge people by how much fun they yield and are to be with, then this makes sense.

A good novel, however, traditionally honours the truths of different people, and in this the good novelist may play as much the domestic drudge as the dandy-wit: that is, working towards a patient understanding, rather than towards a quick and hilarious dismissal. A.T. Ellis is a marvellously, gloriously funny and witty writer, who sees that 'humour comes out of precision' (*UL* 120). Her work is aware of the dangers that accompany the dandy-posture: narcissism, and that cold self-sufficiency evinced both by the brilliant epigram, and by an over-confident matriarchy alike. Extreme and barbarous cruelty, she acknowledges, can have a 'terrible kind of *style*' (*HL2* 58), and she is aware that wit itself must needs often be cruel (e.g. *HL1* 23). The tension between these postures—between drudgery and dandyism—ran through her *Spectator* column 'Home Life' in the 1980s, and might have contributed to its extraordinary success.

The persona she constructed here for herself is an extravagantly 'feminine' one, to the point of conscious self-parody: 'I had a fierce battle with two hamburgers last night' (*HL2* 146); 'one of the things I should be frequently told is how stupid I am' (*HL3* 72). The writer is studiously vague: she cannot remember how much sugar she takes in coffee (*HL3* 20), is baffled by the telephone (*HL2* 65), believes that 'switches and wiring' require a degree (*HL2* 28), boasts of an ability to get lost even in Trafalgar Square 'with no trouble at all' (*HL2* 27), keeps getting side-tracked (*HL2* 127), and suffers from irritating domestic mysteries: 'How did we accumulate eighty odd socks and where do the teaspoons go?' (*HL1* 11).

This unworldliness partly belongs to a class-based persona, but is also a gendered one, where menfolk monopolise only the silly world of reason, rather as Mrs Dalloway and Mrs Ramsay wonder quite what a square root is or where the equator might be, with no urgency whatsoever. What they 'really' know is superior, or is at least 'organic' intuitive knowledge, compared with the dry technology of male chop-logic. As with her own heroine, Lydia, it is always clear that we are meeting 'a sufficiently practical person and not the ass she sometimes chose to appear' (*UL* 9). While affecting a 'dippy' persona in the *Spectator*, A.T. Ellis was an efficient fiction editor at Duckworths.

So, while she purports to admire the pragmatism of certain men (*HL2* 144), what emerges is 'rage at men in general for the worry they cause us' (*HL2* 133). It is not merely that 'Someone [i.e.her husband Colin Haycraft] and I reason in different ways' (*HL3* 48) but that, secretly, 'the much vaunted quality of reason can lead one straight up a gum tree, and I think we should drop it in favour of common sense' (*HL3* 51). So when she dutifully and humbly asked 'Someone where the notion of progress had arisen and he told me, but I've forgotten again' (*HL2* 118), this reasonable knowledge was clearly not worth remembering anyway. Intelligent scepticism about 'progress', and a pity-filled contempt for many aspects of modern living—'I have never come to terms with the modern world and I never will, since I cannot see the need for violent and ruinous change' (*W* xv)—fill everything she writes, as does the attempt, more persuasive in some novels than in others, to suggest an alternative space beyond modern rationalism.

The world of male 'reason', which is presumably to blame for the modern world, is largely sterile and dead. In *The Birds of the Air* Barbara comes to understand that if she passes over the edge of despair into death her husband 'would still be immovable, *because he was an entirely reasonable man*' (149, my emphasis). Against this sterility, and the idiocy of experts who contradict each other and are mainly male (*HL2* 69 and 135), inconsistency is to be delighted in because it alone is fully human. She herself 'never had much trouble simultaneously entertaining diametrically opposing propositions' (*HL3* 57), a negative capability which can also lead to discovery. Having asserted how similar the Welsh and the Egyptians must be, because both go in a lot for *aunties* (*HL2* 132), she is later awed to discover that Welsh and Berbers do in sober fact share a common blood-group and many words from the Hamitic (*WC* 79). So intuition may be the vanguard of a truer 'expertise'. . . .

Though purporting to be written in a fit of absence, these *Spectator* columns are, like the fiction, immaculately shaped and finished, shrewdly *observed*, and—doubtless after much hard work—cunningly imitate the swift movement of thought itself. They are not merely whimsical, with their silly news that vultures have constant diarrhoea in order to keep their legs warm (*HL2* 92), but also happen upon brilliant and surprising parallels which yield a truth or a moral. She is bleakly and shockingly wise about love and egotism (*HL2* 101). Though she makes clear how invasive she finds interviews (*HL* 126–8) and hence how private she is, she none the less befriends the reader with a movement of equivocal gallantry—'I'm sure you're not yourself intrinsically boring' (*HL3* 106)—constructing a version of domesticity, and therefore privacy, in front of an audience of thousands. The return within the column of recurrent anxieties itself also recalls the rhythm of a conversation among friends: the strangers in the London garden and the ghosts in the Welsh one, the visits from the bailiff, the eloquence about depression—'sometimes life seems so short it's barely worth putting one's name in the telephone directory' (148)—and about breakdown and the death-wish, sometimes triggered by seasonal gloom over Christmas, that particularly maternal problem (141).

The world, the flesh and the female spirit

Her first novel *The Sin Eater* (1977), an elegant and truthful fiction, is set in Wales, 'so close to England and so different' (*W* xii). Rather as the woman's world is set against the man's, so North Wales appears in her thinking as an antidote to England. There are suggestive parallels between Wales and femininity; like Ellis's women, the Welsh are constructed as a people of 'fantastic imaginings' (*SE* 43), being both superstitious and intuitive. Ellis's North Wales, where she grew up, is a feminised pre-industrial world, a romantic alternative to England and modernity, with a deep sense of tradition (*W* 29), not class-ridden but 'outside the tradition of man and master' (*SE* 31) and where 'Once upon a time nobody locked their doors' (*W* 101).[8] England, by implied contrast, means rationalism, industrialism, secularism, class-snobbery, creeping suburbanisation and tourism.[9] The Welsh, who have a genuine and ancient culture, have been perceived as savage and backward by the insular English, who have lost theirs (*WC* 69).

This is the back-drop for *The Sin Eater*, and provides its title. Rose, the book's heroine, though born elsewhere, belongs to this landscape. Rose is the daughter-in-law of the Captain, whose function in the novel is to die in such a way as to point up the indifference and mediocrity of the members of the family or court that surrounds him. They compete with each other for influence and material gain. His army back-ground underlines the novel's view of the competing spheres of influence of the sexes: 'Men were made for war. Without it they wandered greyly about, getting under the feet of the women, who were trying to organise the really important things of life. When they couldn't make war men made money—and trouble and a dreadful nuisance of themselves . . . '(70). This is Ermyn thinking, but it could be any heroine in any Ellis novel: it amounts to a received view.[10]

Rose competes with Angela, the Captain's other daughter-in-law, who is loud, opinionated, snobbish, entirely unoriginal and conventional, and thus predictable, typified by the Banker's Regency decor of her over-filled London home. Rose wins by being colder, cleverer, more ruthless, and more willing to stare uncomfortable truth in the face. Rose is the classic female 'dandy', Irish and not top-drawer, but with the ultimate or true patrician's dandy-wit nonetheless to unmask the superficiality of all *bien-pensant* bourgeois attitudinising. She hates fools and can speak as she pleases. For example, *vis-à-vis* servants, Angela mouths the usual sentimental clichés about their staying with the family out of 'loyalty', and is shocked by Rose's hard-headed estimation that it is a matter of being willing and able to pay enough. Rose sees without illusions, and this is one source of her power. It opposes her in the novel's scheme to her *ingénue* sister-in-law Ermyn, who finds reality too painful to deal with, and who thus denies much that is palpably happening around her, which includes a dying man's thirst, an attempted murder, and a possible attempted rape. Ermyn's ingenuousness is partly there in order clearly to focus Rose's finally equivocal worldliness. Rose was 'not a philanthropist' (96), but a 'terrorist, a secret deadly fighter' (159), Ermyn correctly sees. Neither Rose's nor Ermyn's seem adequate responses to the presented world, and though we may prefer Rose's warriorship, the book also silently judges us for doing so. In the final twist of plot, the most terrible of punishments awaits her: so self-sufficient is she, that she can be hurt only through her children. She seems scarcely married to Henry at all, and their only moment of intimacy in the entire novel is wholly insincere on Rose's part.

When asked by Angela why she does not return to higher education, Rose says only that she does not want to (182). The kitchen is her place of power, from where she exercises her magic, 'being greedy and clever and cynical, qualities essential to a good cook . . . '(17). She explicitly distances herself from any idea of domesticity as a sphere of 'lovable muddle'. Not for her the 'endearing smudge of flour on the cheek' (17), but a capacity to perform tasks carefully and well and to look cool while doing so. Like many of Ellis's self-sufficient women, she has some attributes of a witch, using cookery as a means of cruelly funny satire (102) or control.[11] She arbitrarily decides that in the annual village gentlemen-versus-players cricket match, the gentry shall lose, and cooks a horrifyingly over-rich meal to dampen their chances. Containing three duck, the meal may also have caused the consequent failure through a species of sympathetic magic ('out-for-a-duck'). 'I've poisoned [Edward]'(156) Rose is able truthfully to say.

Rose influences events through wit and cookery. She employs irony and self-consciousness and theatricality in her house-keeping, 'staging' elevenses, for example (94). Rose is interested in power (82–3) and good at getting it. As the novel proceeds, and her sheer intelligence enables her to win too easily, she starts to appear frivolous, a moral anarch, treading on a beetle 'for fun' (151), lying for fun (163, 164) or for an easy life (166). Her views—for example, that the Reformation led to the Industrial Revolution, which led to the British Empire which led to the public schools which led to the class system which led to socialism which 'by bad luck arrived just as it couldn't be afforded' (122) and has thus led to the collapse of the world economy—mirror her author's *faux-naive* wisdom. Like her author,[12] Rose too sees the world from a kitchen-eyed point-of-view, so that the narrator views the class-war in terms of cuisine,[13] and Rose has so fully mastered the class-determined semiotics of English cookery that she can manipulate these at will to achieve her effects.

The opposition of an awful England to a kinder remembered Wales also haunts the next novel, *The Birds of the Air* (1980), in the form of Melys y Bwyd ('Life is sweet'), where the 'doors had never been locked' (56). What I earlier termed Ellis's continuing baffled attempt to enclose a space outside and safe from English modernity, looks in this book simultaneously poetic and despairing. It chiefly takes the form of Mary's central daydream of resurrection, in which a Welsh saint at a medieval feast literally and magically revives the 'birds of the air' from a complex dish. This daydream fails to intersect with or in any way to vivify the sheer horror of contemporary English reality.

This novel, and the next, are grim: their eloquence resides in the detail of their satirical depiction of modern England. Here Great Pan has left the deserted places and 'gone on the streets to become a mugger' (18). The downs are 'flasher-haunted' (32) and walkers are as likely to stumble on 'the tights-strangled bodies of young women thrust into plastic bags and bound with electrical flex' (61) as to find winter aconite, or peace with each other. In Innstead, on the estate where the book is mainly set, retired policemen live next door to retired criminals, 'from whom they were indistinguishable in dress, tastes and overall attitude to the world' (106).

The novel is savagely satiric—recalling Huxley or Wyndham Lewis—as a chronicle of the moral poverty of modern English living. Mrs Marsh assembles her family for a suburban and snow-bound Christmas. Her daughter Mary is sick from mourning the death of her son, and in love with death. Her daughter Barbara is working with the imminent collapse of her marriage. Barbara's cold, arrogant, stupid, impatient and generally horrible husband Sebastian—'an entirely reasonable man' (149): that is, a monster—has started an affair. Barbara's son is a punkish drop-out, and her daughter is vain and attention-seeking. Barbara reaches out in her isolation towards the publisher Hunter, not realising that he is gay. Passing acquaintances—the American Mr Mauss, from an America representing 'heresy, genocide and greed' (113)—and neighbours—the 'artistic' Evelyn, and a retired police-inspector and his wife—are included in the party. Christmas is the time you invite people who are lonely because they are 'unpleasant or boring and no one liked them' (123). No-one sees or responds to anyone else's needs. Meaningless presents, or unpleasantly pointed ones, are exchanged. Generation, class and basic selfishness island everyone in their own unhappiness. Much comedy ensues, of the black and bleak kind. Although it is God's birthday, the Lord of Misrule holds sway instead. Comedy is all that is left. 'Forgive us our Christmasses' says Mary aptly, 'as we forgive them who have Christmassed against us' (33).

A seasonal academic party resonates with the tones of the English upper-middle classes at their most horrible; indeed England's class-system is throughout displayed as tragi-comic in the ways it condemns its inhabitants to further lonely incomprehension. Each layer feels 'slight fear and hostility, mixed awkwardly with wondering respect' for the layer just above it (55). And 'this dimension of madness took the form of a grateful tenderness towards the unimaginably rich and privileged; a tearfully joyous, knee-sore loyalty to the witless descendants of ruthless, incompetent, raging tyrants and murderers' (139). England is suburbanised, and given to the fetichism of toy-animals, as well as of the upper orders. 'Winnie the Pooh vied with the Queen (God trailing in the distance) for the forefront of the mind of the English middle class' (60).

Where social connection fails, love too can have no confident destiny. '*Lerve*,' says Evvie, in the next book, *The Other Side of the Fire* (1983), 'It makes me laugh' (79). This book's only act of coitus is when an exasperating and 'almost human' bitch is 'taken' by the dog from the lodge in a distant field (150). That aside, the love-theme is sterile. The wittiest characters are, as always, self-sufficient women, and the one woman who defies the prevailing law of self-sufficiency to fall in love—Claudia—is punished for her stupid optimism. For Claudia falls for her son-in-law Philip without seeing that he is gay; here this is the heart of the book, not one grimly comic strand of it. The title refers both to purgatory (69, also 144), after which you come out cleansed, and to the purgatory of sexual desire. Ellis is, throughout her career, beady-eyed about sexual love. Here she makes use of the story employed by Euripides, Virgil, Seneca, Racine. In the original, both Phaedra and her step-son Hippolytus perish. But for Ellis all sexual love conduces to comedy, not tragedy. Four out of five of her early novels contain at some point a revelation of homosexuality, a sexual temperament she seems to find laughable because of its *evident* sterility,[14] but it could be argued that she displays heterosexual relations in a fashion scarcely more sanguine.

This is her most literary and self-reflexive fiction. Evvie fears that 'every concept capable of expression in the English tongue had long since taken cliché form' (52–3), a fear of banality and unstylishness as the worst of all sins in the dandy's catechism, and also a fear alive in our time as so-called 'postmodern' anxiety. To her mother Sylvie also, 'life was like a novel that she knew by heart, crammed with minor characters whose names she couldn't remember and whose fates did not interest her' (65). Claudia is just such a minor character, a classic upper-middle class wife, of a limited and old-fashioned kind, who is to learn what lies on the other side of hope. Like women in novels generally, it is her destiny to discover discontent and then work through it.

Claudia has exchanged her life and freedom for 'the apron, the milk-soaked blouse, the blood-stained knickers, the coat made of the skins of animals that was her reward for conjugality' (9), an uncomfortable description which assimilates Claudia both to the animal and to passivity. Her husband Charles is a patriarch who can scarcely differentiate between women and children (125). Charles refuses to see the relevance of Claudia's experience. What women really want, the novel asserts, is to be recognised, accepted and appreciated as separate and distinct from men. Men, however, (Freud included) believe that women are incomplete men, and therefore racked with rage and jealousy.

Sylvie and Evvie are this novel's dandy-witches, and provide a Greek chorus to the tragi-comic action, self-sufficient and clever and ironic and sometimes wise. Evvie, Sylvie's clever and unillusioned daughter, is writing both a thesis on Latin Love Elegy, and also a rubbishy pastiche romance, a self-confessedly 'terrible book' (17) set in Scotland, to make money. These writings provide comic parallels with the progress of Claudia's doomed love. Evvie comes to be taken over by her make-believe world and its absurd characters and to feel life and art interpenetrate, not in a way that undercuts our belief in either, but rather in a way that reinforces our sense (just) that both have claims on us.

This is a novel acutely aware of sex-war. Claudia discovers that 'somewhere in the relations between the sexes there lay a huge murderousness' (120). Sylvie believes the sexes to be incompatible, and that the less time they spend together the better. And with deadly wit she notes that 'Unhappiness was a feminine trait. When men wore it they were unmanned, as though they had donned silk knickers and suspender belt. Perhaps that was why the whole of society was weighted in favour of keeping men happy' (140). Evvie sees men as 'a nuisance with more or less nothing to be said for them' (33). When Claudia finds out that Philip is gay, her pain is made real and touching, if not poignant, and this saves the book from its own despair, a despair both about the form and subject-matter of fiction—about, as it were, the *déja lu*—and the empty repertoire of human emotion. The only womanly happiness appears to lie in the by now familiar idea of self-sufficiency, with its concomitant slur of being a 'witch'. A rhetoric about the latter runs through the book.[15]

Aunt Irene is the self-sufficient heroine of the next novel, *The 27th Kingdom*. She is a White Russian aristocrat and also an artist, her skills lying in cooking and house-keeping. Irene mothers her world, which also means feeding it, albeit on occasion with horse-meat cunningly doctored to taste like beef. To her the Ten Commandments seem almost insignificant compared with the astonishing miracle of what you could do with an egg (84). Her kitchen has 'the innocent importance of an essential place'(25). She is psychic. Since she cannot recall names, she refers to everyone as 'Darling' (37), has 'no side' (45), and is, indeed, an innocent. She is surrounded by two bad people (at least), and one saint, the nun Valentine. Much loved and much missed when away, Valentine is also a calming and cheering presence, to be found when needed; she knows much without having to be told, and is quiet because she is happy. She levitates to collect the highest apples in the convent orchard, which subsequently decline to rot; and flies, too, to save a vengeful victim of her own sister's carelessness. She also helps another woman discover her religious vocation. Unusually for Ellis, here the ideal world of spirit throughout interpenetrates the fallen world, the 'upside-down' (40) world of gross matter to which we appear condemned; the safe space outside ordinary life which Ellis pursues is vouchsafed by a religious vocation.

No such transcendence is to be found in *Unexplained Laughter* (1985). It is one function of the dandy to eschew definition through the use of wit. She is the definer, not the defined. In two senses the dandy-wit petrifies or bewitches the world around her—frightening, and also solidifying it. In *Unexplained Laughter*, as in *The 27th Kingdom*, this becomes a theme. Lydia is smart, stylish, self-sufficient, witty, contrary; she is perceptive and intuitive to the point of accurate prescience, another version of the dandy-wit and witch. Her friend Betty is altogether more prosaic, 'a good little thing' (53) in Lydia's condescending view, but also morally nicer.

The story turns on the defeat of the odious Doctor Wyn, a breaker of hearts, through the botched staging of a public scandal, which looks forward to a similar peripety in the trilogy. The 'plot-interest', again as in the trilogy, hinges on the humiliation of a sexually predatory and morally inadequate male. A happy ending turns out to be one in which the sexes can decently separate. Beuno the minister is a good man, married to God and therefore celibate. He it is whose 'ruthless innocence' (82) can exorcise the 'unexplained laughter' of the title. This laughter has a choric function, and may possibly be one apt response of the principalities and powers to the comi-tragedy of human affairs.

The debate between a feminised Wales and a suburbanising England continues through the Molesworths, who represent everything Ellis hates about England: suburban, prudish, narrow, 'refined'. But the book also paints an unillusioned picture of Welsh life, with its own lonely narrowness and bitter, petty, feuding, its chapel-rooted misogyny (66) and its suffocating matriarchs ruining their sons' lives. The mute and backward Angharad represents one aspect of this latter Wales, being simultaneously 'taken care of' and marginalised. Her narrative complements and completes Lydia's story. She criticises Lydia as one of those who, needing to *know* everything, make the world into a smaller place.[16]

Celebration despite despair

For all her wit, it should by now be apparent that Ellis is not a consoling writer, nor one who points to any easy solutions. 'I seem to have thought, all my life, of little but death,' she once wrote (*WC* 106), and I want to end by briefly addressing her pessimism. In few worthwhile writers—certainly not in the cases, for example, of those august pessimists Beckett, Kafka, or Woolf—does the charge of pessimism rest unqualified. And Sylvie surely speaks for Ellis when she wonders why 'facing reality' should always mean ignoring what is beautiful and poignant about human life (*OSF* 69). It needs to be asserted that she seeks a place for these too in her brilliant and densely packed miniatures, as she does for comedy.

This essay began by suggesting that Ellis's apparently 'fey' but actually fierce use of a comic voice provides opportunities for brave originality and defiance of the Zeitgeist. It certainly offers few for easy comfort. Ellis is a devout and picturesquely old-fashioned Catholic[17] whose fiction contains a protest against the importance given to sex in the modern world.[18] In a century in which sex has been overrated, self-sufficiency is also likely to be neglected. These uncomfortable and unfashionable themes are also to be found in her impressive recent trilogy.

Perhaps the note of 'celebration-despite-despair' which Ellis achieves, notwithstanding her investment in 'discomfort', comes over best at the end of her autobiography, where the perception that 'some of this world is so beautiful that it cannot be described' recalls Shelley. Shelley's idealism, like Ellis's, is intensely dissatisfied with the status quo and has its own (very different) fierce impatience with the conventions governing relations between the sexes. The yearning of such idealism for something better threatens, in the end, to reject the given world we must share. Yet it also starts with the awareness that 'at each moment of joyful consciousness comes the knowledge that it will pass; and as time passes, you realise that it will never come again',

. . . and, greedy and grasping as we are, we want not only to enjoy it but to tell it— so that it listens, and in listening becomes fixed . . . No wonder we dream of death, of a true consummation where longing ceases and the earth itself embraces us until we cannot be told apart, cannot be discerned, and have no more responsibility. This, perhaps, is why we dream of Heaven; this perhaps is what is meant by *hiraeth*[19]: a lifelong yearning for what is gone or out of reach.

NOTES

1. Virginia Woolf, *A Room of One's Own*, London, Flamingo Modern Classics 1994, pp. 80–1 (first published Hogarth Press 1929).
2. Alice Thomas Ellis, *The Other Side of the Fire*, p. 53. All subsequent references to works by Ellis will be cited parenthetically in the text, with the following abbreviations: *The Birds of the Air* (Penguin 1983) *BA*; *The Clothes in the Wardrobe* (Penguin 1989)* *CW*; *The Fly in the Ointment* (Penguin 1990)* *FO*; *Home Life* (Fontana 1987) *HL*; *More Home Life* (Fontana 1988) *HL2*; *Home Life Book Three* (Fontana 1989) *HL3*; *The Other Side of the Fire* (Penguin 1985) *OSF*; *Pillars of Gold* (Penguin 1993) *PG*; *The Sin Eater* (Penguin 1986) *SE*; *The Skeleton in the Cupboard* (Penguin 1989)* *SC*; *Unexplained Laughter* (Penguin 1986) *UL*; *Wales, an Anthology* (Collins 1989) ed A. T. Ellis *W*; *A Welsh Childhood* (Penguin 1990) *WC*; *The 27th Kingdom* (Penguin 1982) *27K*. Works marked * comprise the *trilogy*.
3. We associate this triad with Nazi ideology, but I believe that it pre-dates the twentieth century. In the *Catholic Herald* (18 March 1994), 'Wary of taking equality too far', Ellis wrote 'I am perfectly happy with *küche, kinder, kirche* [sic]—so long, that is, as I can have an occasional good gossip and a trip to the pub with a couple of the blokes to make a bit of a change'.

4. *Catholic Herald*, 18 March 1994, 'Wary of taking equality too far'.
5. Gabriele Annan, 'A comedy of morals', *New York Review of Books*, 23 June 1994, review of *The Summer House* (published in UK as *The Clothes in the Wardrobe*), p. 46.
6. See also *HL* p. 75 and *HL2* p. 27.
7. See R. Sales, *J. Austen & Representations of Regency England*, London and New York, Routledge 1994, p. 74 and Ch. 3 passim.
8. See also *WC* p. 57: 'Wales was not class-ridden'.
9. See also *WC* p. 112, where the British try to make everything resemble a suburban sitting-room, a *lounge* . . .
10. See, for example, *OSF* p. 11: 'men thrive on competition, deceit and destruction, women who bear the burden of continuing the race find it necessary on the whole to behave in a limpid and straightforward fashion'; and *OSF* p. 116 where men have 'that terrible urge to make war all the time'.
11. A leading theme of a later novel, *OSF*.
12. 'I am almost as interested in what people eat as in what they say', *W* xv.
13. *SE* pp. 58, 152, 141.
14. Compare Barbara's 'love' for the gay Hunter in *BA*, Kyril's ambiguous sexuality, which he may have employed to help cause a suicide in *27K*, and Michael's lust for Gomer in *SE*.
15. See, for example, pp. 22, 24, 44, 47, 78, 96, 134, 139, 142, 148.
16. Knowing everything is not a danger for Ellis herself. In *27K*, for example, Middlesex (charmingly) has a border with Kent (p. 14).
17. See, for example, her polemic against all aspects of the modernising of the Catholic Church in *The Serpent on the Rock* (1994), and her column in the *Catholic Herald* in the 1990s.
18. See note 5.
19. *Hiraeth*: 'an intense and passionate yearning for that which we have not, for dead friends, vanished youth, the peace of heaven, some satisfaction that life can never give', *W* p. 114, quoting Sir Idris Bell in *The Development of Welsh Poetry*, Oxford, Clarendon Press 1936.

4 Public power

13 Gender and trauma: HD and the First World War

Trudi Tate

At the beginning of August 1914, the modernist writer Hilda Doolittle learned that she was pregnant. The baby was stillborn in May 1915—killed, HD believed, by the Great War. Not long before the child was born, HD had been shocked by some bad news: the sinking of the passenger ship *Lusitania*, in which 1200 civilians died. Whether medically true or not, HD's view of her child's death is a significant response to the trauma of the Great War. It posits a direct relationship between violent public events and the private lives of civilians during war time, and suggests that civilians, like soldiers, may have been subject to crippling war neuroses—an idea which recurs throughout her war writing.

It might be tempting to read this as specifically a woman's response to the Great War, a feminist protest against a public violence which permeates even the most private of spaces: the unborn child in the womb. Yet HD's work resists precisely this kind of rigid gendering. Rather, she explores the peculiar effects of trauma on both women and men, and the uneven ways in which the war penetrates civilian society. She does this partly through her representations of war neurosis: a disorder usually associated with soldiers, and commonly, if inaccurately, known as 'shell shock'.

Did civilians suffer from war neuroses during the Great War? The medical journal *The Lancet* did not think so at the beginning of the war. As late as September 1915, it was arguing that no-one, whether soldier or civilian, would suffer any long-term mental problems as a result of the conflict. Indeed, it argued, because civilian neuroses were caused largely by boredom, the excitement of the war ought to make them diminish, if anything. For civilians, *The Lancet* argued, 'the spectacle of millions of men abandoning home, family, ambition, money, and laying down their lives for a principle is so glorious as to transfigure "the pictures of mangled bodies and human beings gasping in their dark struggle against death" '[1] (the quotation comes from the superintendent of a lunatic asylum). The term 'spectacle' is striking here. Soldiers—men—are seen to have a symbolic function; their bodies form a grotesque 'picture' whose meaning transcends and redeems its own horror. Civilians do not see this 'picture', of course; they imagine it. And when civilians actually did imagine some of the horrible sights of the Great War, they became susceptible to war neuroses, as *The Lancet* found itself reporting only a few weeks later. Women whose sons were wounded, soldiers' wives, young recruits who had not been to battle, as well as civilians subjected to air raids or caught in battle zones: all these categories of non-combatants produced documented cases of war neuroses.[2] In other words, civilians were at risk of 'shell shock' from two sources: the experience of war (air raids, etc.) and the act of imagining, or witnessing, the war experiences of others.

We find, then, that the idea of civilians suffering from war neuroses was by no means unknown during the Great War. Later work on what is now called 'post-traumatic stress disorder' draws explicit parallels between civilian disaster survivors and combat veterans: their symptoms, it is argued, are often remarkably similar. For example, a study of American Vietnam veterans by Bruce Goderez notes that 'severe stress can compromise subsequent psychological functioning in previously normal adults'. There are 'common factors found in syndromes displayed by survivors of rape, floods, combat, the Hiroshima bombing, the Nazi Holocaust, and a variety of other natural and man-made disasters'.[3] In *Beyond the Pleasure Principle*, published not long after the end of the war, Freud too noted the similarities between civilian survivors of railway disasters and shell-shocked soldiers.[4]

What Freud and Goderez describe is the civilian experience of violence, whether public and shared (railway accidents, floods, war) or individual and private (rape). Direct experience of pain, loss of autonomy, and fear of mutilation or death can produce mental disturbance, often expressed in the body, for many years afterwards.

Does this help us to understand HD's view that her child was killed by the trauma of war? If the shock had been caused by the air raids on London, for example, then the models of war neuroses or post-traumatic stress disorder might readily be applied. But HD's case is striking precisely because it is *not* a response to direct violence. 'I had lost the first [child] in 1915,' she remembered many years later, 'from shock and repercussions of war news broken to me in a rather brutal fashion.'[5] It was a *story* which did the damage.

HD was deeply troubled by her memories of the Great War and the death of her first child, and she rewrote them many times throughout her life.[6] In *Asphodel*, an early memoir of the war years, she states bluntly of the protagonist's stillborn child: 'Khaki killed it'.[7] In a letter to Norman Homes Pearson in 1937, she wrote:

> In order to speak adequately of my poetry and its aims, I must, you see, drag in a whole deracinated epoch. Perhaps specifically, I might say that the house next door was struck another night. We came home and simply waded through glass, while wind from now unshuttered windows, made the house a barn, an unprotected dug-out.[8]

This might be the 'carnage on Queen's Square' imagined but never described in *Bid Me to Live*, HD's best-known war novel. Though the damage to London was minor compared with the devastation of the battlefields, it nonetheless had a profound effect on those who lived through the aerial bombardments—the first of their kind in Britain.[9] 'What does that sort of shock do to the mind, the imagination,' HD wrote to

Pearson, '—not solely of myself, but of an epoch?' Her analysis with Freud, she wrote some years later, was partly to gain skills which might help 'war-shocked and war-shattered people' from the Great War in the period leading up to the next war.[10]

In 'Magic Mirror', an unpublished memoir written in the 1950s, HD remembers receiving the news of the *Lusitania*, recounting the memory through the characters of Rafe and Julia in *Bid Me to Live* (originally entitled 'Madrigal'):

> Rafe Ashton [though not stated in Madrigal] destroyed the unborn, the child Amor, when a few days before it was due, he burst in upon Julia of that story, with 'don't you realize what this means? Don't you feel anything? The *Lusitania has gone down.*'[11]

We should be cautious about accepting this at face value, however, as Friedman notes:

> Here and later in a repetition of this memory, H.D. added to the typed manuscript the pencilled words: '(But this never happened. Surely this was fantasy.)'[12]

HD's memories of the war were written and rewritten over a period of more than forty years, the act of writing itself compounding them with fantasy. Fantasy might be constituted differently from the memory of real events, but it can be equally disturbing. And as time passes, the distinction between real and fantasised memories can become blurred.[13]

But whether memory or fantasy, HD's response to the news of the *Lusitania* provides some useful insights into her war fiction. Though almost forgotten today, the sinking of the *Lusitania* became one of the great scandals of the war, forcing civilians in Britain to realise that they too were serious targets. Though the event had little military significance, the sinking of the *Lusitania* became a key symbol in the British propaganda campaign to bring the United States into the war. It was widely reported in all the British papers, with much outraged commentary on German barbarism. It was debated widely in the United States, too, and was later seen as a key factor in the United States' decision to enter the war on Britain's side in 1917. In Willa Cather's war novel, *One of Ours* (1922), for example, one of the characters cites three reasons for enlisting: Belgium, the *Lusitania*, Edith Cavell—all represented in propaganda and the newspapers as examples of a violated 'femininity'. However, the sinking of the *Lusitania* was less the *cause* than the *justification* of the American entry into the war; its function was imaginary or ideological.

And this is precisely its importance in our understanding of HD's response to it. As I have already argued, it is well established that civilians, like soldiers, can suffer from war neuroses if they are subjected to violence. HD takes this point further, however, to suggest that violent events can cause physical or psychic shock even to people who are not present. Witnessing such events at a distance, or being exposed to them indirectly, discursively, through stories, can cause a form of war neurosis, just as some soldiers suffered from shell shock without ever going into battle. In other words, HD's response to the *Lusitania* suggests that the stories which circulate in society, especially in wartime, can damage people's bodies, or send them mad.

It is this imaginary effect of war that HD addresses in her war fiction. I want to look at two of her prose works about the Great War: 'Kora and Ka', a short story about a man who is still suffering from the war in the late 1920s, and *Bid Me to Live*, a novel about a woman's war experiences in London in 1917. Both works deal with the problem of being a witness, indirectly, to the violence of war, and ask how this interacts with structures of gender. But neither work posits a simple parallel between gender and violence. Nor do I agree with critics who argue that 'the war at home is also a war in the home' in HD's work.[14] We need to resist the urge to find simple parallels and causal relationships between gender conflict and military conflict.[15] Nor do I want to argue that HD is trying to define a 'women's experience' or 'women's consciousness' of the war. Increasingly, feminist criticism is challenging the idea of a single experience, common to all women, both in history and in writing. Rather, it is more fruitful to explore *how femininity is constituted* in relation to the war. More than this: if we are to understand gender, we need to pay attention to the ways in which masculinity is constituted, too.[16] Otherwise we imply that gender is somehow peculiar to women, while men are simply human—an idea which feminist criticism surely seeks to challenge.[17] 'Kora and Ka' is a particularly interesting story in this context: a story written by a woman which explores a man's reactions to the Great War. Like *Bid Me to Live*, this story demonstrates that the collective trauma of war spreads far beyond its immediate time and place, and can have a profound effect on the lives of both women and men.

'Kora and Ka' (1934)

'Kora and Ka' was written in 1930 and published privately in 1934.[18] It is a strange piece of writing, and has received very little critical attention. The story is worth looking at in some detail, however, for it specifically addresses the relationship between gender and war neuroses in the decade following the war.[19] 'Kora and Ka' has two main characters: Kora, a woman who has left her husband and children, and John Helforth, the man she lives with now. (The name John Helforth was also one of HD's writing pseudonyms, under which she published a short novel entitled *Nights* in 1935.) The story tells of Helforth's belief that his mind has been occupied by what he calls the 'Ka', a spirit from Egyptian mythology which lives on after the body has died. The story is narrated by Helforth in two interwoven voices: his own and the Ka's. This makes it difficult to follow, partly because it is a representation of a nervous breakdown, narrated from within.

The story opens with a struggle between Helforth and the imaginary spirit, as it tries to take over his mind. The struggle is centred on the act of looking, an act which is mentioned many times in the first few pages of the story. 'Helforth must see everything', we are told, but his eyes trouble him. He suffers from hallucinations, some of them very like Septimus's visual delusions in *Mrs Dalloway* (1925). He decides to have his sight checked by a doctor, but the problem lies in his mind rather than his eyes. The doctor diagnoses 'nerves' and recommends that Helforth stop working. But work is not the cause of his nervous disorders, though this does not become clear until half-way through the story. Helforth's illness dates from the war, some ten years earlier, and its symptoms are uncannily similar to war neuroses: hallucinations, a sense of dissociation, loss of certainty about his sexual identity. What is so striking about this, however, is that Helforth has not in fact been a soldier; his distress arises not from battle experience, but from the lack of it.

Out of the confusing chronology of the story and Helforth's disordered mind, one thread clearly emerges: his memory of the war. Both of his older brothers went to the front and both have been killed. Helforth was meant to avenge them, but the war ended before he was old enough to enlist. He blames their mother. 'Mother could have kept Larry at home,' he says:

> I was too young. Larry was of course vicious to have told me, in precise detail, all that he did. It was a perverse sort of sadism. I loved Larry. I would have gone on, loving men and women if it hadn't been for Larry. How could I love anyone after Larry? My mother used to say, '*Bob* would have been too noble-minded to have regretted Larry.' Bob? But Bob went that first year, dead or alive he was equally obnoxious. He was the young 'father', mother's favourite. I was sixteen. By the time I was ready, the war actually was over. Mother reiterated on every conceivable occasion, 'Larry is only waiting to get out there.' I don't know what mother thought 'there' was. It was so near. It was 'here' all the time with me. Larry was sent to avenge Bob, I was to be sent to avenge Larry. It was already written in Hans Anderson [sic], a moron virgin and a pitcher. We were all virgin, moron. We were virgin, though Larry saw to it that I was not. Larry. (197)

Larry has initiated Helforth into various kinds of adult experiences, providing him with an identity as a bisexual man. But when Larry is killed, war stories and sex stories become confused, and Helforth regresses into an angry, infantile state, raging against his dead brothers, his mother, Kora's children.

Helforth hates the war, yet it remains a measure of his own failed gender identity. In compensation, he attempts to assert an unambiguous masculinity:

> I will to be John Helforth, an Englishman and a normal brutal one. I will strength into my body, into my loins. (194)

> I have meant to be robust; I have meant to smash furniture. I find myself seated on the low rush-bottomed arm-chair. I beat my hands on its sides . . . I say 'when are we going back?' I can't stay here forever. It is her [Kora's] turn, at this moment, to retaliate, she does not. Then I sway. Ka is coming . . . I hear a voice, it is only Kora but still I say, 'Ka shan't get me.' . . . I go on, I say 'cow', I say 'mother, mother, mother.' Then I fling myself down, anywhere, head on the table, or head that would beat through the wooden floor to the rooms that lie beneath it, 'Larry'. (195–6)

Helforth is both dangerous and self-destructive, like a disturbed child. He is undergoing psychoanalysis for his problems, and he is encouraged to speak about them with Kora. 'Kora says my attitude is fantastic'—a product of fantasy—'and linked up with mother-complex.' Helforth disagrees, and tries to explain to Kora how his problems have been caused by the war:

> I say I do not think so. I explain it lucidly, as if she herself were a complete outsider, and herself had never heard of that war. I demonstrate how,

167

systematically, we were trained to blood-lust and hatred. We were sent out, iron-shod to quell an enemy who had made life horrible. That enemy roasted children, boiled down the fat of pregnant women to grease cannon wheels. He wore a spiked hat and carried, in one hand, a tin thunder-bolt and, in the other, a specialised warrant for burning down cathedrals. He was ignorant and we were sent out, Galahad on Galahad, to quell him. His men raped nuns, cut off the hands of children, boiled down the entrails of old men, nailed Canadians against barn doors . . . and all this we heard mornings with the Daily Newsgraph and evenings with the Evening Warscript. The Newsgraph and the Warscript fed out belching mothers, who belched out in return, fire and carnage in the name of Rule Britannia. (199)

Helforth speaks as if he were an ex-soldier, explaining the war to a civilian. He tells Kora horrible tales from the war, but they are instantly recognisable not as real atrocities, but as famous propaganda stories from the newspapers: raped nuns, mutilated children, crucified Canadians.[20] A key aim of propaganda was to produce support for the war. British propaganda in the Great War was extremely successful, generating the right kind of disgust and hatred towards the enemy. Yet HD suggests it might also have another effect, producing a profound kind of sickness—a war-neurotic response to stories which were simply unbearable to imagine. More than this: her war writings raise questions about true and false stories of the war, and she explores the ways in which civilians are placed distant from the actual events and unable to tell the difference.

As a young man, Helforth equates manhood with soldiering. But the war ends before he is old enough to go, locking him into a state of eternal childhood—'a small lout in my mother's drawing-room' (195)—struggling against a sense of guilt and the imaginary power of his now-absent mother, for whom Kora is partly a substitute. Helforth's war fantasies lead him to the 'mother-complex' he denies. He sees the newspaper stories as producing monstrous women ('belching mothers') who in turn produce more propaganda ('fire and carnage') to keep the war going. 'I did not realise,' he says later, 'that *nothing* depended on me, that a row of aunts was choros out of Hades, that the "family" was only another name for warfare and sacrifice of the young' (200). Some of Helforth's hatred is directed towards Kora, too, a mother who has left her husband and children to be with him. Kora misses her children, which makes Helforth jealous and resentful.

Perhaps the most curious aspect of this passage is Helforth's use of 'we'. If he is a man, he must have experienced the war; if not in reality, then in fantasy. For the war isn't just 'out there', but is 'here all the time', in Helforth's head. His identity keeps merging with the dead men he has loved, to the point that he feels he really has shared their war experiences. He fantasises about his own body in pieces, his feet as amputated lumps (185), his face seared away. These fantasies challenge familiar representations of war as a shared masculine 'truth'—an idea satirised, particularly, through the use of images from propaganda. It also reminds us that there was no single masculine experience of war—an obvious point which is overlooked in most readings of war fiction. Approximately six million British men served in the war, a vast mobilisation, but still a minority of the entire male population. The remaining men—the majority—were located in an odd position in relation to the discourses of soldiering and masculinity. In 'Kora and Ka', HD suggests that some men enacted a masquerade of masculinity, imitating the illnesses of men at war.

Bid Me to Live (1960)

Bid Me to Live was written and revised during the late 1930s and 1940s, but not published until 1960, shortly before HD died.[21] It is a survivor's account of the First World War, written and revised in the years surrounding the Second. The novel focuses on one character, a woman named Julia, and it explores specific aspects of the war's disruption of civilian lives in 1917, from the direct experience of the Zeppelin raids on London, to the indirect and imaginary effects of battles taking place out of sight—in the sea off Cornwall, for example, or in France, where Julia's husband Rafe is a soldier. (The central characters are based closely on HD and her husband Richard Aldington, from whom she became estranged during the war.[22]) The war is also felt indirectly through the presence of a 'multitude' of soldiers in London: 'heroic angels' who are really doomed men, waiting to face injury, madness, and death.[23]

Bid Me to Live sets up Julia and Rafe, a civilian woman and man, living in comparative harmony and equality when the war begins. The war transforms the city of London, both physically and imaginatively. Zeppelins, frightening figures out of science fiction, appear like whales in the sky (11). Though they did relatively little damage, especially when compared with the mass bombings of the Second World War, the air raids of the Great War were a new, unpredictable and often terrifying experience for British civilians. Houses were destroyed and people were killed in a number of areas around Britain. These were reported in the papers, sometimes with photographs, and had an effect on the imaginations of thousands, perhaps millions, of British people: many more, in short, than those directly affected by the bombing. This is an important context for reading the works of civilian war writers such as HD.

The experience of a Zeppelin raid is described near the beginning of the novel:

> Superficially entrenched, they were routed out by the sound of air-craft; she stumbled down the iron stairs (that was the Hampstead flat) and bruised her knee. Just in time to see the tip-tilted object in a dim near sky that even then was sliding sideways and even then was about to drop. Such a long way to come. It drifted from their sight and the small collection of gaping individuals dispersed.
>
> Leviathan, a whale swam in city dusk, above suburban forests. (11)

When the Zeppelin ('Leviathan') attacks the city, Julia receives a minor injury as she runs for shelter. The very insignificance of the injury—in a book about a war which killed and mutilated people in their millions—directs us towards a more important aspect of the passage, in which Julia imagines such a fall with a child in her arms.

> Suddenly, . . . her mind, which did not really think in canalized precise images, realized or might have realized that if she had had the child in her arms at that moment, stumbling as she had stumbled, she might have . . . No. She did not think this. She had lost the child only a short time before. (11–12)

Like HD, Julia has lost a newborn child during the war, and she has the peculiar sense of fearing its loss a second time, through the violence of war.

At the end of this scene, Rafe decides to enlist. This decision takes Rafe and Julia into separate worlds, where gender difference and the distinction between combatant and civilian seem to be symmetrical. When Rafe returns later, now an officer on leave, Julia realises that they have both been completely changed by their separate war experiences. He is no longer the same person she married (16); he is a stranger, 'not-Rafe', an uncanny presence who looks like her husband but is somehow not the same.

Rafe has been altered by his experience of being a soldier, while Julia has been changed by the loss of her child. At the beginning of the book, Julia sees the experiences as parallel, and resents being told about the men's suffering. 'I spared you what I went through,' she thinks, but 'you did not spare me. I did not tell you; my agony in the Garden had no words' (46). Such a loss, specific to women and kept in the private sphere, has no shared language to express it—unlike the suffering of war, which Rafe has tried to describe to her. It is striking that this text, written and revised long after most fiction of the Great War had been published, directly refutes the familiar claim that soldiers' sufferings were indescribable. More than this, it appropriates the idea of an unrepresentable horror specifically for women's experiences.

Is this an example of the 'battle of the sexes' which critics such as Gilbert find running as a counter-narrative to the war?[24] Is Julia cast as Rafe's victim; is this a novel about women's suffering at the hands of men? It seems to me that from the very first paragraph, Bid Me to Live problematises precisely these issues:

> Oh, the times, oh the customs! Oh, indeed, the times! The customs! Their own, specifically, but part and parcel of the cosmic, comic, crucifying times of history. Times liberated, set whirling out-moded romanticism; Punch and Judy danced with Jocasta and Philoctetes, while wrestlers, sprawling in an Uffizi or a Pitti, flung garish horizon-blue across gallant and idiotic Sir Philip Sidney-isms. It was a time of isms. And the Ballet.
>
> They did not march in classic precision, they were a mixed bag. Victims, victimised and victimising. Perhaps the victims came out, by a long shot, ahead of the steady self-determined victimisers. (7)

Out of a nightmarish vision of history, flung out of chronology into a spatial, anachronistic, violent dance (Punch and Judy, Jocasta and Philoctetes), the relationship between victim and victimiser is rendered uncertain. Who is the victim, who the oppressor, in this scene? It is by no means clear, and remains ambiguous, despite the sympathetic focus on Julia, throughout the novel. Julia and Rafe—woman and man; civilian and soldier—are simultaneously victim and victimiser, in their marriage, in the war, and in their relationships with others. Rather than reading Bid Me to Live as an expression of sex warfare, or as a competition in suffering, I would argue that the novel shows how the war, as both experience and discourse, *interpellates* women and men differently, constructing them differently as gendered subjects.

But the difference is endlessly modified by other structures of power and difference. When Rafe comes home on leave, for example, he dreams about the war and mutters about ghastly sights in his sleep. He is suffering from a mild form of war neurosis, an illness which makes him seem even more of a stranger to Julia. The difference between woman and man, soldier and civilian, seems to extend even into the unconscious. But this structure is disrupted only a few pages later, when Julia wakes from a brief sleep with a 'muddle of poisonous gas and flayed carcasses' in her head (39). These are *Rafe's* nightmares which have spilled into *her* unconscious, just as traces of poisonous gas are transferred from his body into hers when they kiss (39). Rigid distinctions between woman and man, civilian and soldier, are broken down even as they are invoked. Traces of the horror faced by soldiers overflow into civilian lives, just as HD believed that the distant suffering of the *Lusitania* victims had a concrete effect upon her body and killed her child. But the suffering is not the same, and the novel tries to articulate the difference.

As the war progresses, Julia too begins to suffer from war-neurotic symptoms, dissociated from her surroundings, at times on the verge of madness. She is most disturbed by a big group of soldiers in London, men 'who might be ghosts tomorrow, the latest vintage (1917) grapes to be crushed' (119). Watching them from above at the cinema, Julia feels she is 'gazing into a charnel-house, into the pit of an inferno' (126), and alternates between seeing them as objects—spectacles—and identifying with them.

Like 'Kora and Ka' and HD's memory of the sinking of the *Lusitania*, *Bid Me to Live* is concerned with the problem of being a witness to the slaughter of war, but a witness who does not actually see the worst of what happens. As witness, Julia can only imagine what the soldiers have to face. She is indirectly, discursively exposed to events which are terrifying yet mainly harmless to her as a civilian. How can the suffering of others be represented? Does HD, a woman, civilian, and survivor, have the right to write of such things? Her war writings are troubled by these questions, torn between guilt and self-righteousness; staking a civilian claim to war experience—and suffering—yet strongly aware of the greater suffering of the combatants. Helplessness in the face of others' suffering, whether witnessed or imagined, was a cause of war neuroses in both civilians and soldiers during the Great War.

Throughout her war writings, HD explores and often seeks to break down the boundaries of gendered subjectivity. At the same time, she represents subjects (Julia, Helforth) who feel extremely threatened and mentally disturbed by the shifting boundaries of difference produced by the war. Not all changes and transgressions of boundaries are liberating, either for women or for men.

NOTES

1. 'Insanity and the war', *The Lancet* 2, 4 September 1915, p. 553.
2. 'Incidence of mental disease directly due to war', *The Lancet* 2, 23 October 1915, p. 931. See also 'War shock in the civilian', *The Lancet* 1, 4 March 1916, p. 522; Eric Leed, *No Man's Land: Combat and Identity in World War I*, Cambridge University Press 1979.

3. Bruce I. Goderez, 'The survivor syndrome: massive psychic trauma and posttraumatic stress disorder', *Bulletin of the Menninger Clinic* (Kansas), 51 (1), 1987, p. 97.

4. Sigmund Freud, *Beyond the Pleasure Principle* (1920), Pelican Freud Library 11, Harmondsworth, Penguin 1984, p. 281.

5. HD, *Tribute to Freud*, rev edn, Manchester, Carcanet 1985, p. 40.

6. See Gary Burnett, *H.D. Between Image and Epic: The Mysteries of her Poetics*, Ann Arbor, UMI Research Press 1990; Burnett, 'H.D.'s responses to the First World War', *Agenda*, 25 (3–4), 1988, pp. 54–63.

7. HD, *Asphodel*, ed. Robert Spoo, Durham NC, Duke University Press 1992, p. 108.

8. HD letter to Norman Holmes Pearson, ed. Diana Collecott, *Agenda* 25 (3–4), 1988, p. 71.

9. These are described in a strange, uneasy scene in Woolf's *The Years* (1937). See Gillian Beer's discussion of aeroplanes and air raids in Woolf's writings: 'The island and the aeroplane: the case of Virginia Woolf', in Homi Bhabha (ed.) *Nation and Narration*, London, Routledge 1990, pp. 265–90.

10. HD, *Tribute to Freud*, p. 93.

11. HD, 'Magic Mirror' (1955), quoted in Susan Stanford Friedman, *Psyche Reborn: The Emergence of H.D.*, Bloomington, Indiana University Press 1987, p. 29.

12. Friedman, *Psyche Reborn*, p. 310, n. 20.

13. This point is explored by Lynn Hanley in *Writing War: Fiction, Gender and Memory*, Amherst, University of Massachusetts Press 1991, Ch. 1.

14. See Susan Stanford Friedman, *Penelope's Web: Gender, Modernity, H.D.'s Fiction*, Cambridge University Press 1990, p. 139.

15. Here my argument is opposed to Sandra Gilbert's reading of the war as a metaphorical version of the 'battle of the sexes'. Her interpretation is misleading, it seems to me, and fails to engage with the specificity of the war as an historical experience, both for women and for men. Gilbert 'Soldier's Heart', in Sandra Gilbert and Susan Gubar, *No Man's Land: The Place of the Woman Writer in the Twentieth Century*, Vol. 2, New Haven, Yale University Press 1989.

16. For recent discussions of masculinity see, for example, Peter Middleton, *The Inward Gaze: Masculinity and Subjectivity in Modern Culture*, London, Routledge 1992.

17. For an extended discussion of this issue see my forthcoming book on subjectivity, gender, and the Great War. For discussions of current directions of feminist criticism see, for example, Judith Butler and Joan Scott (eds) *Feminists Theorize the Political*, London, Routledge 1992; Sally Ledger *et al.* (eds) *Political Gender*, Hemel Hempstead, Harvester Wheatsheaf 1994.

18. Reprinted in Bronte Adams and Trudi Tate (eds) *That Kind of Woman: Stories from the Left Bank and Beyond*, London, Virago 1991. Page numbers cited in the text are from this edition.

19. For the history of war neuroses, see: Martin Stone, 'Shellshock and the psychiatrists', in W.F. Bynum, Roy Porter and Michael Shepherd (eds) *The Anatomy of Madness: Essays in the History of Psychiatry*, Vol. 2, London, Tavistock 1985; Leed, *No Man's Land*; Ted Bocagz, 'War neurosis and cultural change', *Journal of Contemporary History* 24, 1989, pp. 227–56; Elaine Showalter, *The Female Malady: Women, Madness and English Culture, 1830–1980*, London, Virago 1987.

20. See, for example, Peter Buitenhuis, *The Great War of Words: Literature as Propaganda 1914–18 and After*, London, Batsford 1989.

21. My dating of HD's works comes from Friedman, *Penelope's Web*. For a detailed discussion of *Bid Me to Live* as a war novel see Claire Tylee, *The Great War and Women's Consciousness: Images of Militarism and Womanhood in Women's Writings, 1914–64*, London, Macmillan 1990.

22. See Caroline Zilboorg (ed.) *Richard Aldington and HD: The Early Years in Letters*, Bloomington, Indiana University Press 1992.

23. HD, *Bid Me to Live* (1960), London, Virago 1984, pp. 123, 126. All page numbers are from this edition, and will be cited in text.

24. Gilbert, 'Soldier's heart'. For a detailed critique of Gilbert's argument see Claire Tylee, ' "Maleness Run Riot": The Great War and women's resistance to militarism', *Women's Studies International Forum* 11 (3), 1988, pp. 199–210.

14 'Violent times': Janette Turner Hospital's art of memory and the history of the present

Julian Cowley

Allusiveness is a striking feature of Janette Turner Hospital's fiction. Explicit or tacit reference to other works of literature and art is characteristic of her narratives. An aesthetic embracing allusion might seem to place her work squarely in the wake of modernism. Modernist allusion was grounded in concern for tradition, largely a response to a perceived crisis in knowledge, with established beliefs losing ground and cherished assumptions being found untenable. Tradition constituted a resource of authority in a world anxious at the prospect of chaos and decline.

The context for Turner Hospital's use of allusion is very different. As an Australian, she is necessarily conscious of the notorious 'cultural cringe', in which the creations of Australian artists are deemed inherently second-rate, paling beside European cultural achievement. As a woman writing fiction, she must locate herself against a canonical conception of literature which has been predominantly male.

She writes in a postmodern context where challenges to authoritative knowledge have grown steadily. But while she has manifest familiarity with the history of Western art and science, the recuperative notion of tradition is unsuitable to the situation in which she works. From her position of double exclusion, or at best marginality, she instead raises questions about inheritance, the givens of experience and of understanding in the late twentieth century. Formations through which power is exercised, technologies and institutional channels through which information is transmitted, increasingly assume the appearance of a global network, but in what sense can we talk of this as realisation of a shared inheritance? What values, what perceptions do we hold in common, on account or in despite of this transcultural configuration? And how is authority established and preserved while bodies of knowledge change shape or dissolve altogether? Such questions lead her to interrogate the nature of that collective memory that we call history, and to test it against the individual's experience of recollection.

There has been a tendency in recent fiction to show concern for the assumptions of conventional historiography, for the manner in which the past has been represented by professional historians. Graham Swift's *Waterland*, for example, addresses the sense that we inhabit a world that has lost its historical dimension, resulting in collective amnesia, and entrapment within 'the prison of idiocy'.[1] In postmodernity, the grand narratives of religious salvation, political liberation, and scientific progress may have lost their authority, as Jean-François Lyotard claims, but the practice of storytelling, the art of narrative, is in Swift's view crucial to the reinstatement of history as a mode of comprehension charged with ethical responsibility.[2]

The historian Hayden White has argued that narrative can be taken as a solution to the problem of 'how to translate knowing into telling, the problem of fashioning human experience into a form assimilable to structures of meaning that are generally human rather than culture-specific'. He is suggesting that narrative is a means for transmitting messages 'about the nature of a shared reality'.[3] He equates the absence of narrative with a refusal of meaning. Swift conveys postmodern anxiety through the voice of a schoolmaster. For Turner Hospital, pedagogues and comparable figures of authority lack the resourcefulness to escape the prison of idiocy. Their impotence is proportionate to their reliance upon tradition for the derivation of their authority.

In her novels *Charades* and *The Last Magician*, acts of storytelling are foregrounded as the matter of the fiction.[4] Characters strive to locate themselves in the present through efforts to grasp the past. Their means is the experience of narrative itself. In *Charades*, a young Australian student, Charade Ryan, emulates Scheherazade and spins tentative tales through the anxiety-ridden fields of postmodern efforts to know.

Charade enters the world of Koenig, an American professor of physics. His name meaning King, he is doubly identified as an authoritative figure, yet he works within the paradigm of radical uncertainty established in physics by Werner Heisenberg. His specialist area of research is the first second after time began. His is a statistical realm, speculative and abstract. Koenig has jettisoned 'sweet vulgar heavy Newtonian mass. *Substance*' (*C* 77). His knowledge drives him to insist that 'a sense of the solidity of matter, is one of our most persistent illusions. The presence of matter represents nothing more than a disturbance in the field at a given point, the figure in the carpet, as it were' (*C* 19). Koenig's training and his instruments of research lead him to this conclusion, yet he is distressed by a sense that Charade is insubstantial, that she is a mere hologram (and to compound his fears, she features in the holographic experiments of a colleague, whom Koenig disdains as a superficial applied scientist).

For Koenig, a word is 'an infinitely unstable element'; but within quantum physics, one may look to waves for consolatory continuities. In language, he suggests, 'talk is what glues one minute to the next' (*C* 28). Inasmuch as continuity affirms solidity, talk matters, despite Koenig's professional convictions. The King's discomposure contrasts with the resourcefulness of Bea Ryan, Queen Bea, whose frontier existence in an intensely physical Australian environment is remote from the urbanity and refinement of Koenig's New England. Charade, who knows this woman as mother, inhabits both worlds liminally; she carries into the sophisticated world necessary lessons learnt from Bea. Watching her, Koenig becomes aware of his own alienation:

How to begin again? How to recover the knack of swimming smoothly from one
minute to the next, to keep on fitting each new day into the puzzle the way
everyone else does without thinking. Without thinking, probably that is the crux
of the matter. Talk is glue, and thought is the great and terrible solvent.
Everything falls into the well of too much thinking and comes apart at the seams.
(C 31)

Charade talks to discover, but also to communicate and share. Introspection risks isolation; for Charade, intelligence must be responsive to community.

Koenig is notorious for his seduction of female students. In this way he asserts his
power over them, while meeting narrow and selfish sexual desires. He is himself
seduced by this woman who remains enigmatic, yet grants a security he needs
through 'spinning a safety net of talk' (C 30). In her tales, certainty remains elusive
but talk is a form of contact that counters alienation and despair. A crucial distinction
exists between the kinds of seduction in which they engage. The same distinction
exists between the male, professorial voice that speaks monologically from a position
of power, and Charade's mode of storytelling that generates mutuality, fostering a
dialogic situation. Her relationship with Koenig may be illuminated by Susanne
Kappeler's insight that

> in a political perspective, sexuality, like language, might fall into the category of
> intersubjective relations: exchange and communication. Sexual relations—the
> dialogue between two subjects—would determine, articulate a sexuality of the
> subjects as speech interaction generates communicative roles in the interlocutors.
> Sexuality would thus not so much be a question of identity, of a fixed role in the
> absence of a praxis, but a possibility with the potential of diversity and
> interchangeability, and a possibility crucially depending on and codetermined by
> an interlocutor, another subject.[5]

The seduction is sexual, but also narratorial, as Koenig is drawn into the storytelling
situation as interlocutor. Charade teases him for his reluctance to leave his body
uncovered. His defensive concealment says much about the precarious relationship
between his claims to authority and the processes of discovery. Still, Charade shares
with him her explorations of the past, including the possibility of multiple versions
within her provisional narratives.

The difficulty of understanding events that occurred before one's birth or in one's
absence is at the heart of Turner Hospital's concern with memory, and its articulation. In *Charades*, 'hologram' is connected verbally but also thematically to
'Holocaust'; the removal of the body as a site of value is the issue that links atrocities
committed in Nazi death camps to the glacial pleasures of postmodern technologies.
The trial in Toronto of an historian who denies the reality of the Holocaust is one of
the nodal points where the diverse threads of narrative converge. The presence of
this trial in the novel highlights the moral urgency of recovering human contact
within a context of epistemological indeterminacy. Such a critical divergence
between events and their transmission as historical knowledge shows how an act of
telling can be a violent act, and how expertise may slide into abuse of power.

The Toronto trial is personally significant to Charade, for Verity Ashkenazy (her

175

actual mother) lost her parents, removed to Nazi camps where they were murdered. Again Turner Hospital risks dangerous wordplay, Verity as Truth propelled into madness and catatonic isolation by the unthinkable violence of a calculating structure of authoritarian power. What does it mean that the horrific event took place? *Charades*, in its complex and convoluted treatment of the meshing of personal and public circumstance, makes the vital point that historical occurrences mean only according to the nature of their telling. Turner Hospital examines, here and elsewhere, key narratives of patriarchal society, the stories that tacitly sanction perpetuation of violence in the exercise of public power. Not only does she explore how women are placed within these narratives, as characters, or beyond them as silent auditors, but she offers models of specifically female storytelling that disclose very different possibilities for structures of social relationship.

Charades is prefaced by a quotation from *The Book of the Thousand and One Nights*, concerning our capacity to learn lessons from the past. Scheherazade's strategies for survival are counterpointed against the cultural model furnished by nuclear physics, and Robert Oppenheimer, father of the atomic bomb, provides the epigraph for the novel's first section:

> If we ask, for instance, whether the position of the electron remains the same, we must say 'no'; if we ask whether the electron's position changes with time, we must say 'no'; if we ask whether the electron is at rest, we must say 'no'; if we ask whether it is in motion, we must say 'no'.

Nonetheless, the existence in the world of the bomb may be proclaimed with certainty.

Indeterminacy may have entered the centres of contemporary orthodoxy, but the specialists (predominantly male, as were the priests of old) still speak from monologic positions of authority, inviting no response, no questioning, no alternative view. *Charades* is dedicated to the author's parents, 'who taught me that love is rich and redemptive whatever costumes and guises it wears'. Such is the lesson Charade may learn from Bea Ryan, 'the Slut of the Tamborine Rainforest'(*C* 13) according to conventional propriety, who does not pause to consider the instability of the word 'love', but through her actions and her attitudes bridges the spaces that open between human individuals.

She cares for people, never reducing them to concepts, nor rendering them abstract to fit theories, but accepting them as real physical presences in the world she knows. Her sphere of action is a close, small community; her effect is local and limited. In postmodernity the experience of such specific place has largely dissolved into the distributional space of mass-media and mass-consumption. Charade has left the rainforest, and entered postmodern space. Yet she carries with her Bea's maternal example of redemptive love, coupled with her own understanding of the need for versions of the past responsible to the present.

If Australianness is a resource, it is in terms of anti-authoritarian ethos, and the remoteness and slowness to change of its small communities. A key proposition is that 'once upon a time, geography was stable' (*C* 34). In the woman Bea lies a centre of gravity for the persistence of such stability. 'Once upon a time' is a banal formulation, yet it is tell-tale, for in postmodernity the evocation of place requires the storyteller's skills, as does the conception of human character. Bea has access to authentic (yet not authoritative) knowledge, the continuities in her environment admitting continuities of information unavailable to the touristic citizen of the postmodern. She puts human beings, their needs and feelings, first; they are her measure of right and wrong, not some abstract code or abstruse theory.

Charade's upbringing grants freedom from the conceptual conformity that frames perceptions, and determines behaviour in a patriarchal society. Her recognition of this acknowledges a reality that runs counter to any facile idealisation of Australia: 'I escaped a lot of that caging, the bound-feet business, the stuff that happens to girls everywhere but especially in Australia' (C 13). She has overcome 'the desire to please the teacher' (C 12), and this has produced her particular strength. Charade is a creature of the rainforest and a university-trained city-dweller. Her desire for knowledge draws her from home, but she bears with her resistance to the authoritative posturing of those who deliver that knowledge. She understands how easily the authoritative may elide with the authoritarian.

It is a quirk of historical circumstance that her convict ancestors, having fallen foul of British Law, should have arrived in Botany Bay, rather than 'some plantation in Virginia' (C 23). The histories of Australia and America bear the scars of colonial violation, the traces of European power. In her allusions to early colonial activity, Turner Hospital focuses upon the visual emphasis of the colonists' accounts. Tench in New South Wales in 1790 sweeps the horizon with his telescope in the hope of some 'intercourse with civilized society'(C 93). He does not look to the native population to speak with him. Dampier in 1688 comments on the wretchedness of the aborigines, plagued by flies so that 'they do never open their Eyes, as other People: and therefore they cannot see far'(C 45). And, most tellingly, Charade glosses Cook's response to the native inhabitants:

> '*Quite naked*, Cook wrote in his journal, which would have made the point, don't you think?
> '*Without any manner of clothing whatever*, he added, just a little fascinated, I'd say.
> '*Even the women do not so much as cover their privates*, he wrote. Hmm. *They never brought any of their women along with them to the ship*, the old perv went on to complain, *but always left them on the opposite side of the river where we had frequent opportunities of viewing them through our glasses.*'
> She shakes her head. 'What a bunch of voyeurs!' (22–3)

The critical distance between the viewer and the viewed allows no opportunity for exchange, no mutuality. Such colonial domination sheds light upon the situation of women in an inherited world dominated by certain attitudes and values enshrined as male. There is little room for love, and great potential for cruelty, in the voyeur's realm of self-gratification.

Susanne Kappeler notes how in literature and the visual arts, 'the expert domains of representation', authoritative concepts of realism have encouraged 'our commonsense attitude of dividing representations into form and content, medium and represented reality'.[6] By placing storytelling at the heart of *Charades*, Turner Hospital draws attention to conventions of the medium she uses, without sacrificing the substantial characterisation at which realism excels. In the process, the common-sense divisions are effectively challenged: the telling is evidently inseparable from what is told, and the importance of narrative to our sense of human value becomes a central issue. The early European colonists, with their telescopes and detachment, made the aboriginal Australians objects of study. This effective reification of the natives may be understood in terms of what Kappeler calls 'erecting the sadean barrier against intersubjectivity'.[7] In contradistinction to communicative exchange, we may see in the rarified, intellectual pleasure of this monologic voyeurism a positioning of self and irreconcilable other whose exemplar was the Marquis de Sade.

As with Scheherazade, Charade's storytelling is an act for survival. Scientific and philosophical indeterminacy have been matched by definitive technological implementation and political absolutism throughout the twentieth century. Within the terms of that split, knowledges of human particularity and of the conditions for authentic community have been lost. The storytelling art that Charade combines with sexual allure is a vital challenge to this atomised and dehumanised situation. Kappeler argues that 'the achievement of subjectivity through writing, through self-expression, is a male-gendered project'.[8] The silent woman is, on the other hand, a familiar, traditional figure. It is significant then that Charade confides, 'Stories have their own voices; they speak me' (C 34). Her acts of narration create intersubjective states, rather than confirming inflexible, fixed identities. Against 'the official fictions of the past' (C 90), Charade and Koenig come together to share a sense of 'the weird and wonderful routes to truth' (C 95).

Charades demonstrates how narrative can be what Ross Chambers calls 'a trans-actional phenomenon. Transactional in that it mediates *exchanges* that produce historical change.' Such transaction is made possible, he points out, only through 'enabling agreements'.[9] One such agreement enables Charade to assume the storyteller's role in relation to her auditor, Koenig. Another establishes our own engagement with the text. Turner Hospital engages us with complex fictions, inconceivable without print, while conjuring from the page an experience of oral narration and of the intimacy inseparable from that premodern storytelling situation.

It is through transaction, as opposed to the exclusive discourse of the specialist or élite, that appropriate response to common inheritance may be negotiated. Charade asks Koenig for his authoritative view on 'the possibility of knowing anything'. He replies it is 'a useful fraud', but resists her suggestion that knowing is consequently just a joke—the useful fraud is 'all we've got' (C 94). His pragmatism is not mere defeatism, or nihilism in meagre disguise. At the end of the book, he encounters the expert in holograms; after 'marathons of his colleague's moody predictions, his monologues, his obsessions', Koenig gets to see again the holographic Charade Ryan, 'insubstantial and absolutely real' (C 290). A question posed by Ross Chambers is pertinent here: 'When we are seduced, are we not always seduced into conforming ourselves with an image: the simulacrum of one whom we believe can be loved?'[10]

The hologram is no longer just an illusion, a disembodied body; rather it is a simulacrum, an image of Koenig's love. Unlike his monologic colleague, he has acquired the capacity to communicate in a way that is meaningful identification with another subject, rather than possession of an object. He has telephone numbers for Charade in rural Queensland. 'One day he is going to place a call' but the communicative potential will not slide into possessiveness. Kappeler writes of the classic literary act of reification: 'the message is viewed as complete, perfect, unalterable, not susceptible to the communicative interaction by a listener who might want to clarify, question or comment upon particular parts of the message'.[11] The book's closing paragraph discloses the perversity of those whose response to the twentieth-century paradigm of knowledge is desperate adherence to illusory certainties. Koenig, the teacher, has learnt to live constructively within the paradigm, to understand what it might mean to share this inheritance. He intends to call Charade: 'Actually, quite often, almost every night in fact, he lifts the receiver and begins to dial the numbers. But then he thinks of Heisenberg and the indeterminacy question, and wishes to keep the ending open' (*C* 291).

The Last Magician ends in comparable fashion, with ostensible silence, yet with 'the great beating wings of our absent ones deafening us and filling the air with light' (*LM* 352). Here Lucy, like Charade, returns home to Queensland, to the rainforest, leaving behind the denizens of the Quarry, an evocation of Dante's inferno and a model of urban dereliction lurking beneath the veneer of sophistication in contemporary Australian life. Violence is more graphically present in this novel. In particular the focus falls on Cat, a woman of the rainforest, comparable to Bea, yet wilder.

A literary critic, speaking authoritatively from the comfort of some tasteful drawing room, warns against the dangers of violence in fiction. Her sense of decorum allows her to recognise and castigate those effects produced by writing whose intention is 'titillation of the reader, plus the comfort of horror happening to someone else'. Against such good taste and critical detachment, Turner Hospital offers Cat who 'slashes herself. She sculpts her own body into an artefact of abuse, she makes a monument of her own pain. This is not only ideologically unsound, it is distressingly un-Aristotelian' (*LM* 301). Cat's self-mutilation makes visible psychic wounds caused by persecution, by the action of Law.

In explaining the illusory nature of matter, Koenig referred to 'the figure in the carpet'; we are invited to recognise an allusion to Henry James's story of that name. Cat could never have entered the Jamesian menagerie, but as a living text, an incarnation of her story, she embodies the crucial inseparability of narrative from narration, of tale from telling, that was James's concern. The generation of meaning depends upon situation, and the enabling agreement which engenders Lucy's narration penetrates Cat's self-imposed rule of silence.

The fastidious critic cites Yeats's poetic treatment of the rape of Leda as a classic case of 'the deft touch', the aesthetic 'sleight-of-hand' that keeps bad taste at bay, even in the treatment of brutal assault (*LM* 301). But Lucy asks: 'Have her *terrified vague fingers* found illumination yet? Or are they still scrabbling, gnarled and untransformed and unenlightened, in mud and in her own shit?' (*LM* 302, emphasis in the original). Yeats's mythopoeic figuring of historical process trails off into questions of transmission, but it remains an image of rape and rupture, rather than a model of communication.

'These are violent times' insists a character in Turner Hospital's earlier novel, *Borderline*.[12] The articulation of that violence is central to her history of the present. But how can print reproduce Cat's scars, those self-inflicted traces of the ripping of her flesh by 'rusty razorblades or broken beer bottle necks'? Another, anonymous 'self-slasher' is quoted saying, 'you do it when you need to scream but you can't' (*LM* 258). Yet Lucy believes that art has the capacity to make audible the otherwise silent scream; her evidence is Munch's woodcut, *The Scream*:

> It is composed of every scream the viewer has ever heard, every fear he has ever felt, every nightmare that has ever jackknifed him out of sodden sheets. It cannot be shut off, that scream. It is deafening. It is not just the open *rictus* of the mouth which screams, but the skull, the hands, the whole body. The body is at risk of imploding, the scream sucks the body into itself. The giddy sky screams too, and the contortionist earth writhes in the grip of the same endless shriek. (*LM* 227)

Lucy here projects a male auditor, incapable of not sharing the terror. The stories that speak through Munch's representation communicate through silence. Still, within the picture, there is warning of the executioners' approach; it warns that they are

> deaf, indifferent, sinister, grim as reapers with black scythes, as schoolteachers looming above young children, as bullies hanging about on a corner, as judges. They are unmoved but moving closer, their intentions unswerving, straight as railway lines, straight as the law, relentless as death or the black fact of power. (*LM* 227)

Lucy comments that two worlds coexist here, occupying the same space. One is 'the world that is only scream'; the other, 'where the scream means nothing and is not even heard'(*LM* 227). The polite, civilised world of public office and institutional power grants no acknowledgement to private terror, and, through a consensual strategy of withholding meaning, that terror is effectively denied existence. But the refusal of officialdom, with its protocols and regulatory mechanisms, to countenance situations inviting dialogue perpetuates and intensifies the terror. Lucy perceives that art may make an intervention, but it is art that departs from the strictures of Aristotelian tradition that are here identified with the vengeful imperatives of the Law.

'Humankind cannot bear very much lack of meaning' (*LM* 300); in T.S. Eliot's version it is 'reality' that haunts us, but this formulation identifies absence of explanatory narrative as the real source of fear. What is truly distressing about Cat's seeming madness, as in the case of Verity, is her retreat into silence, her refusal of verbal articulation for her suffering. As Lucy remarks: 'If we have to experience horror, there has to be a point. There has to be. In fact, it is not the horror itself that torments us so much as the need to understand' (*LM* 300). But points and straight lines are not adequate to a geometry of suffering.

As writers have reported throughout the twentieth century, we do not live in an age that can accommodate tragedy, and the status of tragic heroine is not available to us. 'Of course terrible things do happen. Of course the newspapers report atrocities every day', but they are random horrors that afflict our insecure and insubstantial selves. In *The Last Magician* the orthodox view is stated plain: 'A work of fiction has nothing to do with this. It may have had for Sophocles and Euripides, but not for us. Modesty and the intimate domestic scale are the appropriate postures for our time' (*LM* 300). Turner Hospital's novels refuse to adopt these postures.

Lucy, a student, lives a double life. As Lucia she performs the services of a prostitute, posing for photographs, while refusing to be touched. The photograph recurs in Turner Hospital's work as a mode of representation that lends itself to a particular model of knowing. The snapshot freezes the processes of life and so makes them 'knowable', and it transmits an image of the real into the future. But this artifact has no meaning in itself; it needs the dynamic of narrative to flow through it, as it flows through Munch's picture. Charade Ryan studies a photograph which includes her father and Verity: 'every morning a different history came off it like fog and she took deep breaths, gulping down one past after another' (*C* 70).

To Koenig she confides her view that photographs, all those 'droplets of stopped time', are lies. She feels that the camera 'falsifies everything' through various acts of selection. Her conclusion is that 'What's interesting about a photograph . . . is what isn't in the picture' (*C* 68). It is a view derived in part from Bea's recognition that 'a photograph . . . is no more use than a snakeskin after the snake has crawled out'. The figures in the picture both are and are not Charade's father and Verity Ashkenazy: 'Yes and no. It doesn't have his smell, her smell; it doesn't tell you anything at all' (*C* 74).

Charade and Lucy refuse merely to look at photographs; that voyeuristic detachment is, as we have seen, associated with certain forms of patriarchal power. Lucy knows that the police have many of Cat and a veritable archive of official records dealing with her case. Just as Charade cites the accounts of colonists, so Lucy refers to records from Australian history. An 1827 report on a convict woman, made by the superintendent of the Hobart Female Factory states:

> She screamed most violently, and swore that no one should cut off her hair . . .
> She then entered my Sitting Room screaming, swearing, and jumping about the
> Room as if bereft of her senses. She had a pair of Scissors in her hand and
> commenced cutting off her own hair . . . Coming before the window of My Sitting
> Room [she] thrust her clenched fist through three panes of glass in succession . . .
> (*LM* 302–3)

Turner Hospital links the convict women to her own creation, Cat. They leave no journals, no accounts of their experience in their chosen story form. Rather they become case studies, objects of institutional scrutiny. The official accounts are monologues delivered from seats of power; they invite no response. Cat takes no photos but, like Ann Bruin, the convict, marks her own body, suggesting an extreme and radically alternative mode of knowing.

Lucy comments, archly: 'It is amazing, really, how many expert and professional words have accumulated on the incorrigibility and incomprehensibility of the propensity to self-destruct'. She adds, tellingly: 'One could almost see the endless reports and treatises, *words, words, words*, as in inverse ratio to Cat's silence' (*LM* 302, emphasis in the original). For her, as for Charade, talk is redemptive, but its real value resides not in the words, but in the situation, in the enabling agreement and the terms of exchange.

Sonny Blue is the pseudonym of an eminent judge. In conversation with Lucia, he is revealed as a man of honourable intentions, operating blindly, and so destructively, within the strictures of Tradition. They discuss the interesting ways in which the bonds of human kindness are both loosened and strengthened by a glass or two of Four-X beer, of the ways in which *communitas* becomes more elastic, more inclusive, more durable. They speak of the vibrancy of pubs as compared to the modes of community in law courts, say, or in universities. (*LM* 261–2)

But as a judge he wields patriarchal authority, drawing lines of regulation and division within society. Lucy is anxious: 'Doesn't the fact of power create an automatic conflict of interest?'. Sonny Blue assumes a predictably conservative position:

We *inherit* the lines, you see, they are sanctioned by time. We inherit the instinct for when it is appropriate to turn a blind eye. It is tradition, and respect for tradition, that makes the web of civilisation. And it is the bitter zeal of those who want to redraw the lines which destroys. (*LM* 262)

He fails to make a crucial distinction: Tradition is an exclusive delineation; inheritance is what we all must deal with. Without that understanding the deaf, indifferent world will continue to contain the world that is all scream, without registering disturbance, without responding.

Turner Hospital has created in Charade and Lucy characters engaged in acts of communication, women dedicated to the task of closing the gaps that prevent mutual understanding and human interaction. Their positions are far from straightforward, but against those male voices that deliver the authoritative version, they offer examples of shared experience of discovery. In a world where detachment facilitates control, they aim to connect. Without such engagement, the voice of authority is destined to remain a voice that threatens violence. Turner Hospital discloses sadistic forms underlying social relationships in patriarchal society. The history of our collective past is replete with evidence of what follows from such reduction of human beings to the status of objects. Charade and Lucy are characters who, as women and as storytellers, seek to counter this, to establish reciprocity, in short to promote love. Their encounters with confusion, with suffering and difficulty embody the need for an art of memory that is adequate to the history of the present, and to the terms for survival in violent times.

NOTES

1. Graham Swift, *Waterland*, rev edn, London, Picador 1992, p. 108.
2. See Jean-François Lyotard, *The Postmodern Condition*, translated Geoff Bennington and Brian Massumi, (Theory and History of Literature, Volume 10) Manchester University Press 1986 (first published as *La Condition postmoderne*, 1979).
3. Hayden White, *The Content of the Form: Narrative Discourse and Historical Representation*, Baltimore, Johns Hopkins University Press 1990; 1987, p. 1.
4. Janette Turner Hospital, *Charades*, London, Virago 1990; 1989. Henceforth referred to in the text as C. Janette Turner Hospital, *The Last Magician*, London Virago, 1992. Henceforth referred to in the text as *LM*.
5. Susanne Kappeler, *The Pornography of Representation*, Cambridge, Polity Press 1986, p. 198.
6. Ibid., p. 2.
7. Ibid., p. 181.
8. Ibid., p. 181.

9. Ross Chambers, *Story and Situation: Narrative Seduction and the Power of Fiction*, (Theory and History of Literature, Volume 12) Manchester University Press 1984, pp. 8, 9. Henceforth referred to in the text as Chambers.
10. Ibid., p. 15.
11. Kappeler, *The Pornography of Representation*, p. 171.
12. Janette Turner Hospital, *Borderline*, London, Virago 1990; 1985, p. 12.

15 Women and Mother Ireland

Anne–Marie Fyfe

Introduction

> The literature of the Irish literary Renaissance is a peculiarly masculine affair . . .
> it is in society that women belong.
>
> Frank O'Connor[1]

The reader approaching the field of Irish women's writing could be forgiven for expecting a wealth of material, not least because of the standing of Irish male writers in English from Congreve, through Swift and Sheridan via Wilde, Shaw, Joyce and Beckett to Heaney. The reader might also be thinking of the homage paid to 'Mother Ireland'; the significance of women in the Catholic tradition (the Virgin, numerous saints and abbesses); the power of women in peasant lore; the images of women in Irish mythology as warriors, queens, banshees; the roles of women in the Celtic Literary Revival and in the uprisings of the early twentieth century.

Yet the absence of any real tradition of women's writing in Ireland becomes immediately apparent when one attempts to recollect the female names which should sit alongside the male writers listed above. A brief look in any canonical anthology will confirm the initial impression and render credible Elizabeth Smart's 1960s claim of continually hearing men, 'mostly Irish men, declaring that women were incapable of creating works of art'.[2]

There are certainly parallels here with problems encountered by women writing elsewhere. But there are also factors which are peculiar to the twentieth–century Irish condition, North and South, and which have their origins in politics, economics and religion: in many ways the roll-call of significances outlined above merely asserts the general rule that there is an inverse relationship between the exaltation of *images* of women and their actual degree of *power* in any society.

Obviously there is no one single explanation for this phenomenon just as there is

184

no one Ireland. But in exploring several 'Irelands' (the Anglo-Irish in the nineteenth century, the rising Catholic *bourgeoisie* in the early twentieth, the rural conservative South after the Rising, the Protestant North before and during the current Troubles and so on), one finds remarkable similarities in the ways in which gender perceptions in society inhibited and prohibited women's writing and the ways in which such writing has been simply marginalised by a variety of patriarchal establishments.

Regional novels and Celtic revivals

The dearth of women's writing in modern times stands in sharp contrast to the fact that Maria Edgeworth (1767–1849) is regarded as having written the first regional novel in English and as having considerably influenced (by their own admissions) both Jane Austen and Sir Walter Scott. Austen describes, in *Northanger Abbey*, the novels of Fanny Burney and Maria Edgeworth as 'work in which the greatest powers of the mind are displayed and in which the most thorough knowledge of human nature, the happiest delineations of its varieties, the liveliest effusions of human wit and humour are conveyed to the world in the best chosen language'.[3] Indeed Edgeworth's *Castle Rackrent* (1800) has been described as 'probably the single most influential piece of narrative prose to appear in England between the death of Smollett in 1771 and the publication of Waverley in 1814',[4] and Turgenev was to acknowledge her importance in his own artistic development and in the evolution of the Russian novel.

It should be noted that Edgeworth, daughter of Richard Lovell Edgeworth of Bath and a cousin of the then Lord Longford, is of the 'Ascendancy', an imprecise term referring to the landlord class, predominantly Protestant and largely English in origin. *Castle Rackrent* is, therefore, the first Big House novel, a genre that exists to the present day, dealing largely with relations between the Ascendancy and a stereotypical indigenous population. While Edgeworth was driven by a moral imperative in her biting satire on these conditions, her successors in this form, two cousins writing as Sommerville and Ross, adopt a lighter touch, most notably in *Some Experiences of an Irish RM* (1899). In *The Real Charlotte* (1894), however, they take more serious issue with the unfair treatment of women, even in the leisured classes.

Parallels exist here with the emergence of women's writing in the middle and upper classes in England and with the evolution of the novel form as the medium for exploration of the subtleties of a settled society. For the landed gentry (despite the presence of a sometimes comical, sometimes threatening, peasant class), Ireland was just such a settled society. Moira O'Neill (Agnes Nesta Shakespeare Skrine née Higginson, 1870–1955) uses her poetry to move outside the confines of the demesne, but her observations on nature and her capturing of native accent and wit are essentially a brand of rural romanticism, politically complacent and with no awareness of a specific woman's voice.

Changes begin in the latter part of the nineteenth century, as much a result of the artistic and scholarly exploration of romanticism, which led to the Celtic Revival, as a consequence of political and economic agitation. While the names most associated with this era were Yeats, Synge, Douglas Hyde and AE, the role of Lady Gregory is of major importance. Her interest in both mythology and fairy lore and her later plays about the fight for freedom are more significant for their influence on others than as works of artistic merit. What is of interest here is both that Augusta Gregory effectively assigns herself a lesser role as patron and facilitator to 'great' male writers and that in her choice of subject matter (fairy tales, folklore, the romance of the Rising) she avoids gender realities even more surely than her Ascendancy predecessors had done.

Ethna Carbery and Alice Milligan, both from the North of Ireland, are romantic nationalists in the Celtic Revival vein. Their work in editing the journal *Shan Van Vocht*, and in writing ballads and poetry based on Irish legend, shows similar concerns to those of Augusta Gregory. (Even the title of their periodical, which in English means 'the poor old woman', reflects the notion of Ireland as the sentimental female victim of colonial occupation, yet little nationalist rhetoric at that time or since addressed the real lives of poor old women, or indeed women of any age or economic status.)

The other dominant visual image of Ireland in this period is that of the young maiden dubbed 'Cathleen Ni Houlihan' or 'Roisin Dubh', names which infuse the work of Yeats and other Revivalist writers as much as they infect the poetry of the revolutionaries Pearse and Plunkett. Ireland is portrayed as a beautiful young girl, rivalling the Virgin Mary in purity, who is about to be set free by her heroes. The metaphorical notion of Irish freedom as a form of cosmetic surgery or hormone replacement therapy, potentially restoring the 'crone' to a state of nubility, is essentially male fantasy and is therefore, surely, inimical to women.

The Rising and the fall of the Big House

The events of 1912 to 1922, resulting from political agitation and the nationalism of the Celtic Revival, ended in the creation of two states, both nominally within the Empire but with the southern part moving rapidly to a greater degree of independence with its own symbols, constitution and language. The six northern counties conversely strove for ever greater integration within the United Kingdom. In the South the political changes which enfranchised the rural peasantry (and the campaign of burnings which had accompanied the Troubles) resulted in the decline—and in many cases retreat to England—of the former Ascendancy. Since this had been virtually the only class to contribute Irish writing by women in the previous century, naturally this decline was to become a major literary theme. John Cronin identifies its foremost chronicler: 'If Somerville and Ross celebrated what Conor Cruise O'Brien called *the Indian Summer of the Irish Ascendancy*, we may say that Elizabeth Bowen commemorates its sad, autumnal moments'.[5]

Elizabeth Bowen (1899–1973) was born in Dublin to parents of long-standing Ascendancy pedigree, one branch of her mother's family including among its descendants the Duke of Wellington. With ten novels in all between *The Hotel* (1928) and

Eva Trout (1969), her work deals with love and its hazards, exploring sensitively the emotions of naive young women while simultaneously criticising the societal impulse towards marriage and domesticity. She deals, unusually for her time and place, with lesbian episodes in *The Hotel* and other novels and with strong friendships between women in her 1929 novel *The Last September*. This latter work is regarded as the lament for a dying tribe. The dilemma of Lois, the daughter of the house, in her inability to choose between an aged and ineffectual potential lover in Hugo and the more dynamic Gerald Lesworth, stands as metaphor for the inability of Bowen's own class to choose between their Englishness, a faded thing from the past, and the notional dynamic of identification with the new Ireland.

In many ways Bowen's writing and her life as a writer—coming, as she did, from the upper classes—are not significantly different from that of her contemporaries in England. The fact that she has been under-recognised may owe something to the fact that in England she is regarded as vaguely Irish, the social content—the real function of the novel—being diluted by political sensibilities which are essentially foreign; and in Ireland her contribution is largely ignored since she was not one of those Anglo-Irish writers who chose to support the new nationalism, preferring to write about her own class and in fact setting many of her works in London society.

Bowen's contemporary, Molly Keane (the daughter of the poet Moira O'Neill), born in 1904 into the same landed background, wrote numerous plays and novels between 1928 and 1956 dealing with class, sex and in particular a lesbian relationship in *Devoted Ladies* (1934). Keane published under the pseudonym M.J. Farrell; her reasons, echoing those of Currer Bell and George Eliot a century earlier, stand as a corrective to the notion that writing was easier for middle-class women: 'For a woman to read a book, let alone write one, was viewed with alarm. I would have been banned from every respectable house in Carlow.'[6] Her achievement is perhaps at its best in chronicling the straitened circumstances of women, young women in particular, in the etiolated and moribund society of the Anglo-Irish gentry after 1922. Eclipsed for the same reasons as Bowen, Keane has enjoyed considerable success since the appearance of *Good Behaviour* (1981). Although set in the same post-1922 era of decline her more recent novels attack the pomposity of that class from a distance with a wicked and subversive humour.

The Ulster contribution to this genre is Caroline Blackwood's *Great Granny Webster* (1977), set in the same decaying mansions, though the Ascendancy is much less relevant in Northern Irish culture. Like the rest of Ireland, the North had been in the hands of an essentially Anglican landed gentry, but differed in that it had been settled by Scottish small farmers or Planters, mostly Presbyterians. Belfast by the end of the nineteenth century had become a not untypical northern British industrial city, famous for its engineering and evangelism.

Patricia Craig, in her anthology *The Rattle of the North*, observes: 'It is well known that conditions in the North of Ireland, from Plantation times on, were never sufficiently settled to foster literary activity and that the development of the novel, in particular, was consequently retarded'.[7] Yet following the divisions of 1922, with the North remaining a part of the United Kingdom, Belfast had its own, settled, prosperous middle class, recorded in the novels of Janet McNeill. Born in Dublin in 1907, McNeill was educated in England but spent most of her adult life in Belfast

187

and its suburbs. Her 1956 novel *Tea at Four O'Clock* deals with a society far from dying, but stolidly and suffocatingly established in its patriarchal oppressiveness. McNeill's sensitivity in this novel, a portrayal of a girl's awakening, does not fail, however, to identify the girl's psychological dependence and, to an extent, her complicity in her own imprisonment.

What is unusual about *Tea at Four O'Clock* is that it offers a picture of Northern Ireland society which is undifferentiated from English counterparts, or at least North of England society with its industrial and Protestant overtones. Ireland when it appears is simply the charming rural backdrop, and the tensions within the new state and 'over the Border' have no visible impact. By contrast, male Northern Irish novelists, poets and dramatists of the period, such as Sam Hanna Bell, Sam Thompson and John Hewitt, focused unrelentingly on the cultural and political anomalies of the Northern Irish situation.

New beginnings: the South after 1922

All the writers considered above belong to the English tradition, both the landed gentry in the South and the Protestant merchant class in the more prosperous North. Given that the newly-independent state in the South was born out of the idealism of the Celtic Revival, with female sponsors such as Lady Gregory, Ethna Carbery and Alice Milligan, and was created by the revolutionary activities of the likes of Maud Gonne, Constance Markievicz and Hannah Sheehy Skeffington, it should reasonably have given scope and space to women writers of the native Irish tradition who had so long been marginalised and denied educational opportunities.

The male writers of the period, Sean O'Faolain, Frank O'Connor and Liam O'Flaherty, all wrote of the 'thatched cottage' view of Ireland which was to dominate the new society as markedly as the Big House concept had presided over the old. Kate O'Brien (1897–1974) chose significantly different territory from either. Born into a Catholic middle-class family in the thriving seaport of Limerick, O'Brien, in her first novel *Without my Cloak* (1931), related the saga of an emerging, confident, mercantile family whose politics are decidedly neutral if not actually pro-British in outlook. The poet and critic Eavan Boland has commented, 'This was Catholic Ireland. It was never Nationalist Ireland'.[8]

In one sense O'Brien was flying in the face of the Nationalist domination of the new political entity, as she was later to offend Catholic sensibilities by the brief male homosexual incident in the opening pages of *The Land of Spices* (1941). Her outlook had no doubt been broadened by the opportunities afforded to her by a middle-class education (in a convent run by French nuns) which, though narrow in outlook, enabled her then to teach in London and in Spain. *The Land of Spices*, however, was to earn her the honour of being banned by the Censorship Board, a notorious piece of small-mindedness which typified the repressive, conservative, even puritanical atmosphere of the new Ireland. Despite the fact that *Without My Cloak* achieved considerable recognition (the Hawthornden Prize and the James Tait Black

Memorial Prize), O'Brien went largely unrecognised in her own country—the banning of one book was sufficient to discourage reading of any of her other works—and it was a novel on a Spanish rather than an Irish theme, *That Lady* (1946), which achieved most recognition for her, being subsequently dramatised on Broadway and filmed.

A more typical chronicler of the farms and small towns in the 1930s and 1940s was Mary Lavin, who had been born in Massachussets of Irish parents and who returned to live in Dublin. Educated at the National University, the new alternative to Ascendancy-dominated Trinity, she began to write in 1938 with the encouragement of Lord Dunsany and her short stories and novels, focusing particularly on love and on the lives of women, enjoyed considerable popularity.

A strange aspect of the post-revolutionary period, with its official espousal of rural Ireland and its Gaelic heritage, is the dearth of women's writing in Irish. One exception is Peig Sayers, a storyteller from the Blasket Islands off the south-west coast, whose autobiography *Peig* was published in Irish in 1936; her later work, *An Old Woman's Reflections*, was published in 1939. Both were subsequently translated into English. Sayers was not a product of the new culture of compulsory Irish in education but was the last of an authentic but dying tradition. The first new writers in Irish begin to appear much later.

What is surprising in the period from 1922 onwards is not simply that there were so few women writing in Ireland (despite a flourishing male literary world) but that Virginia Woolf was to comment in 1929 in the English context that 'there are almost as many books written by women now as by men'.[9] It might also be noted that while the women cited write realist narratives of family life, the mode of Irish writing which had the most impact in international terms was the non-realist narrative invented by Joyce and developed by Beckett and Flann O'Brien. This form, which allowed interrogation of the impositions of Church, empire and nationalist myth, is clearly, in Joyce's own terms at least, a product of the conflicts between his Catholic schooling and the study of the liberal arts at university. The lack of similar educational opportunities for women prior to this time may, in part, account for the failure of women to explore such experimental routes.

The 1960s

Even realist narratives had to deal with the same influences, however, and the work of Edna O'Brien achieved a sudden prominence by dealing with the typical subject matter of 1960s novels, but uniquely from a small-town Irish Catholic perspective. Able to write frankly about the sexual (and romantic) desires of *The Country Girls* (1960), she naturally had much to say about the repressive effects of convent schools and of the puritanical hypocrisies of small-minded communities. Needless to say her novels were praised in England but offended the sensibilities of rural Ireland. The notorious Censorship Act meant that this offence resulted in her books being banned, putting her in the elevated company of Joyce, Gorki, Lawrence and Shaw (and Kate O'Brien) and making the work even more attractive to a younger generation. Edna O'Brien has commented on the acceptable images of Irish Catholic womanhood at the time, 'devoid of sexual desires, maternal, devout, attractive . . . I offended the Catholic Church. I betrayed Irish womanhood . . . I showed two Irish girls full of yearnings and desires. Wicked!'[10]

O'Brien's writing began in London, exile having played a significant part in much of Irish writing from Joyce to the present day; this is not simply due to the influence of the Church or censorship in Ireland, both of which have recently waned somewhat, but to the need to escape the oppressive hold of community. O'Brien went on to write prolifically, not always about her background, but always about love, desire, relationships and loss. She is, however, conscious of the double disadvantage that characterises modern Irish women writers: 'Women's lot is hard anywhere, but an Irishwoman's lot is ten times harder'.[11] This echoes the less strident comment of Iris Murdoch (born in Dublin): 'I think being a woman is like being Irish . . . everyone says you're important and nice but you take second place all the time'.[12]

Jennifer Johnston is possibly the only other Irish woman novelist to have achieved such widespread recognition. Yet her novels, while centring on women's lives for the most part, frequently deal with the remaining Anglo-Irish in the context of a new Ireland. *How Many Miles to Babylon* (1974), for example, is a classic tale of master-servant loyalty in the Great War; similarly, *The Railway Station Man* (1984) has a reclusive woman artist in Donegal meet a war-veteran railway enthusiast in a middle-aged encounter against a backdrop of her student son's radical politics, and his manipulation by terrorists.

Interestingly, although Johnston writes about the Northern Irish Troubles, she was born into a Dublin literary family with Ascendancy connections. What is noticeable in the period after 1922 (with the exception of Janet McNeill who was also born in Dublin) is the shortage of Northern women writers of either Catholic or Protestant background commenting on life in Northern Ireland. Among the dominant group, some of this absence may no doubt be traced to the ambivalent position of women under Calvinist Protestantism; some to the reputation of the Northern Irish Presbyterians for dourness; and some to the perceived state of siege under which the new political entity was created. Arguably the same controls as in the South—Church and rural piety—applied to Catholics in the North, although no Northern Irish Edna O'Brien was to appear in the 1960s to defy these. This suggests that Northern Catholic women were, to extend Edna O'Brien's notion, triply burdened, by their womanhood, by the Church and conservative pieties and by being part of a disadvantaged political minority.

Contemporary developments

The period from the 1960s to the 1990s has seen very gradual change in society in the South of Ireland. Politically the country has begun to put its Republican past at a distance in the attempt to be seen as a modern European nation-state. The position of women has shown some improvement following the birth of feminism in the 1960s (although major issues such as divorce and abortion are still on the agenda); and the difficulties of the writer have been eased with tax concessions and public subsidy. Writers such as Kate O'Brien have been rediscovered and are more acceptable to a forward-looking, pluralist element in society which can now accommodate versions of the past other than the simplistically nationalist. New writers emerging since the 1970s include Julia O'Faolain, Eavan Boland, Maeve Kelly, Clare Boylan, Evelyn Conlon, Mary O'Donnell, Mary Dorcey, Eilean Ni Chuilleanain and Nuala Ni Dhomhnaill who, uniquely in this list, has chosen the Irish language to explore contemporary women's experience.

Eavan Boland, born in 1944, published her first collection of poems, *New Territory*, in 1969. Also an essayist, she has attempted to explore and understand the ways in which women's writing is not merely something different from or subservient to male modes of writing: 'An Irish poet is a male poet, and the Irish poet who is a woman has to be described as *an Irish woman poet*'.[13] Outside the Irish context Boland has been much influenced by Adrienne Rich, who wrestles with the separation of selves, of woman and writer: she 'begins to unite the two identities and in doing so confronts the need for a new language and new images with which to express herself'.[14] In Boland's search for new language and new forms to represent woman's experience she is conscious of the idea of the nation and the poetic tradition or pre-existing structures as essentially male constructs out of which—or against which—she is compelled to write.

The objection to the idea of nation is largely centred on the way in which poets from the romantic period onwards converted the Ireland of strong feminine images (warrior queens and saints) into two weak remembered images of the oppressed Ireland either as a betrayed and burdened poor old woman or as an innocent young girl. While these were no doubt effective and sentimental devices with which to sell romantic notions of revolution, Boland recognises that their use—and the equation of womanhood with nationality in Ireland and elsewhere—reduces real women to abstractions and deprives them, in the case of the two examples above, of positive role-models. A key turning point in her perceptions is recorded in her polemical pamphlet *A Kind of Scar*.[15] As a young Trinity student she is spending Easter studying English 'Court poets of the Silver Age' on Achill Island; she is visited by an old woman who speaks of the courage of women during the famine and who shows her how the sense of their greatness is preserved only in the oral tradition, something which had been invisible to Boland in the literary world.

Despite her objection to the appropriation of woman as national symbol, she finds an interesting conjunction in disadvantage: 'Womanhood and Irishness are metaphors for one another. There are resonances of humiliation, oppression and silence in both of them and I think you can understand one better by experiencing the other'.[16] Here Boland has found a positive potential in a concept which Edna O'Brien found merely obstructive.

It could be argued that although there are many obstacles to women in society, women's writing in the South of Ireland is now on a par with its position in many other countries; changing perceptions of woman's role have, for example, been given impetus by the election of a woman as President. Conversely the publication in 1991 of the *Field Day Anthology of Irish Writing*, an attempt to construct a representative canon, showed by its almost total omission of women writers that change is gradual: the apparently accidental nature of the omission says more about the narrow views of Irish male academics than a deliberately constructed exclusion could have achieved.

The same period in the North of Ireland has been marked by a renaissance of (male) writing, coinciding with, and possibly gaining in importance from, the recent political Troubles. These arose from the partitioning of the country in 1922, which left an inbuilt Unionist majority looking towards England and feeling threatened by the South, and a significant Nationalist minority who felt betrayed by the settlement and as oppressed under the new regime as southern Catholics had done before 1916.

Thus Seamus Heaney, who was first published in 1962, has been seen as the first of a line from both political traditions, including Michael Longley, Derek Mahon, Paul Muldoon, Tom Paulin and Ciaran Carson, who write of life under this regime and of what Muldoon describes as 'unfinished business'.

Noticeably the list is entirely male except for one noted writer, Medbh McGuckian, who was born in 1950 and whose subject matter avoids the externally political, embracing the domestic and the experience of women. There is a current and continuing debate as to whether McGuckian's poetry is understood in any real sense or, indeed, whether it expects to be understood. Her opacity contrasts with the work of male poets from Heaney onwards whose international fame is widely believed to be due to an unchallenging accessibility. In some senses McGuckian's acknowledged obscurantism meets the needs of a critical establishment which is ready to attack feminist writing at any level.

McGuckian, however, makes no claim to a feminist position, decrying many women writers as being content to be second rate. Much of the achievement in the South and elsewhere has been as a result of the encouragement (by editors, academics and women's groups) of women's writing, allowing good writers to develop out of a non-hostile ambience. McGuckian appears to make no allowance for this process, her attitude reminiscent of those women who achieve power despite the obstacles but who then do little to remove those obstacles for others. Indeed, so male-dominated are perceptions of Irish literature generally, that McGuckian has defined her desire to write thus: 'I basically see the role of the poet as a male role which I have adopted . . . I wanted to do something that would make me into a man, or give me the status of a man'.[17]

One writer who is an advocate of empowerment through writing and supports the 'writing as therapy' element in women's development, is Ruth Hooley, editor of *The Female Line*, a collection of writing by women in the North of Ireland.[18] Coming, as she does, from neither of the main traditions, Hooley is comparatively optimistic that there is a female line, and that both in politics and literature it can operate in the North as elsewhere. Her own work arises primarily out of her experience, and is conscious of the burdens of domesticity while remaining positive about family relationships: 'A lot of poets use female imagery to convey beauty or fertility or feeling, and yet women have really strong qualities as well. I don't want women to be more like men. I just want them to have a fair share of recognition'.[19]

Despite McGuckian, the scarcity of women's writing in the North, particularly in a situation of civil disturbance of which women bear much of the brunt, has puzzled many critics but is in line with a general failure to develop a strong women's movement and to achieve a high level of representation for women in the structures of that society.[20] This under-representation contrasts with current political trends in the South and in the rest of Britain. One might expect that women from the Catholic community in the North would have made as much progress in countering the effects of a hierarchical Church and male-dominated societal structures as their counterparts in the rest of Ireland. That this is not so must surely owe something to the sense of unsettledness and the group solidarity arising from the Troubles: to be seen to attack any of the (male-dominated) institutions which define the community could be seen as disloyalty to that community. In the same way any attack on the male structures of the dominant Protestant community—churches, Unionism, the Orange Order, militarism—would be seen as being pro-Republican.

What is ironic from the standpoint of women's writing is that the part of Ireland which has most brought recognition for male writers in the contemporary period has seen least advancement for women's writing and women's politics. This might be seen as paralleling the political disturbances in the first two decades of the century, which brought many male writers to prominence but did little for women.

Taking Virginia Woolf's comment that the essential difference between men and women is not that men write about battles and women about children, but that each sex describes itself, one might attempt to explain the prominence of male writers by suggesting that the writing which was visible and popular in these two periods was inevitably about male phenomena: politics, terrorism, intrigue and adventure. In fact this analysis applies as little to the works of Joyce or Beckett as it does to, say, Paul Muldoon. Critics such as Katie O'Donovan and Nuala O'Faolain have attempted to explain the difference in prominence between Irish men and women writers by emphasising modes rather than subject matter, and contending that Irish male writers from Joyce to Flann O'Brien have been notable precisely for their experimentation in the non-realist mode (the same is true of Muldoon) and their eschewal of the conventional novel form with its essentially female origins.

This argument is clearly supported by the significant presence of women writers in the comparatively settled Ascendancy period (suitable for the novel) and by their absence in subsequent periods where men deal either in a realist mode with masculine themes or in a non-realist mode with more sophisticated themes, both options being conventionally denied to women.

It could be argued therefore that the absence of women in the North's political disturbances of recent years has rendered some women's writing invisible or irrelevant, while the comparatively stable situation in the South has allowed women to begin to develop their own realist narratives. At the more experimental end it appears from the work of some Southern women writers that non-realism may no longer be the exclusive preserve of the male. Women are now actively questioning the impositions of Church, state, history, myth and legend, and both experiential narrative and experimental modes provide vehicles for this development. There is clearly both the opportunity and the need in Ireland for women's writing of women's lives, though the necessary societal changes face a variety of substantial obstacles, North and South, which have seriously hindered development in the past and may yet continue to do so.

NOTES

1. Frank O'Connor, *The Lonely Voice*, London, Macmillan 1963.
2. Rosemary Sullivan, *By Heart, The Life of Elizabeth Smart*, London, Flamingo 1992, p. 292.
3. Jane Austen, *Northanger Abbey*, 1818, reprint Penguin, Harmondsworth 1984, p. 58.
4. Patrick Murray, *Maria Edgeworth, A Study of the Novelist*, Cork, Mercier 1971, p. 38.
5. John Cronin, *The Anglo Irish Novel*, Vol. II 1900–40, Belfast, Appletree 1990, p. 127.
6. Polly Devlin, Introduction to Molly Keane, *The Rising Tide*, London, Virago 1984, p. v.
7. Patricia Craig, *The Rattle of the North*, Belfast, Blackstaff 1992, p. 1.
8. Cronin, *The Anglo-Irish Novel*, p. 142.
9. Virginia Woolf, *A Room of One's Own*, London, Grafton 1977, p. 76.
10. Julia Carlson, *Banned in Ireland*, London, Routledge 1990, p. 76.
11. Ibid., p. 77.
12. Daniel J. Casey and Linda M. Casey, *Stories by Contemporary Irish Women*, New York, Syracuse University Press 1990, p. 2.
13. Gillean Somerville-Arjat and Rebecca E. Wilson (eds) *Sleeping with Monsters*, Dublin, Wolfhound 1990, p. 85.
14. Ibid., p. xi.
15. Eavan Boland, *A Kind of Scar*, Dublin, Attic 1989.
16. Somerville-Arjat and Wilson, *Sleeping with Monsters*, p. 84.
17. Ibid., p. 4.
18. Ruth Hooley (ed.) *The Female Line*, Belfast, NI Women's Rights Movement 1986.
19. Somerville-Arjat and Wilson, *Sleeping with Monsters*, p. 171.
20. 'Currently there are no women among the seventeen Westminster MPs or the three MEPs ... a Northern Ireland male politician in 1985 ... observed only half jestingly, *Well, someone has to stay home to mind the kids!*', Catherine B. Shannon, 'Recovering the voices of women of the North', *The Irish Review*, 12, Belfast, Institute of Irish Studies 1992, p. 28.

FURTHER READING

Blackwood, Caroline , *Great Granny Webster*, London, Duckworth 1976.
Boland, Eavan, *New Territory*, Dublin, Allen Figgis 1969.
— *A Kind of Scar: The Woman Poet in a National Tradition*, Dublin, Attic 1990.
Bowen, Elizabeth, *The Hotel*, London, Constable 1927.
— *The Last September*, London, Constable 1929.
— *Eva Trout*, New York, Knopf 1968; London, Cape 1969.
Craig, Patricia, (ed.) *The Rattle of the North*, Belfast, Blackstaff 1992.
Edgeworth, Maria, *Castle Rackrent*, 1800, reprint London, Oxford 1964, 1982.
Hooley, Ruth, (ed.) *The Female Line*, Belfast, NI Women's Rights Movement 1986.
Johnson, Jennifer, *How Many Miles to Babylon?*, London, Hamish Hamilton 1974.
— *The Railway Station Man*, London, Hamish Hamilton 1984.
Keane, Molly, (M.J. Farrell) *Devoted Ladies*, 1934, reprint London, Virago 1984.
— *Good Behaviour*, London, Deutsch 1981.
McGuckian, Medbh, *On Ballycastle Beach*, Oxford, OUP 1988.
McNeill, Janet, *Tea at Four O'Clock*, 1956, reprint London, Virago 1988.
O'Brien, Edna, *The Country Girls*, London, Hutchinson 1960.
O'Brien, Kate, *Without my Cloak*, 1931, reprint London, Virago 1986.
— *The Land of Spices*, 1941, reprint London, Virago 1988.
— *That Lady*, 1946, reprint London, Virago 1985.
Sayers, Peig, *Peig: The Autobiography of Peig Sayers of the Great Blasket Island*, 1936, translated Bryan MacMahon, Dublin, Talbot 1973.
— *Peig Sayers: An Old Woman's Reflections*, 1939, translated Seamus Ennis, London, Oxford 1962.
Somerville and Ross (E.O. Somerville and Violet Martin) *Some Experiences of an Irish RM*, London, Longmans, Green 1899.
— *The Real Charlotte*, 1894, reprint London, Quartet 1977.

16 Sizing up: women, politics and parties

Elizabeth Maslen

Because novels not only speak from their cultural moment but take issue with it, imagining new versions of its problems, exposing, albeit by accident as well as by design, its confusions, conflicts and irrepressible desires, the study of fiction is an especially inviting and demanding way into the past.

Alison Light[1]

True hearts, clear heads will hear the note of glory
And put inverted commas round the story . . .

W.H. Auden[2]

In this essay I shall be looking at some of the ways in which women writers engage, in their fiction, with the history of their time during the decade after 1927 when women were finally given the same political voting right as men. Most of the women I shall discuss have known commitments to political parties of the Left; all are clear-eyed about the continuing struggle for social justice for women, and about the cost of their newly won place in society; and all, when they want to put ideas across, have to frame a narrative mode which will offer these ideas in ways acceptable to their readers.

But first, to set their fiction in context. The 1920s had seen the rapid rise of the Labour Party as a serious independent political force. However, it was a party which was having to work hard on what it stood for: up to 1918, it had been purely federal, with over one hundred affiliated trade unions and such divergent affiliated socialist societies as the Independent Labour Party, the Fabian Society, and the British Socialist Party. Such a mixed inheritance was inevitably both rich in ideas and potentially explosive. Crucially, most of the party leaders envisaged the transition to socialism as a gradual process of social reform within the capitalist framework, while a minority within the party saw the first step in this transition as revolution, with the working class seizing power. In 1920, this ideological difference led to the British Socialist Party breaking away from the Labour Movement and linking up with other

Marxist groups to form the Communist Party of Great Britain. But there remained many divergent views among members of the Labour Party, and when Labour came to power in 1924 and 1929, they were still working on aspects of their identity in the face of inherited problems of massively rising unemployment and economic depression. And, it must be said, they offered very mixed views on roles for women both within the party and in the community at large, conservatism often obstinately vying with more progressive thinking.

It is hardly surprising, then, that women writers in the 1920s and 1930s offer very different views of socialism. Moreover, the confusions confronting them increase when party allegiances tangle with divisions in the women's movement. In her article, 'Feminism and fiction between the wars: Winifred Holtby and *Virginia Woolf*' (1988), Marion Shaw describes two strands of feminism:

> The Equalitarians, as Holtby calls them, who politically aligned with a Centre/Liberal position, demanded parity with men in rights, treatment and responsibilities. Theirs was a classical feminist position, their most characteristic body was the Six Point Group and their champion was Margaret Rhondda. By contrast, those who called themselves the 'new' feminists and who were largely trade union women like Eleanor Rathbone, were conscious of the special disabilities and requirements of women, particularly in regard to maternity, and sought to legislate for their privileged treatment.[3]

Sadly, there was considerable hostility between the factions which Holtby and other women writers had to negotiate while coming to terms with what some, like Storm Jameson, perceived as the conflicting demands of physical involvement with the many active women's groups and their roles as writers. And if this were not enough, they were also faced with the long-standing debate over what mode of writing lends itself to women's particular concerns.

For what constitutes 'women's writing', both in subject-matter and narrative mode (at times, indeed, extending into how women ought to write) has been an issue for most of this century. Marion Shaw explores Holtby's position, as expressed in her book on Virginia Woolf, on whether women's fiction 'could or should be distinct from established literary practice'.[4] Such practice refers primarily to realism, since realism was perceived by many feminists to have been taken over by men and the establishment, and used to sanction a social status quo. Many feminists therefore urged the need for new literary modes (such as the 'stream of consciousness' in Dorothy Richardson's work, which was named and acclaimed by May Sinclair) to map 'the largely uncharted territory of women's subjective lives'.[5] But such urgings were seen by some, including Holtby, as bringing their own dangers. Shaw perceives Holtby, given the remaining areas where women suffered social injustices, as ultimately

> a committed but reluctant feminist, resenting the divisions feminism wrought and its threat to the ideal of a common humanity she held to . . . To her, the threat from the 'new' feminist novelists, as from the 'new' feminists like Eleanor Rathbone, was that gender would usurp humanity as a primary condition.[6]

How typical was Holtby's position? It is well worth spending time over the question

196

of why, when realism had come under such determined attack from the 'new' feminist novelists, so many women writers in the 1920s and 1930s, committed to the Left, still used it as a narrative mode, albeit, as I shall be arguing, adapting and experimenting with it, when they engaged with the history of their time. The divisions for and against its use were, as Shaw implies, as deep as those between opposing strands of feminism and, it is tempting to add, mirror the debate which divided the socialist movement in 1920 between those who wanted all-out revolution and those who preferred gradual, evolutionary change within an established system.

Certainly the debate about the use of realism and what it stands for has been and continues to be a contentious one. And the debate is complicated by disparate definitions of realism often underlying contemporary discussion as well as, one suspects, being concealed within the debates of earlier years. In her influential article, 'Listening to Minna: realism, feminism and the politics of reading' (1991), Jan Montefiore demonstrates this problem.[7] She examines Sylvia Townsend Warner's *Summer Will Show* (1936),[8] in which Sophia, her children dead, abandons her socially conformist, privileged life to go in search of her absent husband in Paris. There she forms a passionate relationship with his erstwhile lover, Minna, chooses poverty alongside her, and takes part with the communists in the revolution of 1848. Montefiore ends her article with a consideration of her own and Terry Castle's interpretations of the novel. Castle, in her article 'Sylvia Townsend Warner and the counterplot of lesbian fiction' (1990), explores, among other things, Warner's rewriting of a number of incidents culled from English and French nineteenth-century fiction and shows how she revises 'the seemingly indestructible heterosexual narrative of classic European fiction'.[9] However, Castle takes, it seems, a fatalistic view of society (and, by implication, realism) saying:

> By its very nature lesbian fiction has—and can only have—a profoundly attenuated relationship with what we think of, stereotypically, as narrative verisimilitude, plausibility or 'truth to life'. Precisely because it is motivated by a yearning for that which is, in a cultural sense, implausible—the subversion of male homosocial desire—lesbian fiction characteristically exhibits, even as it masquerades as 'realistic' in surface detail, a strongly fantastical, allegorical or utopian tendency.[10]

This conclusion seems to assume that a freeze on social change, never mind narrative mode, is normal and inevitable, and that there is no such thing as evolution.

Montefiore agrees with much of Castle's argument but pauses, importantly, on what she identifies as their differences which, she asserts

> stem partly from different notions of realism, which she defines in terms of a plausibility of story . . . whereas I use the term to mean a method of fictional writing which can be read as 'transparent', as presenting a social and material world as if it were or could be readily knowable and known by the reader. In other words, she is thinking in terms of plotting, I of narrative mode. But the difference is, finally, political: for her lesbian-feminist reading what is important about the book is that it goes beyond plausibility . . . My own socialist feminist interpretation values the novel for the way it enables the reader to share in the transformation of

197

a woman's consciousness, not only of her own erotic desires (though these are crucially important) but of the material world of struggle . . . These opposite interpretations are, as far as I can see, irreconcilable: either *Summer Will Show* engages with history, or it does not. But either way, feminist critics clearly need to stop dismissing novels like Warner's to an unread limbo of supposedly phallocratic bourgeois humanism.[11]

This is an arresting conclusion. I want to bear both Castle's and Montefiore's interpretations in mind, since they show how the term 'realism' can refer to story line or narrative mode, to engagement with history or to a disguise cloaking fantasy. For if realism shows itself able to offer such very different readings, may it not equally have the potential to evolve into a mode capable of serving differing concerns in the hands of inventive and independent-minded writers?

Both Castle and Montefiore base their conclusions primarily on analyses of just one of Warner's novels. But I would argue that an exploration of a broader range of her fiction shows a number of experiments with realism which, rather than offering uncritical support to the status quo of a literary or political establishment, accommodate undercurrents within a changing society. Realism, it would seem, can be wrested from past conventions just as surely as other modes; it is the definition of the term that needs continual revision, if it is to keep pace with what is acceptable as the reality of any period's modernity.

If we look, for instance, at some of Warner's fiction which predates *Summer Will Show*, there is plenty of evidence to suggest that she is 'sizing up' realism as a vehicle, just as she is teasing us with the story line articulated by it. As early as 1926, in *Lolly Willowes*,[12] she uses realism to trace the quiet, spinsterly life of her protagonist, daydreaming of independence, but for many years filling the traditional role of family servant to her demanding bourgeois family, taken for granted but outwardly uncomplaining. However, halfway through the book she breaks away, taking lodgings in a country cottage where she can begin to evolve an identity of her own fashioning. At this point, she gradually becomes aware of a witches' coven in the village and, as a final sign of her liberation, meets someone who is, for her as for the 'witches', the devil.

So this novel leaps off from what was seen by the 'new' feminist novelists as traditional realism into a two-tier mode which can be read as realism transformed by Lorna's imagination, or as pure fantasy (the tension between materialism and fantasy, Montefiore asserts in a footnote, is present in all Warner's novels, while Castle refers to a 'hankering after the fantastic' in her work). Does this novel engage with history, allowing us to 'share in the transformation of a woman's consciousness'? Yes, it does engage with history, as the world Lorna inhabits for half the book is a well-documented, recognisable middle-class home of the early part of the century, with Lorna playing a traditional role. But then both protagonist and novelist write new versions of reality, with a secondary level of interpretation as to what Lorna experiences in the cottage and surrounding countryside, a psychologically plausible level of fantasy interpretation woven around a Joycean epiphany. It could of course be argued that this novel is therefore not an expansion of the bounds of realism but some other narrative mode. But this seems to me a perverse reaction which would insist that realism is only realism when it supports, in Montefiore's memorable phrase, 'a phallocratic bourgeois humanism'.

The suspicion that Warner is experimenting with what can be done with realism, shaping it in parallel with the ideas it articulates, is, I think, strengthened by a subsequent novel, *The True Heart* (1929).[13] This work, situated in 1873, tells the tale of Sukey Bond, an orphan placed, true to period, as maidservant to a farming family on the Essex marshes. The plot follows the struggles of the girl to marry the simpleminded son of a middle-class family. The period and its rigid class distinctions are vividly portrayed, the Essex countryside and those who inhabit it meticulously described. The plot may contain elements which are, according to Castle's argument, implausible, but it fulfils Montefiore's definition of what constitutes realism: it engages with history; it 'enables the reader to share in the transformation of a woman's consciousness, not only of her own erotic desires . . . but of the material world of struggle'. Yet, as Warner has herself revealed in her 1978 preface to the novel, it is a retelling of Apuleius's tale of Cupid and Psyche. As she says, 'These disguises were so efficient that no reviewer saw what I was up to. Only my mother recognised the basis of the story.'[14] So here is myth dressed up as historical realism with a young woman fighting for a vulnerable lover against the conventions of her Victorian society, but also reflecting the aspirations of 1929 feminism, with a woman taking her destiny into her own hands, against the odds. The engagement with history is being played very skilfully here, in ways which have become familiar in the literature of recent decades. A story of the past blends with a myth which needs recasting if it is to speak to contemporary audiences in terms of their own concerns.

In a later work Warner, by now a member of the Communist Party, again shows her skill at engaging with history on more than one level, historicising legend in *After the Death of Don Juan* (1938).[15] This novel is set at the end of the eighteenth century in a vividly evoked Spain, and explores wryly and wittily the aftermath of Don Juan's death, with Doña Ana and her party travelling through rural Spain to bring the news of his son's supposed death at the hands of demons to Don Juan's father. Doña Ana's motives are enigmatic, as it is by no means clear whether she believes her fantastic story or is pursuing her own erotic fantasies. What is clear is the hold which superstition has on the consciousness of many of the local peasants, while some are none the less experiencing a transformation as they become aware that, whether Don Juan lives or not, their traditional oppression at the hands of Church and aristocracy will not be eased without their own efforts. Legend, or rather superstition, about Don Juan's death and the manipulation of that superstition by the oppressors can only add to the realistic evocation of a rural, backward Spain, and has much to do with the roots of the Spanish Civil War. For, as Warner herself explains in a letter written to a friend in 1945, the novel is:

> a parable if you like the word, or an allegory . . . of the political chemistry of the Spanish war, with the Don Juan—more of Molière than of Mozart—developing as the Fascist of the piece.[16]

The way Warner blends fantasy and history as part of the operations of the real world, the way she can operate fluently on more than one level in the three fictions I have been exploring, albeit briefly, throws light, I think, on the differing readings of

Summer Will Show discussed above. It seems to me that on this evidence Montefiore's and Castle's readings can indeed co-exist, reconciled by the expanded use that Warner makes of realism as a narrative mode capable of containing the games minds can play and the impact of those games on what can be observed objectively. In the age of psychoanalysis, such an expanded notion of what constitutes reality seems ultimately reasonable. Furthermore, as Wendy Mulford comments in her 1989 introduction to *After the Death of Don Juan*:

> All Sylvia Townsend Warner's novels are rich in evocation of place—one might compare the treatment of revolutionary Paris in *Summer Will Show*—and paradoxically, in their unique registration of a time and a place, capture a remarkable quality of timelessness. Here is the Spain of the familiar . . .[17]

If 'timelessness' can be interpreted as 'familiar', this implies a certain meeting point between a world of then and a world of now, and so, it seems to me, space is made for the aspirations, even the fantasies of one age to be recognised as shared or even realised in another. Certainly Warner's experiments with a realism which embraces fantasy and intertextuality suggest that imagined situations can offer quite as much to commentaries of now as the more traditional role played by 'objective' documentation, which in any case is a highly suspect concept.

I have spent so long on what can be done with realism, even in the hands of a single writer, because I think her work does demonstrate how readily the mode can be reshaped and trained to other allegiances than a 'supposedly phallocratic bourgeois humanism'. But as I am reluctant to structure my argument around Warner alone, I propose to explore a sample of Naomi Mitchison's work. Her fiction has a grand sweep, exploring myth and legend, the ancient world and contemporary society. The novel I am going to consider is *We Have Been Warned*,[18] published in 1935 (although written in 1932), because it displays most strikingly both a creative attitude to realism and a 'sizing up' of contemporary issues which is highly idiosyncratic and independent of official Labour thinking, even though Mitchison is ostensibly involved in the Labour movement. The novel centres on Dione, wife of an Oxford don who is the Labour candidate for a working-class constituency. The action covers a wide social range, moving between visits to Dione's childhood home (her mother is a Scottish landowner), her own middle-class Oxford home, her husband's Labour constituency and, memorably, the Soviet Union. Each place with its cast of characters is admirably brought to life (apart from a highly romantic view of idyllic existence in the Soviet Union, a view shared by many socialists at the time Mitchison was writing). So far, realism of a traditional kind seems to triumph, particularly as in much of Dione's life she conforms to a traditional, strictly subordinate role as wife and mother, worrying about the children and supporting her husband, while keeping up good relations with the 'new' feminists who cross her path. But there is much in the novel that does not uphold convention of any sort. For instance, Dione has more than a passing flirtation with communism (or rather, an unacknowledged anarchism), dreaming of the barricades while continuing to check the linen and administer tea to undergraduates. But this leads to incidents which would not have been tolerated by the British Communist Party: Dione condones a murder committed by a Scottish comrade whose parents she knows, helping him to escape to the Soviet Union disguised as her brother, because the murder was of a class enemy. Once in the Soviet Union, her priorities are distinctly confused: she visits an abortion clinic with a 'new' feminist activist, is horrified by its primitive and dehumanising state, and offers graphic description to share the horror with the reader. But at the same time she is preoccupied with the notion of free love as a necessary test of her allegiance to socialism, urging her adored husband into a love affair with a Soviet girl, only to find, unsurprisingly, that she has difficulty with her own emotions when the affair prospers. Subsequently, wanting to prove her equalitarian comradeship within the Labour constituency, she walks trustfully into a situation where she is nearly raped by one of the communist workers, is deeply shaken but eventually forgives him, socialism taking priority over feminism, according to her own assessment of the situation. Later, when pregnant (by her husband), she considers abortion of this fifth child but rejects it, as her smallest infant is no longer a baby.

There is much here which is conservative, much that engages with the modernity of the 1930s and, in explorations of contemporary issues, the costs as well as the rewards of freedom are examined with some sensitivity. But there is also much, as in the condoned murder, attempted rape, and promotion of free love within marriage, which goes way beyond what the mainstreams of socialism or feminism could sanction. All in all, it is not very surprising that Mitchison had trouble getting the book as a whole into print. It took her three years to find a publisher, and even then she had to add a foreword which began:

> In deference to the intensive criticism which this historical novel about my own times has already received, I wish to state most earnestly that the views on socialism and in general on social morality expressed by the main characters in the story do not represent either the official Labour Party attitude nor the views of any Left-wing or 'intelligentsia' group. Nor do they, to the best of my knowledge, represent the views of any person in the dedication of the book.[19]

As there are some twenty-eight dedicatees, including her husband, W.H. Auden, Victor Gollancz and Walter Greenwood, Mitchison's disclaimer is impressive. However, as Alison Light suggests in my first epigraph, this novel does offer some of the 'confusions, conflicts and irrepressible desires' being discussed, if not accepted, at the time it was written.

So much for the storyline. But the narrative mode is also teased beyond the traditional bounds of realism, introducing many instances when elements of fantasy seem to manifest themselves physically, at least in the eyes of Dione and her children. More importantly, the novel begins with Dione reading about a seventeenth-century witch, Green Jean, and ends with the witch in person offering warnings to Dione by means of vividly life-like visions of a Fascist takeover (and they are presented very realistically, as invasions of the 1930s world we have become familiar with in the novel). As in Warner's *Lolly Willowes*, a protagonist breaking free of convention sides with the powerful but feared outcast women of the past, an eloquent response to the restraining pressures of social conformity and a comment on how such restraints can endanger freedoms that vision helps to safeguard.

Mitchison's novel offers a heady blend of conservatism and modernity pushed to its limits, as well as driving wedges of visionary perceptions into her largely traditional realist mode. Ellen Wilkinson, as a young Labour MP, also blends conservatism and modernity within a realist mode in her novel, *Clash* (1929),[20] but the effect is utterly different. In this novel, covering the period of the General Strike, there is a self-conscious confrontation between several of the classic ingredients felt by many feminists to belong to realism as presented in the radical career of a Labour activist. The result is refreshingly vivid, as the protagonist Joan, a young trade union organiser and brilliant orator, contends with the lures of good living, epitomised in the home and character of a Bloomsbury woman friend and political sympathiser, and struggles to maintain her Labour priorities in the face of a too demanding love. The novel is strikingly open about the pressures on a politically committed woman. There are urgent debates weighing marriage against career (and the underlying assumption for her lover in the key debate is that the two are incompatible). The anguish of the choice confronting Joan is made plain, as she eventually turns to the committed Labour man (still of public school background, a sop perhaps to the conventions of popular romance) who will marry her and her socialist commitment.

The unwillingness of the novel to romanticise political commitment is impressive. Certainly Joan is equalitarian in her dealings with colleagues and workers but when, during the strike, she travels north to organise relief for strikers' wives and families, she shows herself increasingly sympathetic to the views of 'new' feminists, only to find herself dismayed at how the privileging of women's needs undermines the morale of the men on strike, a salutary reminder of how complex such issues can be in practice. Certainly the novel is eloquent on Joan's dynamism as an activist, her passionate oratory, her inspiring dedication, and the background detail of conference, negotiations and life in the provinces is vigorously drawn. But it also shows how the tug of conservatism constantly dogs Joan, the private individual, and how she can never be complacent about the effect of her activism as a woman on the strikers she helps, as when, carried away by enthusiasm, she mistakenly uses her personal appeal to call a strike leader to a 'safe' area, so hurting the local man who has kept his area squarely behind the strike.

Wilkinson uses realism to convey a passionate fight for social justice, simultaneously showing how a woman constantly faces traps, triggered by pressures either social or self-made, in situations offering no guiding precedent. Wilkinson's realism is imbued with precise documentation, in ways which anticipate Holtby's *South Riding*, published seven years later.[21] I have concentrated on the diversity of ways in which the three writers I have discussed use realism because so many women writers do use it when engaging with the history of their day. As socialists and feminists, they do not always fit smoothly into the compartments that might be anticipated, often revealing 'by accident or by design', as Light says, the conflicts and confusions that dog both movements. They also show the powerful pull of conservatism, not only within society at large but within individual men and women. And in their experiments with the realist mode, they show considerable ingenuity in luring readers in with what had come to be expected of realism, only to surprise them with a visit to fresh territory once they are involved with the narrative.

The need to lure readers and publishers in cannot be underestimated if ideas, socialist and feminist, are to reach a wide range of novel readers. And the need to reach out to a readership must be present, given the priorities of these novelists, or why write fiction about such matters? Arguably, non-fictional books and articles on party politics or feminist issues tend to appeal to an already committed or, at the least, interested audience. But fiction, certainly the fiction of women writers, has the chance, if shrewdly presented, of invading the more popular preserves of public libraries. Commercial publishers are alert to the need for acceptable routes of appeal, and by no means all the works mentioned above were published by avowedly political houses such as Gollancz or Cassell. They have been able to convince an impressively wide range of publishers of their worth as entertainment, whatever the potentially didactic underlay. Two valuable books, published in 1991, give insight into a broad range of readers' tastes: Bridget Fowler's *The Alienated Reader: Women and Romantic Literature in the Twentieth Century* explores the reading habits of women of working-class background, while Alison Light, in *Forever England: Femininity, Literature and Conservatism between the Wars*, explores the work of Ivy Compton Burnett, Agatha Christie, Daphne du Maurier, and *Mrs Miniver* to see what they reveal about the priorities of their largely middle-class audience.[22] The conclusions both writers reach certainly suggest why a theoretically conservative mode like realism was chosen by so many writers with a stake in modernity, bending a reassuringly familiar narrative mode to their purposes without alienating potential readers at the outset.

But of course I am not suggesting that the familiar is the only route to a wide readership. For example, Aldous Huxley produced one of the most popular futuristic dystopias in English in 1934, and a number of women writers adopted this variation on a mode which engages with history, though none achieved the fame of Huxley's work. There are two particularly powerful ones which I shall close with, both written after Hitler came to power in 1933 and Nazism had shown its teeth. Storm Jameson's *In the Second Year* was published by Cassell in 1936, and tells of a Fascist takeover of Britain.[23] All the activists are male. The only woman is remembered as vivid and intelligent before her marriage, but is subsequently consumed and diminished by her love for her macho husband, committing suicide when he is shot by order of his former friend, the dictator. It is a bleak work, terrifying in that the England so vividly described is recognisably the familiar place of the 1930s, an engagement with history where defamiliarisation subtly increases as the novel progresses. The following year, Katherine Burdekin (under her occasional pen-name, Murray Constantine) published *Swastika Night* with Gollancz.[24] It tells, largely through dialogue, of a desperate attempt to keep alive suppressed truths expunged from rewritten history under a Nazi régime which has swallowed the Western hemisphere centuries before. The fate of women is extrapolated both from certain post-Darwinian theories which argue for the genetic inferiority of women and from the Nazi policy of 'Kinder, Kirche und Küche', which barred women from education and the professions. It is devastating. Women have become barely distinguishable from apes, are caged and used entirely for breeding purposes. They are underfed, unintelligent, and uncomely. The English protagonist who, with a Teutonic Knight of the Nazi aristocracy (intriguingly a descendant of Rudolf Hess), represents the one hope of keeping the record of forgotten truths intact, and who shows a remarkable sense of the possibility of democracy despite centuries of servitude, can still barely cope with the idea that women may be equals. He manages to force himself, intellectually if not emotionally, to recognise his baby daughter but, when dying, can only say to his son:

203

'Edith,. . .'
'Who's that?'
'My baby girl.'
'But what do you want me to do with her?'
Fred was almost convinced his father was wandering, and yet his one eye looked still intelligent.
'Don't know. Nothing—to be—done. Must be left. In time—'
Alfred's whisper died away.[25]

Confused and complex as relations among socialists and feminists may sometimes be in the 1920s and 1930s, they offer at the very least aspirations for the future. The alternatives, as Jameson and Burdekin perceptively insist—well before the Second World War—are, quite simply, untenable.

NOTES

1. Alison Light, *Forever England: Femininity, Literature and Conservatism Between the Wars*, London, Routledge 1991, p. 2.
2. W.H. Auden, 'The truest poetry is the most feigning,' in *Collected Shorter Poems 1927–1957*, London, Faber 1966, p. 317.
3. Marion Shaw, 'Feminism and fiction between the wars: Winifred Holtby and *Virginia Woolf*' in Moira Monteith (ed.) *Women's Writing: A Challenge to Theory*, Brighton, Harvester 1986, pp. 171–91. (p. 176).
4. Ibid., p. 177.
5. Ibid., p. 177–8.
6. Ibid., p. 190.
7. Jan Montefiore, 'Listening to Minna: realism, feminism and the politics of reading', *Paragraph* 14 (1991), pp. 197–216.
8. Sylvia Townsend Warner, *Summer Will Show* (1936), London, Virago 1987.
9. Terry Castle, 'Sylvia Townsend Warner and the counterplot of lesbian fiction', *Textual Practice* 4 (2) (1990), pp. 213–35 (p. 224).
10. Ibid., p. 229.
11. Montefiore, 'Listening to Minna', p. 212.
12. Sylvia Townsend Warner, *Lolly Willowes or the Loving Huntsman* (1926), London, Virago 1975.
13. Sylvia Townsend Warner, *The True Heart* (1929), London, Virago 1978.
14. Ibid., Preface.
15. Sylvia Townsend Warner, *After the Death of Don Juan* (1938), introduction by Wendy Mulford, London, Virago 1989.
16. Sylvia Townsend Warner, *Letters*, London, Chatto and Windus 1982, p. 51.
17. Warner, *After the Death*, p. vi.
18. Naomi Mitchison, *We Have Been Warned*, London, Constable 1935.
19. Ibid., p. v.
20. Ellen Wilkinson, *Clash* (1929), London, Virago 1989.
21. Winifred Holtby, *South Riding: an English Landscape* (1936), introduction by Lettice Cooper, London, Virago 1988.
22. Bridget Fowler, *The Alienated Reader: Women and Romantic Literature in the Twentieth Century*, Hemel Hempstead, Harvester Wheatsheaf 1991; Light, *Forever England*.
23. Storm Jameson, *In the Second Year*, London, Cassell 1936.
24. Katherine Burdekin (Murray Constantine) *Swastika Night*, London, Victor Gollancz 1937.
25. Ibid., p. 287.

Index